D0759082

BabyHouston

BabyHouston

A NOVEL BY

J U N E A R N O L D

Texas Monthly Press, Inc.
P.O. Box 1569
Austin, Texas 78767

A   B   C   D   E   F   G   H

Library of Congress Cataloging-in-Publication Data

Arnold, June, 1926–
   Baby Houston.

   I. Title.
PS3551.R53B34   1987   813'.54   86-30089
ISBN 0-87719-063-1

Book design by David Kampa

June

JUNE MADE NO bones about it. She'd move back to Houston to write about her mother. Not a biography and not for therapy's sake. Always cranky about trends, she did not mean to exorcise the past or settle old scores in order to find out who she *was* and why. She came home—moved, bought a house—to write a novel from the point of view of her mother: first-person no less, as if she had become her own mother, thinking her mother's thoughts, wearing her mother's perfume, bearing her mother's children—including of course herself—imagining her mother's dreams and passions and death without breaking character to step outside the curtain wearing sandwich boards saying it's really me writing this, June, smart and wise and modern and I know how silly all this is, the Tabu perfume, the face cream and flower arrangements and Revlon Fire and Ice lipstick, but what can I do? Her intent was not to comment on her mother's time but recreate it. She meant to enter the realm of her own mother's dreams.

At the time—I had just met June—the idea seemed shocking, not just psychically, though of course there was that. As literary strategy too, I had to wonder. Nobody comes right out and says they're writing a novel about their mother. When questions are asked implying a connection between real life and fiction, fiction writers get very nervous . . . especially in advance of writing the thing. Yet here was June making the announcement herself. "I came back to Houston to write about Mother." In that blithe tone she had, with its underlay of perverse, rapscallionish glee.

We were having dinner at a fancy French restaurant just west of Post Oak Road in Houston, four novelists and a lawyer . . . friends but for the most part, just barely. We didn't know each other that well. (Which June didn't much care about, how long she'd known someone or what their politics were. She liked putting people together, seeing if how old friends and new acquaintances got along, what kind of conversation and tone they'd come up with. She liked—always—freshness and surprises.) The evening was an occasion celebrating June's past. June's mother had once lived in the house that had become the fancy French restaurant. The room we were eating in had been the living room. ("The front door used to be there," June explained.) Having been told in advance who June was, the waiter was paying us particular attention. The new owner came by to make certain we were well taken care of. After the meal, he provided complimentary brandy. June seemed delighted by everything that night: the company, the food (even though it wasn't first-rate, which June knew), the attention she was receiving, the place itself.

The lights were appropriately low, down to a semblance of candles. As the restaurant was brand new, it was practically empty. Waiters stood against the walls smiling, hands behind their backs as they waited to pounce on empty plates and dirty ashtrays. Yet in the way restaurants seem prone to, the *maitre d'* had seated us only one table away from a largish, well-dressed couple who were just finishing their main course.

Coincidentally, all five of us had worn bright silk blouses that night. June's buttoned to one side and had large soft, Cossacky sleeves. In the soft light against the starched white tablecloth we felt pretty swell, like jewels in a ring. June's delight was contagious. It was like being at a children's party with hats and balloons. As if nothing bad would ever happen to any of us.

We ordered, drinks, appetizers, a full meal. Soon after the first course was served, the man and woman at the next table began to disagree. Something personal. Who did What to Whom. By the time their coffee came, they were furious. Meantime, our table grew quiet. The novelists strained their ears. The lawyer rated arguments, points won and lost. In whispers we discussed who the two might be to one another. Husband and wife? Illicit lovers? June was certain the man was capable of violence. "He beats her," she said. "I'm sure of it. And yet . . ." she looked again . . . "maybe she's too big to beat." (June was really small. After she died I took some of her clothes as a special remembrance, including a terrific striped linen vest with twenty-four tiny buttons down the front. She was wearing the vest the first time I met her. I could not begin to close the vest without looking like the fat man who's regained all the weight he's lost. I hadn't realized. The way she dressed and carried herself, you couldn't tell. She gave the impression of size.)

Finally the woman stood, tossed her honey-colored mane of hair over one shoulder, and as if it was what she'd meant to do all along, in a single, graceful motion, picked up her water glass and dashed the water across the table into the man's face, then turned and walked away. Her high-heeled boots clicked against the floor. The door slammed. The waiters smiled. We were gaga. The man wiped his face and drank his coffee. In a few minutes the woman returned. She held out her hand. "The keys," she said. They left together.

"That's the trouble with Houston," June declared when they were gone. "You storm out in a beautiful, dramatic huff, then get to the parking lot and there you are. You've got no way to get home."

I believe the *maitre d'* actually came over and apologized to June for the scene, as if she'd hired him to be in charge of customers' behavior. June just laughed. After dinner, she took us into the back rooms, beyond the dining area. "This is where the bedroom was," she said. "Here is where Mother used to sleep. That's where the armoire was. Out there beyond the parking lot and the bayou, were the stables." I don't think I ever saw her any happier, there with friends in what once had been her mother's house.

As June Davis, June had lived in Houston during most of her childhood. Her mother was a Wortham and during those early years, she was a proper little, privileged Texas girl. She showed horses at Pin Oaks Stables and went to Kinkaid and Shipley. She even made her debut with the other Allegro girls . . . reluctantly we are told and I believe that. (I also imagine June finding a sweet spot of pleasure somewhere in the fluttery proceedings, although there is no telling where, June did love to amaze, surprise and shock.) Her teen years were spent with her mother Cad and her sister Fanny in a small house on the far edge of what Houstonians now call shallow River Oaks. She went off to Vassar for a while but, hating the north, came back home, went to Rice and eventually got her master's in literature. All four of her children were born in Houston. "Everyone was having big families then," she once told me. "We thought we were supposed to."

When her marriage foundered June fearlessly took her children and up and went to live in Greenwich Village, like that. "The Village was all the rage then," she explained. She enrolled the children in schools, met new people. She listened to jazz at the Village Vanguard, introduced herself to Miles Davis, studied writing at the New School. One night, watching a pottery factory near Sheridan Square burn, she had another bright idea: why not buy the factory when it was in disrepair, then fix it up. She bought the factory for a song and became one of the first loft-dwellers in Manhattan. She began writing novels. McGraw-Hill published her first, *Applesauce*. Then with her partner Parke Bowman June decided to up and move again, to Vermont this time, where she and Parke dabbled in the rural experiment and established a publishing company, Daughters, Inc, which became quite respected and well-known for publishing a distinguished list of women's novels. Then June got restless again. From Vermont—"We'd done rural"—she and Parke moved back to Houston. June needed to write that novel.

She was like water, June. It was her mind. It moved so fast. Some people you know are smart, but it's a quiet thing. In company they breast their cards. In June's presence you could see it happening— she was not shy—her mind leaping and skating, never predictable, always supple, on the track of a new idea. If there is any truth to F. Scott Fitzgerald's theory that one measure of intelligence is the ability to hold two opposing thoughts in the mind at the same time, then June was a genius. She had earned every feminist credential in the book, but people expecting a textbook response were often brought up short. She was loyal, but no sheep. She sometimes got this look on her face, the way musicians do when they play a particularly difficult passage, as if their fingers are a shock to them too. She was capable—always—of surprising herself. This was the source, I think, of her rippling, endless capacity for delight.

"Let's start playing bridge again," she once announced. And after twenty years of abstaining, she returned ardently, devotedly, brilliantly to the table, a standing game every weekend, rubber after rubber, far into the night.

No good writer sees life straight on. June's vision came from as admirably oblique an angle as I have ever been witness to. I miss that a lot, her *take* on things, and how her mind worked. There are stories I know she'd get a kick out of. I miss sharing them. And I swear, I have no idea what she'd have to say about a one of them.

Baby Houston is the book June moved to Houston to write. When the book opens, the central character, Baby, is the same age as the century, 39. And Houston is a baby too, barely more than a hundred years old, not yet the brash boomtown it would become but a smallish, gossipy, very Southern city, easy to get around in. June's babies—her city, her mother. Both of whom raised her. Houston's been looking for its novelist for a long time. June may well be it, its own daughter, come home.

Beverly Lowry

PART I

1939–1941

I AM THE widow called Baby.

I am the widow who came back to Houston a year ago with two daughters.

And this is the house that Oscar rented for us.

Why would a big brother choose such a house for his sister? Because he thought it would be convenient—for my dates to pick me up (it is three blocks from Main Street), for the children to get to school (two miles), for him to drop by on his way home to the Warwick Hotel? He said it was a stopgap house. Friday I will tell him that the gap has broken wide open again.

I cleaned this house last year and I am tired of it; an ugly house is only interesting at first dirty sight. Last year I cleaned the windowsills, the panes, the woodwork back to a mottled white; cleaned behind the radiators, wiped off the kitchen mucus as I would the nose of a runny child, wiped the whole place down with ammonia—behind the stove, the toilet, the kitchen cabinets; I spent a month cleaning in the ninety-plus heat of September while the Germans reduced Poland to rubble.

I was already up cleaning when the girls came in for an anxious breakfast, which they would carry like a stone through the terrifying school day; I cleaned to protect them from those halls of loud strangers, from Texas twangs echoing off concrete walls when their ears were used to soft, wooden Memphis speech in an old one-house school; I cleaned to promise them order, promise them that everything could be stripped back to its honest surfaces and seen for just what it was; I cleaned to show them that I could tackle and control their home even though the father was dead.

Every evening at four I stopped, pulled off the sweaty shirt and shorts and underwear and hung them on a towel rack to drip, bathed and dried my hair before a fan, put on pink mock-linen, and had the drink tray ready at five when anyone could drop in.

I smiled and believed I could do it all—I have the constitution of a horse and a famous disposition; I believed I could take a crumbling rent house and immaculate it and still be baby-pie at five—and still pay attention to the girls' separate whines or sobs, and still listen when a friend was troubled, and still keep one fat brown eye out for a suitable husband.

Then Hallie and Mary Cowan began to fight. The house has three bedrooms so they each have their own room, but they have to share a bathroom, a hall, a living room and a kitchen; every time one met the other in the general part of the house there was a fight. They no longer argued, they fought. Mary Cowan is older and taller but Hallie is stronger and reckless; last week she chased Mary Cowan down the hall and threw the iron at her head; Mary Cowan ducked into her room and got her door closed just in time, but the iron made an ugly gash in her door, head height. Estelle, the fourth maid in ten months, waited until I got home to tell me and then said she was quitting.

The house is in a slum. Children live up or down to their surroundings, I told Oscar. Men can walk down the sidewalk and look right into the living room, right into my bedroom.

In winter, of course, I can close the curtains and sleep hidden past daylight—but when is winter in Houston? During all other times I train myself to wake at dawn, get up, and shut my bed off from the sidewalk—watching out my window for curious night strollers, feeling each minute that I can be *caught*—arms up-stretched, in the act of seizing the curtain edge—like a mock Jesus, ridiculous in flimsy night dress. But to cover myself with the curtain and clumsily pull from inside is not possible for my dignity, my insistence that I have a right to be here in my own bedroom, rent house or not, and will not hide. Unbroken sleep is a thing of the past—a thing of two stories or cold climates or marriage.

You can live in a cute little cottage if you have a husband, but a woman alone with two adolescent daughters is given exactly the respect her house gets. Sis agrees with me and she told Oscar, "It is a disgrace that the Baby is living in that house with those children while *you* . . ." Sis is older than Oscar and trades on her temper; he is afraid of her. But she didn't get me another house.

Hallie is my most adolescent daughter; she acts like she is in love with me. Since her bedroom is right next to mine, she can hear me talking in my sleep, sorting out my day. Tonight I protest that I cannot answer the questions because they overlap; I am sitting up in bed saying twiddle-twiddle-twiddle nurnurnur reese-reese-reese, pointing my head in alternate directions, my eyes wide open staring at Hallie as if I were awake. I go to bed lace-enclosed from my marriage; Hallie is wrapped in child's pajamas suitable for sleeping porches or bedrooms where men can look right in from the sidewalk. I wake up with her cotton arm around my shoulders, her nose inhaling Ponds cold cream from my cheek.

Ponds appears on my face every afternoon between four and five while I sit in front of a fan and my dressing table mirror; appears every night at bedtime when I clean my face for sleep. It is a barrier between the respectable distance her nose must keep from my cheek most of the time and the longing of her nose for my cheek—the soft private land of the cheek, which never gives away its secrets. The other parts of the face are shamelessly transparent. Eyes tug at the heart but my cheek catches Hallie's brain. It is my strength. On tiptoe Hallie cannot kiss either cheek unless I bend cooperatively toward her mouth.

But prone she has got me. "I love you!" she announces, breath impatient right up against my cheek. "I love you, Mother." Her weight holds down my shoulder.

I am pinned in a nightmare offering love while Houston growls just outside my window, I am hemmed in by a cotton arm still round with original fat. Her freckles are fearless and no daughter knows how true the color of her eyes shines at midnight.

"When I grow up I am going to get you a house of your very own."

I am staring at seagreen rimmed by black lashes and original love. I imagine that I am captain of a different ark, loading pairs of every species at three months old—that I am looking at all the trusting, adoring animal babies in the world. I cannot believe how much I love her. My mouth reaches out for her smells—cotton, grass, sleep, child. My teeth clench; I want to bite her in two. My eyes squeeze shut. I am maddened: I feel like growling; she is like a pulse in my throat. Her mind covers my mind like fire.

"I promise," she whispers.

I am conscious of my breasts pressing against her chest and let go. I am shuffling her back to bed; patting her shoulder; I kiss her goodnight and shut her door but the need to keep patting her shoulder is glued to my palm like an itch.

I PARK IN front of Cad's house. I want to sit on her side porch
under the old trees dripping with moss—moss hanging like lazy,
gray women. No one seems to be home. I walk in, look in the
kitchen, get a glass of ice water, and go to the porch. It is dark and
cool and very quiet. The moss moves in gray threads like horses'
tails; there is a breeze here near the bayou and the trees rustle like
taffeta.

Cad and I had a party here last April for the women who
helped us work for Oscar's candidate—a big man with the odd
name of Lyndon who was running against Pappy Lee O'Daniel for
the Senate. It was easy to get workers; no one wanted Texas to be
connected with that ridiculous Pass the Biscuits, Pappy politician.

The women had fun at the party even though Lyndon lost;
most of them had never seen a house like Cad's or known a woman
like her. Lyndon came to the party only for a few minutes but that
was long enough for Cad to take him to task. Lyndon was expan-
sively reassuring the ladies that we could avoid getting in the war,
that we could discuss the issues and settle them intelligently if only
we didn't panic. Cad is an amateur historian and, although I've
never seen her lose her temper, she raised her voice to Lyndon as if
he were far more than eight years younger than she. She said if she
were president she would declare war today; that we would have to
get in it and we'd better do it while Britain was still free or we
would never win it. Lyndon said that he was sure this country
could win any war as long as it had ladies with Cad's spirit as its
citizens.

Cad was angry but curiously flushed when Lyndon left. He
has presence, we all agreed. Presence is what Hallie calls brilliance—she means what her mare emanates in the show ring beyond her actual conformation and gaits. Presence isn't sex appeal,
but I too was feeling what Cad felt—both of us at forty responding
to April like fat pillows longing to be pressed down. I don't think

Cad and Johnny do much of that sort of thing any more. Cad laughed in that scoffing way she has when she's embarrassed and said, "Oh, Baby, it's power. You know *that*."

It is slipping under the taffeta of the leaves and sliding into my nose curiously mixed with mildew and mold from the porch glider. Everything needs painting, especially me. I need a new coat of glossy white to reflect and protect my parts, which are showing through all the chipped-off spots; I am rusting in a soft nervous process which sends bright new orange colors through me when air reaches my underparts. My left foot on the floor rocks the glider; I am lying on an unyielding plastic pillow with my chin on my chest staring at my own dress, which is the orange color of rust in Houston—light and airy, flakes piled on flakes. The top flake is lifting in the breeze from the ceiling fan; the bottom flake is just forming; I am porous. I am cool and also melting. I am lying on a support of powerlessness, rusting and rusting.

None of the men I know have presence except Benjamin Falk and he is too old for God.

At almost five Cad drives up and joins me on the porch; it is the hour to have a drink.

We stand for a moment facing each other, letting the nearness of our bodies do the hugging, the kissing, the patting that other women squander in words. Cad pokes me with her eyes, jabbing little slivers of electric charge into my bloodstream; her eyes are spliced gray and crystal.

I tell her the story of the dice game, the forged note. I can tell by her face that she's going to laugh. "Wasn't it Oscar who bought a roulette wheel so the girls would have something to do when they used to come visit?" I watch so hard I miss what she says—but it echoes near my hearing and I think I heard and I repeat to make sure, earning myself a familiar scoff—"Are you taking dictation, Baby?"

I am taking a lesson in heart. I can only live in my attic (what Cad calls brain) for a short time, then only on clear blue days—I can't breathe in that dust. My heart is my living room. Cad yanks me like strings, determined I will move to her level; I hang on her toes like weights, keeping *them* at least down here with me.

"Mary Cowan loves boarding school but Hallie flatly refuses to go." How can I make her go? How can I break her heart?

I am asking the wrong person: Cad deliberately keeps her sons at arm's length—she is terrified of the Oedipus complex. She claims it doesn't apply to mothers and daughters. But I am terrified

8

of Freud—fear stemming from ignorance, I guess. I stare at Cad's hair. Strands stand up in curls like parentheses, like question marks, like pubic hair springing . . . I take a quick sip of bourbon. "I'll never find a husband if I have to cope with Hallie the whole time."

"Why don't you ask Oscar to help? He's paying for it." Cad chuckles. "Do him good to see what happens between writing the check and riding the horse."

Soothed by ice-cold bourbon, I melt back into my famous disposition. It is a disposition kept placid by handing things over to men; Cad's solution meets my inclinations like a bulb in a socket. Oscar should have married Cad . . .

Why should I suddenly remember Daddy's will? . . . "In consideration of the love and affection which I have and bear unto my son, Oscar R. Yancey . . ." I feel like crying. "What time is it getting to be?"

Cad has a successful brother too. "Maybe I can help. I'm not much good at reading minds, though."

"I was thinking . . ." I feel my voice turn pink. "I'm so lucky to have a brother like Oscar, so successful . . . I mean, I'd hate to be a widow raising two girls without him to help me. He's been just wonderful to us . . ."

"Does he get along with the girls?"

"I'm sure he loves them as if they were his own. And they love him too."

"Then he's the one to talk to Hallie about boarding school."

"Oh, I don't think he can *talk* . . ."

Cad snorts with laughter.

"You know what I mean."

"Exactly." Cad reaches for our glasses. "Let's have one more. I know exactly what you mean." She says something else from the kitchen which I can't hear.

"Hallie's the only one besides me who can talk to him," I say when she comes back. "She's the only one who isn't afraid of him." Since Hallie actually did graduate from junior high and isn't in trouble at all, I allow myself to admire the skill involved in her joke. Particularly since it wasn't meant for me. And Cad, my public opinion standard, doesn't think it was bad. The bourbon releases a burst of affection for Hallie and I grin. "I think *he's* afraid of *her*."

Cad crosses her blunt spectatored feet on an adjacent chair. "I've always paid more attention to Mary Cowan—because she's older, I guess. I think I'd like to get to know Hallie."

"Maybe you could talk to her."

"Maybe the D.R. could. Isn't she out there a lot?"

"She's growing hooves." I giggle briefly, catch myself. "No, the D.R. is hopeless. He's weak-minded on the subject of Hallie. If she said she didn't want to go to boarding school that would be that."

"Well, a lot of people we know send their children to Lamar. It's supposed to be a pretty good school . . ."

"It's different with you. You don't have daughters." Suddenly I see the daughters I've loved since birth, the little girls with their curious hands and eyes that blinked to stay awake past bedtime, their darling bodies that moved in unbelievable ways when they climbed, played hopscotch or swinging statue, horsed around in the water . . . bodies now shaping out like grown girls' bodies but still so fresh you were afraid to touch them hard for fear they would bruise—I see them as if they are waiting bodies, decoys, lures, bait for terrible traps where snarling wild animals will converge on them and tear them to bits . . . I want to fling myself into the traps instead but I am rusting to shreds, unsuitable for bait and at the same hideous moment unable to protect them either and I hate myself. But most of all I want to encase them in plastic eggs and keep them safely in the playroom. I have already lost Mary Cowan—while I was nursing the sick man she grew up; her eyes are now scanning the horizon; she knows; she is fifteen; she is looking outward. I feel tears streaming down my cheeks and Cad patting my back and trying to say the right things but I can't stop crying, all I want to do is to grab Hallie and to seal her in a plastic case and to keep her in the back room where I can watch over her and I am ashamed of myself.

The sun is directly in my eyes now, driving west across Houston. Because of it Gaius goes from his office to the Country Club instead of going home; he used to tell his wife he could not possibly drive to River Oaks until the sun set. His wife died this spring, leaving Gaius as a future beau.

I turn down Main Street toward the Warwick Hotel. Since the Duchess is in Santa Fe for the summer, I should have called Oscar first, but if he isn't there at least I can have a drink with the servants before I face the west sun back to my house. Oscar's kitchen is my country club, I think and giggle, feeling better.

The Warwick rises up at the merge of Montrose and Main and looks out over Hermann Park and, in the distance, the Rice Institute. Mother lived here after Daddy's death; Sister and the D.R. lived here until last year, and Oscar and the Duchess occupy a top floor apartment at the end of a wing, giving them three exposures. The lobby is furnished like a parlor in parrots and gilt, with chairs where ladies from fiction sit. Coming in under the porte cochère, leaving my car with the doorman with a familiar greeting, I feel the energy of the rich lengthen my spine.

Etta's elevator is open. She speaks warmly to me and we chat about Mary Cowan and Hallie . . . Etta remembering, as we pass the ninth floor, the summer the girls wrote anonymous poison-pen letters, slipped them under the doors of people's apartments, and brought the FBI to the Warwick.

I am welcomed with squeals and hugs by Julia and the new maid, Betty; a huge grin from William. Even when Oscar and the Duchess are home I always go into the kitchen to say hello. Now, Julia offers me a drink and I sit down with it at the kitchen table and ask her how the orange juice is.

"Oh, Miss Baby." Julia laughs. "I slipped six oranges in with the groceries and fixed fresh juice for Mr. Yancey's breakfast. It was just before Mrs. Yancey was to leave and I figured she wouldn't be looking in the icebox. But she looked at that glass, *and* she looked . . ."

"At noon when she finally got up?" I say.

Julia laughs again. "That's right. I should have known to wash that glass first thing. Well, she saw those pieces of pulp on the glass and said, 'Julia, what kind of orange juice is this? Canned orange juice doesn't have this pulp in it.' And I say, 'Oh, that's a new kind that's made to look just *like* fresh. That's where the pulp come from.' She ask, 'Does it cost more?' 'No, ma'am,' I say. 'It was on sale and it cost less than the regular kind we been using.' 'All right, Julia,' she say. 'But you know I'm responsible for paying the grocery bills and with everything so high I just can't afford to pay for fresh oranges.'"

Betty giggles wildly. "*She* think she pay the grocery bill. Wonder what she'd do if she was ever to walk into a store and see what groceries *cost*?"

"Po' Mr. Yancey," Julia says. "He has to write two checks: one for her to pay the little bill Joe Jett make up for us and one for the rest of the bill I slip to him."

"You'd think she'd be glad she could afford fresh oranges for his breakfast," I say.

"Yes, ma'am, that's right," William says. "That's just what you would think."

I feel a little uncomfortable around William and turn back to speak to the women. "With all the money Mr. Yancey has you'd think he could at least have fresh orange juice for breakfast if he wants it."

"Oh, we see that he gets it all right," Betty says laughing.

"Oh, he gets it all right," Julia says. "It's just that we has to buy some cans of that other to put up on top of the garbage where Mrs. Yancey can look at them."

William hears the step at the door and quickly goes to open it for Oscar. I get up. "Now you'll be staying for dinner with us, won't you, Miss Baby?" Julia says.

Right now I'd agree to stay here for life. I say, "If you're sure you have enough?"

"Oh, we got plenty!" Julia grins again. "We always got plenty during the month of August."

IN GALVESTON MY skin rises up for a touch of air blowing in from the Gulf. It is ten degrees cooler here than in Houston, but warm still. Tar, salt, wet shells mix with my new Tabu and Cad's timid Fleurs Houbigant as our car crosses the narrow causeway onto the island. One whiff of that air and I know I am beautiful.

Cad and I walk down the pier together with the men following; the Gulf is the color of slate and decorated with foam, jellyfish, and an unusual amount of phosphorus, but Cad is talking about me so I don't stop to look.

"Is that Tallulah Jones, please, ma'am?"

Although everyone assumes the Rangers have been paid off, the pier is so long that even at a run they can't reach the Balinese Room itself until the gaming tables have been converted into something legal like billiards. However, we all have an alias in case we are raided and our names must appear in the papers. My mother's maiden name was Jones, her black eyes straight from the Welsh coal mines (from the Spanish Armada, Cad claims wryly).

The glass doors into the Balinese Room reflect my luck, my birthday image: skirts are short and my legs are long and fine with chiffon breaking over my knees like tiny whitecaps. My head is high and back like Tallulah's and I know, as we wait for Johnny and Dutch to swing open the door for us, that I am just right. We are slapped in the face with air conditioning, with plush and mirrors and Balinese lanterns; we are infants jarred into taking deep new breaths.

My date and my brother come from separate corners of their table, Oscar with his arms outstretched like wings, Dutch running like a squirrel to do his duty as escort—hold my chair, order my drink, dance; he learned it all before his wife went into the insane asylum.

"Why, looka there, here comes the Baby!" Oscar says. We hug, hands not sure where to go rapidly patting each other's back.

My arms are on top since I am inches taller than Oscar, even barefoot.

"Brother, this is the best birthday party anyone ever had for me." I bend my knees to dimple at him face level.

"Let me look at you!" Oscar steps back. "If you don't look as pretty as an ice-cream cone at the drugstore counter on a hot Saturday . . . here, sit down, honey." Dutch moves the appropriate chairs and we all sit.

Oscar is built close to the ground like our mother and like her already going to belly although he is not yet fifty. He has the black-brown Welsh eyes and dark hair like Sis but also the big nose, low eyebrows, and padded face that Sis's genes refused. Sis is definitely the family beauty—aristocratic, dark, Goyaesque; I look more like my father—taller, fairer, more everyday English, I hope. I like having a face that can be moved into different arenas when the action changes instead of one which makes a single statement all your life long. Tonight I am caramel—eyes, hair, dress; dabbed with whipped cream—shoulders, rest of dress, and teeth (I hope). I give Oscar another dazzling smile. Pleasing Oscar is how I make my living.

All my friends are here: Boots and Jasper, the Fascinator and Raggedy William (our Texas Lucius Beebe), Drukie and Jim (who have a daughter who is Hallie's only Houston friend), the Tennessee Walking Horse who claims a wife in Tennessee but he's been down here for six months and we haven't seen wife yet, Nanpan, Teensie, Titta, Grandfather (no relation to anybody), the Mogul (our only other intellectual), Bitsy, Jonesy, Trip, and Benjamin Falk besides Oscar, Cad, Johnny, Dutch Nathan and me.

"We are twenty-one, a magic number," I say happily.

"She's free, white, and twenty-one!" Dutch grins and pulls his chair too close to mine. He's been working on his sense of humor since his wife went crazy and hasn't got it yet. Of course, I am forty, the age of the century.

Oscar rattles his ice. "Well, I guess it's up to the Baby and me to get the dancing started," he says, picking up my arm like a fork to signal that everyone can begin.

I tell Oscar again what a darling idea this party is, bending my knees as we begin a small town Southern foxtrot with dips. On the dance floor several men stop to speak to Oscar. While they are speaking we cease moving our feet but not our bodies; we are two couples swaying in place while the men of us extend joviality across the women's backs. My dance with Oscar is over and I straighten my spine.

I walk slowly back to the table so I can tell him how proud we all are of his business success and that I hope he does even better next year because I have to get those children out of that slum. I say, "You've been so wonderful, Brother, but I just can't stand another year of this . . ."

Our table is near. He looks terrified and squeezes my arm. "You call me first thing in the morning . . ."

"We just have to have a better *house* . . ."

"Well," he says to his guests. "Let's get the boys and girls lined up together and bring on the caviar."

After dinner we have the birthday cake. It is carried out blazing with all forty candles and a dozen pink ribbons springing out of it in a circle around "Happy B-Day to the Baby." Oscar has on his rabbit look; his lips make tiny nibbling motions. He tells me that each one of the ladies is supposed to get a slice of cake with a ribbon attached; we see, when the cake is cut, that the ribbons are tied on their hidden end around a twenty-five-dollar chip, gold-colored, of course. We all yelp like happy puppies and I lean over to kiss Oscar whose expression is divided between pleasure at the fun of his idea and disgust at the mess on the money. Disgust wins. He beckons to the waiter: "Now take all those chips back in the kitchen and wash off that cake."

After I've won ten dollars and cashed in thirty-five—enough to buy anything I can think of at the moment—I stand in the bar by the piano Peck Kelley is playing; I have an arm around Dutch and the other around the Tennessee Walking Horse while we sing "In a Little Honky Tonk Village in Texas" over and over again. I feel that this is my Houston. Seen misty-eyed from the sporting palaces of Galveston, Houston appears something to claim, a queendom, even possibly an obligation.

Oscar and Cad do not leave the tables until it is time to go home.

I think Benjamin Falk will be a new beau although he is too old for God.

I'M EITHER GOING to kill someone or have a nervous breakdown. I've always known that people who can't afford it don't have nervous breakdowns; that leaves me with murder. Double murder. Mother strangles teenage daughters in a cute little cottage that backs on Shepherd.

I'm killing Mary Cowan first. In her perfect little rust-colored shorts she asks me if she can take the car to her art lesson. I tell her again how furious I am at their calling the police last night . . . I am screaming again: "You humiliated me in front of rednecks! You subjected Ben Falk—a friend of Oscar's, an important man— to a common police car! I can't even sit in my own house in private—how dare you call the police on me . . ." Blood is exploding in my skull; I think I am having a stroke. I am gasping for breath like Sis when she has an asthma attack. But through watery eyes I see Mary Cowan, my own daughter, standing as prim as a model.

"It's your own fault," she says. "You should have told us when you got home."

"I *what*? I have to announce everything I do? I have to inform you of my every step or else you'll call the police? How dare you!"

"We thought it was a burglar." Her mouth, covered with Raven Red lipstick, gives a little smirk. "There weren't any lights on at all, you know."

"Get out of here."

"May I please use the car?"

"*No.*" I see that mouth quiver back to helplessness and think, *Good.* The car is right outside—William and Julia brought it over this morning. I don't want to use it but I'm damned if she can have it. "Take the bus. Walk. Crawl. But get out of my sight."

"Oh, *Mother . . .*"

"Don't 'Mother' me, Mary Cowan Davis." I wish I could let myself throw something at her. My fists are clenched when she stomps off. I hear her on the telephone, that supercilious teenage voice patiently telling some friend, probably her buddy Brute, that Mother is having one of her fits.

I could die from shame. I was sitting on the porch with Benjie and the lights were out; I think his hand was on my thigh, I think my skirt was up, I know we were so intertwined that we had to scramble when the flashlight shone into our faces. There were two policemen and a man and woman the girls had waked up to use their telephone—the girls said they'd climbed out of their room onto the garage roof and ran down the street because they saw a light go on and then off downstairs and called and no one answered. The man and woman—a middle-aged couple—were fascinated; they stared at everything. The police decided that my blanch of shame was fear, that Benjie had threatened me. They hustled him into the police car, radioed the station to see if he was a wanted man even after he identified himself; they hung around until Ben called himself a taxi; they watched him leave. Ben does look like a character: bushy eyebrows like John L. Lewis, jet-black circles dipping into both cheeks, swarthy skin, massive frame—to an ignorant policeman he looks like a foreigner.

"*Why* can't I use the car? You're not using it." Brute apparently will not come pick her up.

There is no longer any reason. I just stare at her.

"Just give me one good reason . . ."

"No. No, no, *no*."

"That's not a reason." Mary Cowan is going to succeed in life. She has the persistence of a beaver. She will gnaw me into a cone until I topple. I still stare. If she knew how much my hands ache to choke her at this moment she would run for her life.

"It's not *fair*." She is screaming and whining at the same time, contorting her face, failing to make it ugly, tossing her auburn curls as if they could break hearts—there are no hearts around. "Just because the police found *you* sitting in the dark with that old man—just because *you* were bad I don't see why *I* have to be punished."

"Go to your room."

"No."

"Go to your room." I grab her arm and twist it, grip it to bruise it; I slap her face.

Stunned, she screams, "I despise you!" for both of us and runs upstairs stopping only to kick over the telephone table, telephone pad, pencil, ashtray, coffee cup left there.

I am becoming a monster. I can feel my skin leather, fingernails thicken to claws, chest and arms bulge with brutality; my teeth feel sharp as razors and lust to bite, rip, tear into the flesh that I have borne. Every muscle in my body is rigid with rage, paralyzed, frozen senseless like old cold gray lava. But I have no den, cave, hole that I can run to and be dark and safe with this fury; I can only go upstairs to my room where trapped I can only shake with tears where *they* can hear me.

Hallie knocks on my door. Moving as implacably as one of those old whaling ships, she drops to the floor in front of me; she has filled herself with stones and blocks the harbor.

I feel I am looking into the eyes of a sleeping whale: one eye asleep, the other eye watching over its twin. She can see that I don't consider her reworking an old report on Hetty Green to be a good bet if one wants to gain admission to Miss Askew's school; she watches to see how I will manage to persuade her to submit something which will win for her the very thing she wants least. I have the distinct feeling that she is more interested in learning this technique than in the outcome of our struggle over boarding school.

"Since Miss Askew's is a school founded by the Quakers," I begin, "I wonder whether your report doesn't belittle their beliefs—I know you don't want to insult anyone's religion."

She is surprised that Quakers still exist—having left them at the Susquehanna founding their first colony. I assure her they very much exist though not in our part of the country. "They are good people—opposed to violence, materialism, ostentation in dress. They certainly would not approve of Hetty's father, who considered moneymaking the great love and object of his life."

"But Hetty was different. The reason they called her a witch was because she wore a plain black dress and never fixed herself up. She lived in boardinghouses, cooked her own meals, cleaned up after herself. She was famous for her frugality—in fact, somebody used her as an example to argue for an income tax: he said that since she never spent money she probably paid the government less than a day laborer because she escaped sales taxes." Hallie's foot is flapping like a fluke; she is caught in a position where if she defends Hetty and appeases the Quaker school she will lose her freedom. I am loath to use her integrity against her.

"This part is very nice," I say. I want my whale to smile. "You say that she told a woman who had been kind to her to get her money out of a certain bank and when the woman asked why, Hetty replied, 'The men in that bank are too good-looking.'"

I laugh.

Hallie smiles briefly.

"Maybe if you just left out the last paragraph." And I correct the punctuation and grammar, of course. "Somehow that paragraph sounds so . . . mean, I think." I feel that Hallie has switched eyes on me; I look up and imagine that the eye that was awake before now has closed and the one that slept now fixes me with refreshed power. I read the last paragraph aloud:

> She spent her life beating men and proving that she was the proper caretaker of the original Howland wealth. When she died her estate was at least one hundred million dollars. She was called the most detested woman in America. It was said that she was obsessed with pure dollar greed. It was claimed that she ruined the lives of her two children. Of herself she said, "I am in earnest, therefore they picture me heartless. I go my own way, take no partners, risk no man's fortune, therefore I am Madame Ishmael, set against every man." The Witch of Wall Street was held up as an example of what would happen to good little girls if they weren't satisfied with their trust funds. They might end up with a hundred million dollars.

Through the soft, full curves of Hallie's half-child's face I see, as she holds her stare, the other half twitch and tighten, sudden preview of an angry adult. I am alarmed. But I am now convinced that I am right: the last paragraph—Hetty herself—is mean. "What did your teacher say about the report?"

Now Hallie's face is all adult as she mimics the detested teacher. "'Are you in favor of witches? Do you sympathize with a woman who is out to beat men including her own husband? Do *you* believe that the dollar is almighty?'"

In spite of myself, my mother's heart repudiates the teacher on the instant. I put my hand on Hallie's damp, glossy hair. "Well, for heaven's sake, Hetty wouldn't have had to spend her life proving that she could make money if everyone hadn't been against her, would she?"

Hallie nods, totally unconvincingly.

"Let me think about it." I kiss Hallie's even damper forehead and she goes back to her room. I mean I want to think about miscegenation—maybe after all money is too complicated a subject for thirteen-year-olds. I have one other choice: I reread the story she wrote about the turkey queen. A white boy fights a colored boy for talking to her, the crowd beats up the colored boy, an older white man interferes finally and says the queen is the colored boy's half sister . . . I think Hallie has been reading Lillian Smith. Will the Quakers forgive her for writing about illicit sex because she hates racism? Cad will know.

I see that Hetty insisted on making her own money but when it came to the next generation she groomed her son to take over her business just like Daddy did. I have the same headache Hetty used to have—the one that comes from being forbidden to ride astride.

OSCAR CAME BY this morning; he found Hallie waiting for Uncle Doctor to pick her up to go riding. Mary Cowan was still at the breakfast table drinking coffee, I was getting up the laundry; just after Oscar said hello to us we scattered like scared rabbits leaving Hallie to him.

With the bluster, the gaiety, the false heartiness that tells you a shy man is going to deal with a child, Oscar arranged himself in a serious-talk position vis-à-vis Hallie. I could picture her face—when she knows she's about to be manipulated her face divides itself as it did with me the other morning into that of a sleeping whale. Her solid body, not much shorter than Oscar's, solidifies itself even more, looking as round and deceptively placid as a whale's. I find this habit of hers very distracting; I guess that Brother will be thoroughly unnerved to have his chuckles and chatter fall onto a waiting whale; I'm sure he got quickly to the point.

I know how he must have put it—that Hallie wanted her mother to be happy, that her mother had had a great tragedy, sadness, and now needed to rebuild her life, that her mother would naturally want to find in time another husband, that of course Mary Cowan and Hallie would want her to—that their mother was an attractive still-young woman and should not have her search for a husband encumbered by having almost grown daughters in the house . . . phrasing it thus will hurt Hallie most of all.

I told Oscar to assure Hallie that the only reason I want her to go to boarding school—besides wanting the best education for her, of course—is that when she is in the house I naturally want to devote most of my time to her and for *that* reason I could find a husband more easily for all our sakes if she . . . I am now not convinced of any of this. I have assumed that the usual reasons for wanting the girls away at school are sufficient if not a complete picture. I feel now that I have been pushed by some other force, of an invisible nature, which made me hasty, careless, irreversibly shot down a path which could be far different from anything I expect. I feel the sense I often have in barely remembered dreams—that I hold a small girl in each arm and am looking at something which is covered up; if I could put down the children and lift that cover, I would know what I need to know but the dream is occupied—by oceans, cliffs, snakes, those sorts of nightmare things; I am prevented from putting down even one child; I am left futilely trying to pierce the cover with mere eyes. I shiver now; the cover is in the corner of my mind and I cannot reach it; I can only *see* it; as if with a sudden puncture my ball of optimism, inflated by trust in my own instincts, whooshes and goes flat.

I hear Hallie leave with Uncle Doctor and I return to Oscar. He has misjudged her silence, thinking it to be the same total acceptance of his logic, his right view, that he is accustomed to with his subordinates and says cheerfully that everything is settled. He thinks his language, like his perfectly cut suit, streamlines the bumps in the family. Hallie agreed to go to Miss Askew's this fall. Kissing me goodbye, Oscar says he is so glad he was able to have the little talk with Hallie, that he feels so much closer to her now.

That afternoon we cry together. Hallie is crying because she is sad about going away to school and from the dry, crumbling, much deeper pain that her own wishes, reasoning, her own instincts for her life have been discounted, circumvented by sophisticated uses of her love for me. I am crying because I have done wrong but will not correct it. I hold her and my tears mix with her hair.

Hallie's presence acts to deflect romantic urges inside me. I look up and see a daughter and romance won't come out. Acts like its presence would be obscene in the face of her innocence. Or would infect her with its contagion. Or would stop up my eyes and nose and she would burn to death. Around the girls my gears are in motherhood and racing is impossible. I have no clutch.

I am trying to laugh to shake us loose from these tears because I know that I am going ahead—full speed. My self-preservation won out over Hallie. Easily. Much too easily. So easily that I suspect there is death in a different sense at the end of my road. At my age, one can only choose between different lives. At Hallie's, one is choiceless. Somewhere in between for a few heady years—I explain to Hallie that when she is a little older she will be able to choose lives upon lives, she can have everything and give up nothing . . . her tear-scarred, blotched, furious, aching face dares me to believe that I know anything about her at all.

I know that she can have her turn later; this is mine.

24

I hate dirty jokes but I am always inadvertently saying something that sounds perfectly innocent to me only to have Cad burst out laughing and make a big thing over it. I guess that's how Hallie and Mary Cowan learn about sex—through language; at least the linear, verbal facts of sex.

This afternoon I say to Cad, "What is more fun than an ice-cold martini in a halcyon nook?" as I am taking our drinks onto the overgrown porch.

Cad answers instantly. "Not *my* idea of fun." Then she says, "Now honestly, Baby, don't tell me you don't know what you're saying."

"What?" I say guardedly.

"Nook."

Of course I can guess now but I answer from my own innocence *before*. "A nook is a little place partly hidden, like a tiny cave, as in nook and cranny."

Cad snorts. "I am familiar with the cliché nook and cranny."

I know I am going to get dumped into the boiling pot. "Then what's the matter with nook?"

Cad turns to Hallie. "I bet Hallie knows. Isn't it unbelievable that a woman your mother's age could be so *ingenue?*"

I doubt that Hallie knew at all but I'm sure she does now. The other way they learn about sex is through those awful atrocity stories about the Japanese. Lately there's been a deluge of literature about what the Japs do to the Chinese—who are presented as passive, helpless, waiting in tiny family compounds for their sex-crazed bloody island neighbors to find them. They have always just come in from gathering rice and are delicately eating tiny dinners when the door is kicked open and the devil soldiers invade, leering. I don't mind the children reading Pearl Buck but that other trash—and I know they get them from Punchy's grandfather. He leaves them in the bathroom.

I also know that Punchy and Hallie at least aren't quite sure what is being done and why, so they sit around in their underwear working out the details together. Or boldly inventing hypothetical situations dealing directly with each other's bodies under the summer nightclothes on Punchy's sleeping porch. "Suppose I touch your bust here"—I can hear them; I know the touch is made—"I can see that that would feel nice. But how can a bayonet here"—a second touch, longer—"going inside you"—a shudder from the one called *you* and the sentence left dangling.

I missed something. Then I heard Punchy: "I like your mother, too. I like her better than all the parents I know—I mean I love my own mother but I think Baby is the cutest of them all. I think she's just darling. But Hallie, you couldn't mean that . . . I mean, she could never feel about you the way she could about a man."

"She couldn't?"

"You wouldn't *want* her to!"

For a few seconds I was too paralyzed to move. I heard Hallie's "no"—the monosyllable so flat it was impossible to know what it was denying. Then Hallie said, "I get something from what you said when you were imagining. For this particular feeling we're discussing, you have to slip up on someone's blind side. I've been just like a child. I've just been too direct." I heard sounds of a body flopping down onto a mattress. "Let's kiss goodnight."

I heard a second body flop down on the mattress and tiptoed away from the door.

"Do you like your new mink cape?" I begin with how thoughtful and generous Oscar is, but Mary Cowan interrupts: "How do you think you got it?"

That soldier Cad and Johnny brought over told an off-color story last night. He asked, "How does a girl get a mink?" When someone said, "How?" he said, "The same way a mink gets a mink." Of course, he will never be invited back to my house.

"What do you mean?" I ask coldly.

"Hallie got it for you." Mary Cowan plops down on the sofa, watching my face, which I conceal behind motherhood.

"Really? I guess I thought it was Cad's idea."

"Oscar called here Monday around noon and asked Hallie to pick out your present from him. Do you know what the temperature was Monday at noon? Ninety-eight. He had the nerve to ask Hallie to jump on the bus and go downtown . ."

"He probably thought she could use the car."

"You were out in it." Mary Cowan's eyes are not as dark a brown as Sis's are but her hair is red and her eyes can flash just as effectively as if they were black. Was she mad at me for having the car? No, she was mad at Hallie for going downtown in shorts and huaraches.

"I told her to get dressed." It is the exasperated voice of a half-grown big sister. "But she said she didn't have anything suitable for wearing to the Smart Shop anyway and maybe they would recognize the eccentricities of the rich." She gives me a knowing look. "So Hallie walks into the Smart Shop bare-legged and scruffy and takes the elevator to the fur floor—the only customer. She was going to look over the furs first—she'd never heard of anything except mink—but the saleslady came right up as if she were a regular customer . . ." Mary Cowan grins, "or on the wrong floor. 'May I show you something in furs?' she asked Hallie. Hallie waited a minute and then said, 'I'd like to see something in furs,' as if it had just occurred to her." Mary Cowan clearly wishes she had been there to watch. "Of course the saleslady then said, 'Are you interested in a short coat—perhaps a jacket? What particular fur did you have in mind?' Hallie hadn't gotten to look at the names at all so she said, 'Mink.' Then she thought Oscar's charge account might have a limit on it so she added, 'Maybe a short cape since it's so hot.'"

We both laugh. "Ninety-eight is pretty hot for a full-length mink coat," I say.

"So the saleslady says, 'Yes, the winters in Houston are mild and make the short cape the most functional of all fur wraps.' She is talking like a machine—can't you just see Hallie standing there in her shorts practically barefoot?"

Unfortunately I can.

"Then the saleslady has to ask what size Hallie is and Hallie tells her the coat is a birthday present for her mother. The poor saleslady is first so relieved that the mink is at least going to a grown woman that it takes her a minute to be horrified at the size of the allowance this child must get. Unless she's stealing the coat . . ."

"Oh, she wouldn't think Hallie looks like a thief!"

"Well, she wondered, I bet. Then Hallie told her it was from her uncle, that he was paying for it but asked her to pick it out. So they finally decided on your cape—and it wasn't the cheapest one they had either. Hallie told the saleslady that you were tall and slender and the saleslady said, 'Yes, that's just the one that fur is made for.' And Hallie just smiled, accepting that betrayal of her precious animals, because she and the saleslady were pals now, spending Oscar's money." Mary Cowan laughs out loud and I wonder when I can be alone to feel whatever I will feel. "So the saleslady is writing up the charge and asks where Hallie wants her to send the coat. Hallie says she wants to take it because your birthday is the next day. The saleslady says, 'You want to take it.' And Hallie says, 'Yes, please. If you'd put it in a box.' Then the saleslady is muttering, 'Yes. Of course,' and trying to write TAKE across the send-to space as if the pencil were her only weapon for batting down the ugly head of suspicion—and the point breaks. 'I'm afraid I'll have to get an okay on this,' she says, embarrassed, denying their palship. 'I'm sure it'll be just fine but they have a rule here, you know, with purchases which . . .' are mink capes bought by bare-legged teenagers for their mother's birthdays and charged to an uncle and carried right out the door to the bus!"

Mary Cowan, although she is not at all shy in houses, is intimidated by strangers and public places and I can see that she admires Hallie's nerve enormously. I am about to say, She does have nerve, when I remember the last time I heard that phrase was in reference to Hetty Green . . .

"So Hallie tells her she can call Uncle Oscar at his office and gives her the number. In a minute the saleslady comes back all smiles. 'Everything's *fine*,' she says. 'The charge is all in order. I talked to Mr. Yancey himself. He sounded a little surprised . . .' Then Hallie says, 'Well, he didn't know exactly what kind of fur I was going to get her. He'd suggested ermine for evening . . .' she'd gotten to look at the tags by now. The saleslady says, 'I'm sure she'll love this. You can wear mink so many more places than ermine. Although ermine's beautiful too, particularly if you have several furs.'

"So Hallie hints that she might be back to pick out your Christmas present and tucks that huge elegant brown box under her bare arm and hops on the bus on home. I couldn't believe it when she showed it to me. Would you like some more coffee?"

She goes to get it, returning with a folded paper in her teeth; as she unfolds it I recognize Cad's birthday poem to me. From a declamation stance, mid-rug, Mary Cowan reads it aloud to show we conspire:

> The Baby one night had her wish
> For a dinner date—fortyish;
> But he made a mistake,
> Said, "The lady will take
> Something light in a chafing dish."
> Now our Baby was all smiles and dimples;
> "In your style I don't want to put crimples,
> But this lady can drink
> Anything that's not pink
> So to hell with those cute Shirley Temples."
> "And good God," said our Baby with feeling
> And a furious glance at the ceiling,
> "Bring a thick juicy steak
> Or I'll know You're a fake
> And I'll no more to You be appealing."

My daughter's face expresses a beautiful daughter's delight that her mother is different and an equal delight that this fact delights the daughter. My hand cups her head in a kiss. Not so different as you might think, I should be saying to her but what mother willingly throws away a moment when the shine in a brown eye you made is aimed at you?

Holding a large box outstretched like a bad smell, Cad calls from the porch: "Guess who called me this morning long distance and asked me to do her a little favor?"

"The Duchess. She knows perfectly well my birthday was yesterday but she pretends she doesn't." I take the box gift-wrapped we're sure by Julia, tear off the wrapping and lift one end of the lid.

"Is it something you've always wanted?" Cad says.

I raise the lid farther and see cloth that looks like it might become a robe or lounging shirt.

"Is it very beautiful?" Cad's voice is perfect for illuminating the faint colors in common words.

My voice changes with the colors I wear; today I am in ice-blue and white. "Hmm. Not to just anybody. I'd say this particular . . . robe calls for an acquired taste."

"How thoughtful of the Duchess to give you something to wear. I know you've always admired her taste in clothes."

"It's my favorite color too—orange and black studded with green. With my complexion . . ."

"It sounds like Joseph's coat of many colors."

Now I take the lid off the box and hold up what still appears to be a robe or lounging shirt and examine it while Cad gasps. "It does have other colors now that I look closely. Here's red and blue and yellow. I would think anyone could find her favorite color here—if it's a favorite vivid."

"So democratic, our Duchess."

I slip it on over my dress and turn from side to side to model it. "It seems to be cut to accommodate any sort of body, man, woman, or child. Wait, here's a tag. Was Joseph Japanese?"

"Not in my Bible but that could be a typo."

"It can't be a coat. There aren't any sleeves."

"I think that's called a kimono," Cad says, chuckling at her joke before.

"Apparently. A sleeveless kimono."

"How useful!"

I take it off, see the price tag still hanging from the neck, and read it aloud: "Four ninety-nine Macy."

Cad is sitting down now, radiating miff that no one sufficiently appreciated her typo joke. She lights a cigarette and puts on her superior look, which makes her resemble a raccoon with glasses.

"But that could be a typo," I repeat and laugh. Her eyes sparkle again.

"I'll get the table set up," I say. Hearing Cad's familiar chuckle I know that I am once again announcing what I am doing as if, she says, I were writing a dreadful play.

Whatever I am feeling begins to grow insistent during the first rubber. My hands are oiled down to the bone; I deal like a surgeon, a card shark. Did Hallie get the mink for *me* to pay Oscar back for his nefarious role in sending her away to school? She is capable of revenge; she is part Scottish like her father; a clever in-clan trick would satisfy . . . Cad bids two diamonds. The three diamonds in my hand are hard doubled triangles, glittering red, pointed on both ends. I do not want to play the hand in diamonds. My bid is hearts. Can I say "two hearts" with Cad watching? The thought brings a blush of cherishedness to my chest; I look at my hand and see only hearts, round halves cleaving, the point discreetly down, thumping with suggestion: She loves you; she wanted you to have a mink because she loves you. I have to say "two hearts"; it is the only bid my hand will make.

———

I have just tallied the score when Hallie comes in through the porch and I see her hair. Normally it is light brown but not so light that it would avoid the brassy orange color of peroxide when used on brunettes. She and Punchy have cut it short and rolled it up; she confronts the sudden silence of the bridge table.

I gasp. "What happened to your head?" With a sexy tilt of her chin, she turns slowly so we can all get a good look. She dips her head under the bridge light. "Feel it," she says upside down. "We did it very carefully and it's still as soft as ever."

I have a hideous memory of saying just last week what a shame it was that her hair had turned—as a baby she was blonde. I try to touch it but my hand jumps back as if burned.

"It's very distinctive," Cad says looking at the rest of us. Nobody helps her.

"I'm glad you like it," Hallie says, letting an unsexy grin slip off her mouth. She runs upstairs to show Mary Cowan.

I feel slapped. "That color. It looks so cheap."

The Fascinator tells us about the time her daughter cut off her pigtail with one clumsy whack of the scissors but I can't listen. Her daughter's hair has long since grown out. My daughter looks like a . . . like a . . .

"Doesn't it look gruesome?" Mary Cowan says when I go upstairs.

My eyes feel sick. "What on earth possessed you to do that?" Away from the glare of the bridge lamp, in the cloudy dimness of her bedroom shaded by trees, Hallie looks like an almost normal blonde. She looks at least sixteen and exactly like a girl who would get a mink the way the soldier meant. "I simply can't have you going to Miss Askew's school looking like a . . ."

"A chippie," Mary Cowan says.

I am about to ask what *that* is when I guess; I don't want to know where she learns such things. Hallie seems genuinely stunned that I don't like the new sexy her but I can see that within the stun her brain is waving my last sentence: I can't have you going to Miss Askew's . . . "Well," I say, trying a light laugh. "I always wanted to be a blonde myself. You can keep it that way for a few weeks and then before school starts we'll go to the beauty parlor and have them dye it back to its natural color." Of course, unlike every other thirteen-year-old's hair, each strand will be an identical shade of brown and her head will look painted.

OCTOBER 1941

THE GIRLS HAVE been off to school for a month now and I am on my way to lunch with Sister. I live at the beginning of San Felipe Road and she lives at its end—out by Post Oak where it becomes an unpaved, rutted wagontrack.

She is eleven years older than I am. She is my sister and I love her dearly but I wish she wouldn't demand that my daughters be a repetition of the past generation, as if Mary Cowan can't be smart because she is beautiful, as if Hallie will end up as poor as I am.

However, if Sis's prognostications are correct, Mary Cowan will live in one of the prettiest houses in Houston. Sis and the D.R. bought eight acres in the country several years ago—rare acres bisected by a creek; the barn and horse ring are on the flat half, the French provincial house on the rolling, tree-studded half across the creek. With her flair for art and patience with detail Sis created a perfect setting for herself. She has white azaleas scattered throughout the trees—a waste in a way, since she and the D.R. go to bed right after dinner and white is most effective at night.

Although I am dressed in my best daytime clothes—my only real linen dress—I am rumpled when I get there. The house is centrally air conditioned—too late for the linen, which will dry now into its rumples.

Ever since she built her house the children and I and some of my friends have been imagining it in uses other than those to which it is likely to be put. I envision it as a backdrop for an old-fashioned garden wedding (preferably mine), Mary Cowan as a place for a weekend house party with dancing in the ballroom-sized living room, Hallie as a locale for a crazy boy-girl party where they chase each other up and down the hills, shoot craps on the footbridge, and laugh at bad boys throwing towels in the toilet.

The huge entrance hall is a little dark for my taste but the living-dining room, which is the entire middle of the house, double height and huge, with leaded French windows on the front and back and polished beams curving magnificently into the ceiling, makes me feel instantly light-headed. Because this elegance was created by my sister I partake of superiority by birthright. A few soothing minutes on the Louis XV brocade couch dissipate my earlier bad mood.

I intend to tell my sister about our brother's unforgivable forgetfulness—she is the right person to tell; she is two years older than Oscar. But first I have to admire the new Staffordshire dog which has been added since my last visit and secondly I have to offer an opinion on whether she should keep or send back the Hepplewhite inlaid card table (and if she keeps it, is it too plain to sit by itself just inside the door? Yes, I want to say. It should sit by me and be opened out as a bridge table), and thirdly I have to exclaim over the pair of William and Mary armchairs with the original tapestry and pretend they weren't there on my last visit and when Sis remembers and says, "You've seen them. They were right there when you were here last time," I have to think up some reason why they might look different. She has only had this house finished one year and already it is as full of antiques as it can comfortably get. Ever since Sis got sick her main pastime is shopping— I wonder where future years' purchases will go? Sis is reading my mind. "Now I want Oscar to give me a breakfront to go right between those two doors," she says, indicating the wall between the door to the kitchen and the door to the breakfast room. "I've already picked one out at the Shabby Shoppe. The D.R. would give me all of it for Christmas but I think Brother ought to do *something* for this room."

The breakfront will open up a career in shopping for museum-quality china and I agree that Oscar should share the responsibility of perfecting the only work of art this family is likely to create.

I used to wonder why Sis—whose education, such as it was, was in art—never bought paintings or sculpture. I understood immediately when she said she was only interested in art that intersects with her daily life—her humdrum housekeeping existence, she likes to say, not expecting *me* to disagree with her. Her chairs *can* be sat upon, though delicately. Her flowers can be picked, smelled, will fight back with thorns, weeds, diseases, or bugs. Her furniture needs polishing, recovering, regrouping. Since I create people, both of us participate in ephemera; only Oscar will go down in history as having left his name to his accomplishments . . .

It is time to tell Sis that Oscar forgot my house. We sit; she thinks she is listening to me but her black eyes are darting over the room to see if she missed showing me something new and her manicured ring-laden hands are fussing like snakes getting ready to shed.

Sister knows I bought that stock Oscar wanted me to buy and then told him we had to have a bigger house where the girls could each have their own bathroom and the walls separated *something*. I already told her I'd found the perfect house for us on a quiet street two blocks *inside* River Oaks and the rent was only $110—twenty-five more than we're paying on Shepherd. I tell her now that Oscar was supposed to have the lease sent to his office, sign it, and pay the commission and a month's rent.

"So when he called this morning I thought that's what he was calling about but he'd completely forgotten the whole thing. Slipped his mind, he said."

"I hope you gave him a piece of your mind," Sis says, lighting a cigarette, which brings on a brief coughing spell.

"He beats me before he ever gets on the telephone. First he has Miss Hugh call and ask me to hold on, Mr. Yancey is calling. I stand there waiting and wishing I'd picked up my cigarettes. I wait. Finally I decide I'll run grab the cigarettes. I check by saying 'Hello?' when I get back. Still no Oscar. Then I'm just lighting one when his voice comes on all hearty and full of energy and I try to answer and choke on my smoke. Then he says, 'Now you watch those cigarettes—I'm already worried to death about Sister's smoking.'" I look at her for sympathy.

"Why do you give him that control over your life? It's Rusty's money he's spending, which is your money. No, no, Nuisance!" Her voice goes up into the range of a cat's, making *nuisance* sound like the animal itself. "Nuisance!" She catches him just as he springs for the red brocade curtains that hang from the ceiling to the floor. "He pulled them down last week," she explains, sitting him on her lap, rubbing his nose with her rings. "You're a nuisance," she tells him while he waits with eyes closed for her to put him down. "Brother's got you adoring him. Now I love Oscar dearly but it ought to be the other way around."

"Well, I know he's busy . . ."

"He's got two secretaries to help him." Sis laughs. "The pretty one and the ugly one. I prefer Miss Hugh myself."

"Well, Flora's all right but Oscar shouldn't praise her in front of the Duchess—he always says that what he likes is a slim woman in a plain black dress. Of course he *will* say it when the Duchess is at her fattest in fuschia sequins." I feel the lilt returning to my voice; I am enjoying our two against one lineup although no real voting power is involved.

"*I* never had on a plain black dress in my life." Sis throws her head back like in a photograph. She wears beige silk with lace over her flat brassiereless chest and garnet jewelry. Her eyes announce that they are more than enough black for any woman.

"Oscar thinks *you're* the most beautiful woman who ever drew breath."

Sis puts her fluffy Persian on the floor, fussily admonishing him to stay away from the curtains. "Well," she says, her voice soft, "he thinks you hung the moon. He'd do anything for you but you have to know how to play him right."

Suddenly Sis begins to tremble violently; she raises her hand to her face as if she would bite it. "I have to have something to eat! I'm having a reaction!"

I jump up and let her take my arm; she grips it with a claw while I guide her across the slippery polished floor twenty feet to the dining table. Although she has lost forty pounds since she got diabetes she is still heavy in the hips and inches shorter than I am; I couldn't possibly hold her if she started to fall. I'm always terrified that she will fall when she gets an insulin reaction.

"Catherine!" I call.

"Catherine!" Sis calls too in the same high voice she uses for Nuisance. Catherine is immediate; she helps Sis into her chair, puts a plate of crackers in front of her and a glass of juice. "Bring some sugar for Mrs. Davis's iced tea. She doesn't want that saccharin," Sis says.

Catherine and I hug and fuss over each other. Catherine is only about twenty and as pretty as the rest of the house. She came to Sis three years ago and she and Hallie used to go downtown and buy sheet music and sing all the popular songs. She let Hallie eat anything she wanted for lunch—usually ice cream and cake and Dr. Pepper. "Miss Baby doesn't use sugar," Catherine says.

"Well, I forgot." Sis frowns. "Miss Baby! Now what kind of name is that?"

"Mrs. Davis doesn't mind. Do you, Miss Baby?"

The trouble with lunch at Sister's is that I get a whole day's calories at one meal. I have alligator pear stuffed with shrimp with homemade mayonnaise, biscuits and dewberry jelly, and lemon tart for dessert. Before Sis got sick and had to substitute shopping, her main pastime was cooking and eating—especially angelfood cakes, lemon tarts, homemade ice cream. Her dessert is a plain peach and I know she will open her mouth every time I open mine for a bite of my dessert and eat in the air alongside me. To divert her from my lemon tart I say, "What do you think I should do?"

It is every big sister's favorite question. She thinks, first that I should remember that when Daddy gave Oscar the business he'd built up—leaving nothing at all to his daughters, she emphasizes—he stipulated that Oscar would share it with us. Second, my money—from Rusty's life insurance and the sale of our house in Memphis—gave Oscar a chance to buy up a lot of lumber stands very cheap. "Two years ago," she reminds me, "the Depression wasn't over and cash was a great advantage. That's your cash," she says firmly.

In spite of what she, echoing Oscar, believes, I know it is no longer my cash because I'm not handling it. I agree basically with Sister: art is not yours unless you can interact with it. My money is Oscar's art. And he, of course, must be humored, cajoled, *understood* so that his temperamental talent can plunge straight into more art.

"He does give me stock in his company each year." Two thousand dollars' worth a year; if I were very careful, could I live on the dividends? Wouldn't he learn to expect that of me and then produce less? "And he's paying for the girls' school."

"He owes it to you. You've got those girls thinking they have to be grateful—why, Doctor would have paid for Hallie to go to Foxcroft *and* sent her a horse."

"All those girls are so rich, Hallie wouldn't fit into their world." I didn't want to argue with Sis; if she got angry she might have an asthma attack.

"Doctor says Hallie has the best pair of hands he's ever seen handle a horse. He told me yesterday . . ."

I don't want Hallie at Foxcroft. I am a traitor to Mother, who taught us all to support each one's particular talent. I feel like I have loosened the shoe of the lead mare and will get caught. We are caught. We are, or were, a family backed off into separate stalls, as happy with each other's achievements as if we were a herd with all pastures covered.

I am terrified of horses. My hands ache from squeezing the arms of my chair every time I have to watch Hallie in a ring with a dozen beasts. They have blunt angry hooves which pound the dirt like hammers, their eyes flash white with secrets, their uncommunicative mouths snap over bits while their mythical strength builds for a vengeful leap into the audience. Although I'm told they eat only grass and grain, I *feel* that they kill and devour fresh raw meat.

The men (and few women) who live off these beasts are even worse than the horses, as if the violence, the rage that flows as equine blood draws to it the violent and enraged of men. Hallie tells me about the beatings horses take, about hands that yank their bits into their tongues, jerk their heads viciously, dig spurs into their sides and force the recalcitrant into tameness. Of course, she does not treat them this way—yet. She claims they understand through impulses sent them via her hands and body. But even if Hallie herself escapes becoming brutal, she would have to associate with, probably marry, the kind of man who is attracted to horses because of his brutality. I can't forget the one time I went back to the stalls during the Fat Stock Show, through horses veering and balking in the aisles, kicking their stalls: we were surrounded by men drinking from brown paper bags, speaking in stable obsceni-ties, dressed in loud clothes, with eyes unfit for the female sex.

I can't say any of this to Sister because her own husband is a horseman. He also talks with the same country blunt speech he used as a boy but on him it's darling—because he isn't vulgar . . . anyway, he's a very successful surgeon.

I say instead that I do hope Hallie's horse period will turn out to be temporary, that Hallie will willow out and prefer clothes in which she can swoop to romantic music. Riding has already made her upper arms as muscular as a boy's, her view of the correct weight for herself twenty pounds above the fashion. Her walk across Sis's living room sets the china dogs to trembling. I laugh deprecatingly, inviting Sis to laugh too.

Sis declines. She says, "Ethelyn Gouverneer has a good hus-band and two children and she still keeps her two horses right on the place. And, if you *remember,* I rode Myrtle Peavine in the park every day until I got sick."

"I'm not stopping Hallie from *riding.*" The Gouverneers are the richest socially acceptable family in Houston. But there is an-other daughter too, living in New Orleans, who (everyone knows) is a dipsomaniac—who (everyone says) is also a nymphomaniac. Although the family makes it clear that her name is never to be mentioned, the rest of us talk about her constantly, blaming her father and alternately her mother for her unnatural end. I'm not stopping Hallie from riding, seeded in my ready-plowed brain the corollary: if I did stop her she might turn out to be like Natalie

Gouverneer. Of course, to be a nymphomaniac you would have to deaden your sensibilities with alcohol; is excessive horseback riding an early manifestation of nymphomania and at the same time a healthy substitute like football for boys?

"For heaven's sake, Sister, *I'm* the one who told her she could have riding lessons instead of music lessons when there was only money for one kind of lesson. And you know everybody in Memphis was horrified—girls *had* to have music lessons. I've always supported Hallie's riding even though it scares me to death. I'm glad she likes to ride!"

"I know you are, Eudora." Sis is the only one who ever calls me by my name. She speaks so quietly, looks at me so curiously, that I feel I have been excessive—although I'll say one thing for Sister, she's not afraid of emotion. Let it rage and twist through the elegant antiques; she once said, "I'm sure all this furniture has seen plenty of passion in its day, even the English pieces."

"I'm scared," I say, humbled by her unexpected concern.

"What are you scared of?"

I have her attention now. But what *am* I afraid of? Being poor is all I can think of but that is ridiculous, Oscar is doing very well and is helping me and I can find—will have to find—another house almost as good as the one I lost because he forgot. I am lucky to have Oscar; without him I would have to marry immediately or get a job. What kind of job is Oscar's sister allowed?

Sis is still watching my face—this must be a record length of time for her to wait for me to speak. Fanetta McCormick has two teenage daughters and a dead husband; she lives even farther from River Oaks than I do and takes in sewing. I never think of her without mentally addressing her as poor Fanetta McCormick. Sister's silence reminds me of how sick she is and I no longer feel afraid. When you're sick it is so important to be rich that I feel Sis's worldly goods merely balance her body. The converse is even more essential. Good health is money in the ventricle. I hope poor Fanetta McCormick is as vigorous as a horse.

I have to say something into Sis's anticipation. I say, "I've always wondered whether Daddy forgot my name when he was making out his will. You know, after he said 'and to my son, Oscar R. Yancey, in whom I am well pleased' he put in that phrase, 'and my other children.'" I smile and shake my head slightly. "I'm not scared anymore. I know I can always count on you and the D.R." Her staring black eyes blinked with approval. "Do you think he forgot my name?"

"It's certainly possible. How many times in his life do you think he ever heard it?"

Sis's jokes are so rare they always strike me as funnier than anyone's; I burst out laughing.

But my turn is over. Sis's attention is now concentrated on Fussy; she tells the white angora that she will get declawed if she doesn't stop scratching the furniture. Fussy gets lifted by her nape, carried to the door, deposited outside. Nuisance gets scratched on his ruff.

Sis assumes the cat break will lead into a different subject. She wants to talk about the children in a delight-providing way; she wants our words to trace the outlines of their faces, fill in the blank spots of their absence; she wants to perceive them before her, share them with me but hold parts of them off only for herself. I know she sometimes thinks of them as *her* children (when she sees them as finished products needing only a little buffing up, an occasional regrouping). She brags about the way their legs are built: "You can always tell a family by its legs," she says. "Just look at those girls' legs"—and her mind does—"strong and straight." She stares at the Queen Anne lowboy across the room; pictures of the girls are on top of it but she can't possibly see them from such a distance. She doesn't need to. She knows Mary Cowan is a beauty (of the same fine-boned beauty as herself, in fact) and Hallie is so sweet and warm. She is pleased that they are both smarter than she is, smart like their mother, she says—meaning those brains of questionable value which do well in school. They have character in their faces already, and perfect natural manners.

While she talks I feel that my daughters have been accepted into the classiest antique shop for a special window display; and I am pleased but also disturbed, as if without the mess of sawdust and chips that went into their fashioning they have been rendered unreal.

Sis is too nervous to sit still any longer. She leads me to her dressing table so I can confirm the jewelry she has chosen for each daughter's legacy. She has no doubt that Mary Cowan gets the garnets and Hallie the sapphire; she decided that those were their colors the minute they were born and has been giving them velvet dresses and Easter bunnies in shades of red and blue ever since. But is it equal, she wants to know, to leave the emerald earrings to Mary Cowan and the pearl necklace to Hallie?

I always say something like, But you'll live for years, we don't have to decide today, and she always answers, When you're almost sixty it's certainly not too soon to make plans. She is, of course, fifty-two.

We spend a long time over the beds. She wants the Louis XIV twin beds with brocade silk headboards to go to Hallie; she begins telling me that she had Hallie in mind when she bought them ten years ago. They are not even full-size single beds; I can see Hallie of ten years ago in one but my present Hallie, short though she is, would barely fit. I wonder what kind of house she thinks Hallie will live in among her farm animals? Mary Cowan too will need a house with a guest room because she is to get the English Regency suite—twin beds again: does Sis think or simply hope that our daughters' marriages will be morganatic? I am so pleased that I remember the word that a minute passes before I realize I am using it wrong . . . or am I? I think so (only Cad would know), but maybe it's used loosely to refer to any arranged marriage . . .

Unless someone arranges Hallie's marriage it is unlikely that she will wed anything except a horse; I see her overflowing one of the Louis XIV twin beds and a fine horse resting on the other, its mane glossy against the brocade and its immaculate hooves tucked under to avoid tearing the sheet. I laugh and share my vision with Sis.

Sister has the high bony forehead and terrifyingly white teeth of a Doberman; like the dog's, the black of her eyes, viewed alone, invites love not fear. "Well, if there's one thing that child loves more than horses it's her mama," Sis says generously, as if she were leaving me the most expensive legacy of all. "The night you called to say that Rusty had just died—we found Hallie asleep in her cot with her arm around your picture and the covers tucked over you both."

We are standing in the darkness of the entrance hall; the shock I feel on my face is in the shadows. The doorbell rings.

"That must be my nursery man," Sis says, opening the door wide to the hot October sunlight.

Her roses have recently suffered an invasion of aphids which her hand spray is no longer killing. Twice a day she shoots the hose on their leaves' underside, scattering aphids. As soon as they dry out (very soon in this sun) the aphids rearrange themselves on their favorite leaves. The nursery man has a large professional spray gun and I must either leave now or stay inside until the new poison is applied and has dissipated. I go pick up Fussy, holding her so the claws she doesn't deserve won't scratch me, put her inside the door, and kiss Sis goodbye. She is already concentrating on her roses.

I have returned to my city where a road named San Felipe begins at my house and stops at the house of my sister; by a mean twist of fate I have come home close on the heels of Mother's leaving. If only the two deaths (since both had to occur) could have been reversed: Rusty either resting or overworking during his last few years while Mother entered her death day with a full supply of vigor . . . "since both had to occur" stands in my mind like a cold slogan. I am a pushover for self-pity; I have been fighting against it all my life and now it talks back to me: And who, pray, should you extend pity to if not yourself?

Was it Mother's city too or did she just live here, longing for the undulations of Mexia? I had no sooner gotten my growth than I saw how short she was. I imagined that she walked through the crust of the earth like one can through shallow water, her feet several inches below everyone else's surface. But when she sat in her chair after dinner, calling her husband "Mr. Yancey," after the custom, her hands idle because he would not let her have her sewing, he wanted her attention for himself, she appeared as a woman born to a chair, a woman who had never left the drawing room.

Now I picture her in my first house, where Mary Cowan was born. Mother and I sat in the hot shade of South Carolina sewing underpants for my daughter—Mother had brought me her pattern; together we picked out the finest cotton, the cleanest eyelet for the leg holes, the most expensive elastic for the waist. Mother made me sew the first pair without her help; I knew I would never put them on Mary Cowan—they were my practice pair. I sewed as slowly as a child, clipping the seams so evenly not a thread dangled below its neighbor, turning the seam so cautiously not a bump would remain to bruise her tender skin. Then I could not knot my thread. Where could a knot go? Visualizing my little girl's year-old bottom, fine and smooth as homemade ice cream, there was not a spot on it that could bear the pressure of a knot, was there? Mother laughed her rich chocolate ice cream laugh. "Well, then, don't knot it, Baby. Just hold the ends of the thread in your hand." Then she said, "They're just baby animals, honey. Tough as little pigs."

Her voice comes into the car now, reaches across my back like a whip and pulls me into her cheek, into the vinegar smell of her hair. You've always looked down on the farm animals, Baby, she says with a headshake in her voice. She knows; I do. It's because we eat them—because they only exist to become our food, are prisoners of our appetite. Just as the convicts in Huntsville were prisoners of our roads.

The whole time we lived in Huntsville—and I must have been five when we left Mexia—I stared at the convicts working in leg-irons by the side of the road, on the sectioned-off top of the road, with terror. I knew I would not last one day in that heat doing that kind of work. How bad did a person have to be to get thrown away like that? I was told that they stole and they kept on stealing long after they knew they would get caught and punished . . .

There is a letter from Hallie waiting for me at home. Written in her constantly changing handwriting—this time it slants precariously to the left—I fear it will be another essay in grief. Hallie can paint misery as if she were a hundred and had suffered that many years of it unmitigated. The logic of her constructions, the carefully analyzed almost adult explanation of why this particular child is unhappy at this exact school, what she has done to overcome it, and a philosophical (and dreadful) prediction of the outcome if she has to stay much longer—all this makes me feel trapped (as a rational being) into agreement.

But this letter is different. I read a page of self-denigration and apology for what I am not yet supposed to know. The words increase in seriousness; I am alarmed. Suddenly she tells me: she is having her Thanksgiving weekend taken away for smoking. She has been caught smoking? I read quickly. No, another girl was caught smoking and the principal asked all the girls who were also guilty but had not been caught at it to do the honorable thing and confess. It would not be right for one girl to be expelled . . . expelled? I read the second page again, then the last page. No one is to be expelled, there are too many of them. Fifteen, Hallie says.

But I can see her jumping up from the principal's sermon to be first in line for confession hoping to be expelled. I am shaking with fury. *Did* she smoke? It doesn't matter whether she did or not, she said she did in order to be expelled. Not her fault that there were fourteen others who could not endure the pricks of conscience . . . which would hardly bother my daughter, iron-sheeted in her determination to return to me. Boarding school is not a prison, whatever she says; there are no bars that can hold her devious mind.

No mother deserves her badness. Smoking? Can't she do without the cigarettes she can hardly have known for long?—since she won't be fourteen for two weeks. I reread her abject apology again, how she has disappointed me, how she has not lived up to the moral character which I . . . she is still talking about *smoking*. I could shake her to pieces if I could get my hands on her but I am close to laughing. Does she think for one minute that I believe smoking is a sin? I will write to her about behaving, about abiding by the rules of the place where you are; and *then* I will talk to her when she gets here Christmas (if I can keep her there until Christmas) about her attempt to throw herself like a pillowcase over my head.

IT IS MONDAY after Christmas and the children have been home for a week; this is our first dinner with just three of us in our new house. There are always a lot of parties in Houston at Christmas but this year there are even more—as if the war mobilized everyone's sociability. And I have been especially busy since Hyke came back to town and started giving me the rush.

It all happened together in one month: the war, moving into our new house, Cad and I getting a job at the OPA—Benjie is its dollar-a-year head—and Hyke turning up again and turning out to be so different from the night I first met him when he told a dirty joke.

The girls like the house: they each have a regular-size bedroom with a bath between and the upstairs hall goes clear through the house from front to back, so none of us has to put up with a shared bedroom wall. I feel free for the first time since we left Memphis. The downstairs is nice too—although Cad says it looks just like every other house as soon as I put the furniture down the same way it always goes: red rug in the middle of the living room, flowered green sofa atop one end, Mother's green china urns on each side of the mantelpiece and her gold leaf mirror in the middle. I think it's a perfect house: just as good as the one I lost when Oscar forgot and only five dollars a month more expensive. We are one block inside River Oaks.

Now I know what is bothering *me*. My daughters gave me exactly what I've been longing for for Christmas: a string of beautiful cultured pearls with a fine clasp. They must have cost a hundred dollars. I know Hallie thought of it, and practically paid for them because Mary Cowan spends her allowance before she gets it and is always borrowing from Hallie. Since she had her first nickel I've never known Hallie not to have money stashed away. I was so pleased I almost cried but I thought I must have mixed up the cards or forgotten which package I opened—just for a second I was confused and thought they must be from Oscar. I didn't dare hope they were from Hyke, not yet. I guess I said something because Hallie looked amazed and said, "They're from Mary Cowan and *me*."

But I made it up to them and they were very proud during our Christmas dinner—at the Duchess's this year—when the Duchess could not believe children ever gave their mother a string of pearls and Sis looked at me with her I-told-you-so eyes.

But Hyke wasn't pleased. While we were at the Gouverneer party that night Gaius made a joke about if I ever break my engagement to my daughters he'd like to ask for my hand. Hyke laughed much too hard and said, "You'll need money in the bank, that's for sure." Even though he was joking I know he wanted me to think there was something wrong with them giving me the pearls; he's from Connecticut and they don't understand what families are down here.

The photo album comes out. Mary Cowan sees herself in half the faces, especially the one picture we have of the attorney general of the Confederacy's second wife, Lelia Swann. Old George himself wasn't much to look at but both his wives were lovely; I tell Mary Cowan that she is not descended from the Swanns at all—her grandfather was born during the first marriage. "Is that the Swann of *Swann's Way*?" she says as if she hasn't heard. "Well, why not?" I laugh, hugging her. She would much rather come from the decadence of Paris than the swamps of the Civil War.

We are stopped on a picture of George's three sons: George (her grandfather), Junius, and Henry. Henry, the youngest, has a wild-eyed look that intrigues Mary Cowan. "Who is he?" she asks.

"That's Hal. He was an electrical and mathematical genius and, while he was off studying, George and Junius split the family business between them. When Hal came back they told him he was too impractical, he should be a professor or something. Then Hal studied law and got a degree; once again he presented himself to the brothers and said now he would be a business asset. But this time the brothers just told him they didn't want him. Not under any circumstances. Scat, Hal. Poor Hal was absolutely crushed— he was now almost forty since he'd been in the Civil War too, they all had. So he went crazy. Some of the family think he really was crazy—and maybe he was since his brothers knew all along they weren't going to let him in and Hal didn't see it. But your father said he was perfectly sane, just disappointed; he gave up then and went to Atlanta, to a beautiful home for Confederate veterans, where he lived happily with his books and his ideas until just after Hallie was born." She already knows Hallie was named for him.

"Was he in a home for the Southern insane?" She knows he was.

Secure now in the knowledge that her father has been validated, and her sister struck with the crazy genes, Mary Cowan looks me straight in the eye. "Who is this Hyke?" she says.

I imagine I see the glitter in my own eyes reflected in her state. Daughters are merciless. "He's a fine man and I'm sorry you don't like him."

On his first visit Mary Cowan was lying on the sofa reading, her hair in her eyes; Hyke came in and tried to make friends with her. I think Hallie likes him though; she dried his pants. It was the next time he came; he had to wade over from Westheimer—it's not surprising that he stalled the car, Houston streets flood in every downpour. He was sitting perfectly proper with a towel wrapped around his waist and his legs crossed—he still had on his socks and garters—when Hallie came in. Hallie never stalls the car; she prides herself on her water driving. I was so nervous after Mary Cowan's reaction to Hyke that I introduced him to Hallie as a cousin. He is distantly related by marriage to an obscure cousin of Hallie's father; Hyke guffawed and I had to laugh too.

"So this is cousin Baby Hallie," Hyke said, putting down his drink to stand, arranging his towel. "I hope you like me because I like you a lot." Hyke's voice is very deep for his normal size.

"Maybe Hallie knows how to dry pants," I said.

It was impossible to read her expression but she took Hyke's wet pants with a hint of eagerness, as if she understood his importance to me and wanted any information about him she could get, possibly from close scrutiny of his trousers, although they were nothing more than regulation army. I guess they were a disappointment: beige twill with pockets empty and not worn or stained in any informative places. The country had only been at war for two weeks.

She steamed them dry and creased them between two towels and presented them to him. She was on the stairs when I said, "I think Hallie is embarrassed that you're here without your pants on. You'd better go in the bathroom"—I meant the downstairs lavatory—"and put them on." I was counting too much on the thickness of our new walls or the space between floors. At least *I* heard *them:* heard Mary Cowan go into Hallie's room and say (she must have been standing in the open door): "Isn't he yuk? I was lying peacefully in the living room reading yesterday when he came in, sat down, and tried to make friends with me!" And Hallie answering, "He must be dumb if he tried to make friends with *you.*"

And of course I heard a door slam immediately and Mary Cowan stomping back to her room but I think Hallie meant that a man should know better than to woo a woman through her children. Children instinctively dislike the man you're really interested in—which makes it curious that Hallie doesn't seem to resent Hyke at all.

I try now to explain to Mary Cowan that I hadn't much liked Hyke the first time I met him either. I don't tell her that he told a dirty joke and I decided he would never be allowed inside my house again. I tell her that people from different places often behave in a way that *your* set considers coarse but their own set accepts as normal . . . I'm not getting anywhere. She says, "It shouldn't make any difference to you whether *I* like him or not. You're the one who has to see him."

She returns to sorting the pictures, showing a connoisseur's preference for the romantic dead by the angle of her shoulder, the fall of one auburn curl.

I AM LOOKING over the balcony of the Tejas Club. Houston is host to a mist tonight; the outlines of our tiny city are blurred even for those who are not near-sighted, making our downtown look fuzzy and naïve. In this room, which should be used for dancing between courses of delicious food, are now crowded the heads of Houston and at least the shoulders of the United States government. President Roosevelt is not here but Eleanor is. Governor and Mrs. Hobby, Mr. and Mrs. Jesse Jones, Mr. and Mrs. Will Clayton, the heads of Humble, Gulf, and Shell, Todd Shipyard, Hughes Tool, Cameron Iron Works—along with the mayor of Houston and Benjie from the OPA.

Cad and I are official hostesses. My special assignment is to forestall any reference to the great rubber fight between Jesse Jones and our vice-president, Henry Wallace. We are also supposed to separate the Duchess from Eleanor; Oveta Culp Hobby from the religious fool who still believes women should be mummy-wrapped; to support the mayor in his bid for the port of Houston as recipient of war contracts (against some members of Washington who consider port cities too vulnerable).

Cad made me promise that I would surround the Duchess so she can't give Eleanor a piece of her mind on the racial question, but the Duchess currently distrusts me absolutely: Oscar told her he wanted a divorce last month; although they are now back together (gift of our community property laws) the reconciliation is as unstable as tepid Jello. All Cad has to do is remember everyone's political allergies and—if the vice-president should show up—get Oscar immediately. She will hardly be busy at all; I am nervous that she will be watching me.

The power in the room is thundering. Patriotism, the war effort, the urge to produce—quickly, efficiently, full-speed-ahead, especially those products that we have to invent, like rubber—speak directly to our collective energetic Houston hearts. We are on our figurative hands and knees begging for the chance to build ships, produce airplane parts, manufacture aviation fuel, and process chemicals we are just learning to spell like toluene for explosives and butadiene and styrene for synthetic rubber. I can feel it swelling the room: the belief that the city we created was for just this purpose: to prove that excess is our country's greatest asset. And excess is Texas.

Jesse Jones with his mop of white hair towers above the Washington men; Oveta Culp Hobby has a face that is so beautiful and quick and iced with grace that I feel sorry for Eleanor Roosevelt who, the Duchess observes, is long in the tooth like a horse. But Mrs. Roosevelt asked Cad to call her Eleanor and I sidle near when I see the Duchess sitting deep in a charm session with our mayor.

Eleanor is like a magnet; as soon as I am near I am swept into her orbit. The war will at least provide opportunity for the Negro and women, she is saying.

There is no Negro here except as waiter, and I, as an example of wartime woman, feel thrown back a hundred years into my role as bandage-roller and sweet-smiler. I feel this even though Cad and I have gone to work at the Office of Price Administration—even though I have found a job Oscar's sister can take and even though we are dealing with money. We are dealing with prices, I think, as usual.

"They also serve who only sit and wait." I surprise myself by saying that; I speak sweetly though, as usual.

Eleanor turns. "Oh, my dear, I certainly have no intention of sitting and waiting at all. And I really don't believe that our young women do either. They are signing up for factory jobs in droves." She bares her long teeth but she speaks sweetly too—although not nearly as sweetly as I.

"Of course you are right," I say. "What an opportunity for a girl who thought her only chance was the five-and-ten. But I wonder—just a little—if war doesn't always set women back. When the whole country is focused on the soldier, the strong, brave young man . . ."

Cad jumps in at my hesitation. "Have you looked around the room, my friend? There's no one present under forty and I get the distinct sense that the war is being fought right here."

Eleanor reaches out to touch Cad's arm with that gesture so characteristic of Eastern women—deft, glancing, suggesting the choosing of sides rather than warmth. She is winning my best friend away from me. "But when the young men must give their *lives,* surely they deserve the name of hero."

I am isolated; I grow stubborn. "Women give their lives to bring these heroes into the world and we are not given that title."

Cad's stare tells me to stop immediately, I have lost my mind, this is the First Lady of the Land. But Eleanor's face is frozen in a sudden thought; I can almost see the currents whirring in her brain. Her hand is raised palm up toward my face. "You will be!" The sparkle in her eyes is giving me official sanction. "We will institute a Mother of the Year. A four-star mother. An award for the mother with the most sons in service to their country. I can't tell you how grateful I am to you for suggesting it, . . ?" She wants my name again. Am I Eudora or just Baby?

"Baby," I murmur. "I'm Oscar Yancey's sister."

But Eleanor's smile is just for me. "I went to school with a girl from the South—oh, so many years ago! Everyone in her family was referred to by their familial relationship—Brother, Sister, Baby. She was named for her mother but called Ditty—for ditto. I find it absolutely *charming.*"

"Well, I think *you're* absolutely charming." I am blushing and dimpling with pleasure.

Her laugh is shockingly young and strong. Heads turn. I can't believe it: she leans over and kisses me on the cheek.

The Duchess must have seen; her voice is too loud and close for coincidence. "Whatever we have to do to win this war the one thing we must not do under any circumstances is allow colored soldiers to share quarters with our white boys. I hope no one is such a fool as to do that. It would be suicide!"

There are no military men here—presumably they have their hands full; this gathering is to ensure production. Therefore the Duchess has latched onto Jesse Jones as the nearest and most Southern voice in line with Roosevelt's ear.

He says something softly.

"But I mean *suicide,*" the Duchess emphasizes. "Our white soldiers will have to tell them what to do instead of fighting the war—they'll have to protect them on the front lines. Why, they don't even know . . ."

My arm whips through Eleanor's and I firmly walk her over to an opposite clearing where Oveta Culp Hobby is discussing soldiers too.

". . . manpower shortage. Women could fill at least twenty percent of the jobs now done by the army, freeing men for combat . . ."

I leave Eleanor and spin back to the Duchess. With my arm

across Jesse Jones at the waist (I cannot encircle that girth but I am tall enough to reach it) I tell the Duchess what an astonishingly beautiful dress she is wearing, how lovely that fuschia is, how bright and cheerful, how . . .

"Baby, you're just trying to distract me. Thank you but as I was saying to Jesse here . . ."

"Can't imagine where you found that color! It combines the purple of courage with the red of determination, the silk of our brave ally China with the ostrich plumes of Victorian America . . ."

"Hiding its head in the sand?" The Duchess is quick but I am taller; I do not need to bend my knees with Jesse Jones.

"Well, we've pulled our heads up now," I say. "Aimed them right at . . ."

"Just what I was saying to Jesse," the Duchess interrupts with a futile lift of her chin—she is much the shortest of the three of us. "And we mustn't forget that this war will be over someday and that integration of the troops will destroy *your* father's South and *your* father's South and *my* father's . . ."

"South," Jesse interrupts.

"Why, *yes*." The Duchess rests her case.

I am about to remove myself to a new problem spot when the Duchess spies the lieutenant of our Vice-President Wallace (Jesse Jones's announced enemy) standing in the doorway. He spies her and rushes over.

It is happening behind Jesse's immense back. He is not easy to wheel to a safe section of the room; when my arm tries to slide him away as I did Eleanor, it is like sliding an oil derrick. I plead my need for a drink. I am dying of thirst. "My tongue is parched—hanging out," I say with a laugh but of course do not hang it out. Jesse is surprised but merely beckons to a waiter; here at the Tejas Club he doesn't expect to have to go to the bar for me.

Jesse's opponent is kissing the Duchess. He is a handsome Southern-looking man with idealistic eyes. Although Jones is from Tennessee, he stands for the westernness of our state: get it done. With his kiss from the Duchess (on the mouth where the lipstick belongs, she says coyly) still damp, the vice-president's lieutenant picks up an obviously unfinished argument: "We don't need *half* that rubber, Jesse, and you know it. You want to spend the tax-payers' hard-earned money . . ."

"We'll need twice that much by *July*," Jesse says firmly. "And I imagine more of that money is mine than yours since I don't have a church to hide my income in . . ."

"We have freedom of religion in this country, thank God." The idealistic eyes manage to look like they just got off the boat.

"Why, of course we do!" I say sweetly, bending my knees toward our refugee. "And I've always thought the collection plates are so beautiful they should be used for something besides just money . . ."

"Oh, he doesn't have a *congregation*," Jesse says. "Although I'm sure, since he declared his house a 'church,' that he preaches a sermon there every Sunday." His heavy sarcasm alarms me; I sense it is totally uncharacteristic and tug at his waist once more. He won't budge; however, he does brush his hand over the back of his jacket to see what is yanking at him there. I seize the hand.

"Mrs. Roosevelt said she had to speak to you right away." I am pulling his fingers.

"*I* didn't hear her," the Duchess says. Eleanor is a dozen heads away nodding intently to Oveta Culp Hobby.

"Such a beautiful dress!" I wave my free hand and tow Jesse to the ladies.

He is so gallant I am not surprised to see him bow and kiss the hands of both our First Lady and Oveta. Then he looks expectantly at Eleanor's face.

"You wanted to talk to Mr. Jones about his rubber," I say hopefully.

"His rubber?" Oveta looks wary.

"The shortage is quite critical," Eleanor says gravely.

"Oh." Oveta smiles with relief. "Of course. Rubber." She is small and dark with eyes like Olivia de Haviland, and so immaculately groomed I want to check for stray pink threads on my own hemline.

"The President has utter confidence in Mr. Jones and his ability to solve the problem," Eleanor says warmly.

"Because South America has rubber!" I am so pleased that I remember my current events that a few seconds pass before I also remember that this is the exact source of violent disagreement between Jones and the vice-president. "Did you know that rubber comes from trees?" I tell Oveta. "It actually *grows*. But I'm sure *you* knew that." I feel very intimidated between these two career women and sense that they look down on women like me; that knowledge is making me act silly. I straighten up. At least I got Jesse away from his enemy. Now all I have to do is get the conversation off South America.

It's too late. Oveta, thinking to please Eleanor, comments on the vice-president's plan to feed the natives of the Amazon valley in return for their tapping the wild rubber trees there.

Jesse Jones believes in paying them cash for their rubber on the grounds that the natives won't bother to work if they're already fed. He now remarks to Oveta that the rubber governments will resent any patronizing attitude on our part and the implied insult to their native diet.

I am crazy about Roosevelt but none of us understand why he put *both* Jesse Jones *and* the vice-president in charge of solving the rubber shortage, each as head of a different agency. They are opposite personalities: our agricultural vice-president wanting to feed natives, our Houstonian insisting on contracts and money.

Of course, Eleanor can't take sides between her husband's second-in-command and the giant towering over us right this minute; she is wearing gray chiffon and pearls. I was delegated to prevent from happening exactly what is now happening. But when I order my mind to think *rubber* it comes up with a picture of Cad and me in those rubber girdles we bought last summer to make us sweat and lose weight.

"It must be very hot in the Amazon jungle," I say, looking from Oveta (still waiting for her answer from Eleanor) to Eleanor (preparing her nonanswer) to Jesse whose face shows the beginnings of a violent scowl beneath its skin now so cleanly arranged. "What kind of food do we want to send them?"

"Rice." Jesse manages to get something so ominous into that one-syllable word that I am awed. "Eight thousand tons of rice. Coincidentally, Pará—which is a state on the Amazon—exports rice. I am told that they have, at this very moment, an enormous quantity of rice with no buyers. A glut of rice." Jesse is speaking directly to me as if an obsession with rice were evident on my face.

"I certainly want to assure you, Mr. Jones," Eleanor begins in her amazing ability to speak in paragraphs, "that I am in sympathy with and personally appreciate the sentiments behind your recent suggestion that the underprivileged of our own country, the shocking pockets of poverty in the midst of plenty which we still have in the United States, could benefit from governmental concern about *their* nutritional lacks. It is a noble thought and does you much credit."

Jesse bows slightly but is silent. Oveta is wildly alert. She certainly knows what she's in the middle of. At that moment I spy the Duchess, with the vice-president's lieutenant in tow, heading dead for our group. I place my empty glass on a passing tray and reach for a full dark-colored one, hoping for bourbon, willing to accept rye, scotch—anything made from oats, wheat, corn, barley, anything but rice.

"Okay, guy," the vice-president's lieutenant says to Jesse Jones. "I just want you to know that I told Henry"—that's our vice-president—"that there's no way we can give all that food to the Amazon people and still get rubber. I just want you to know that I'm a Texan too and a businessman and I know you can't expect anyone to work on a full belly. It gives them motivation cramps—hahaha."

Eleanor recoils and I'm sure was going to speak but the Duchess thrusts her face right in the First Lady's and says, "You can't go against human nature—I was telling Popsy that just the other night." The reconciliation has produced "Popsy"? "If the good Lord had wanted the black-eyed susans to cross-pollinate with the easter lilies He wouldn't have made one with a root system and the other with a bulb system, I know that." Her smile is dazzling.

"And furthermore, Henry agrees with me that social conditions make it imperative that we conduct further study on the Amazon situation before we even consider shipping them food. BEW is drawing up a plan of study right now . . ."

BEW? Much as I love FDR I think his compulsion for initials is turning the USA into a giant monogram joke.

". . . take the money we were going to spend on food . . ."

"How much money?" It is a question Jones learned at his mother's knee and asks frequently.

"I'm terribly afraid I don't understand the significance of the bulb system and the root system?" Eleanor's voice is as frozen as a Holland winter.

"Five hundred million?" Jesse Jones practically shouts from outrage at the blood of Houston being sprayed out like bayou water.

"I said *under* five hundred million . . ."

"For a *study?*" We are not that hipped on education in cowboyland.

"For the whole project. The study shouldn't run more than four or five million."

"Three generations of Southerners is not long enough to forget . . ."

"Three times the total amount of money which saved the entire banking establishment in Houston in 1933?"

There is no more I can do. I extricate myself and head toward "Popsy." Let them sweat like the Amazon natives, like the figure-conscious women.

Oscar, when I find him, has just noticed the ruckus in the corner—hard to miss with Jones's towering white head shaking in rage over a sea of coiffures.

"Brother, it's such a wonderful party," I say, bending my knees, dimpling pink. "Maybe it would be a good idea to get everyone seated at the table now?"

I catch Oveta's eye as she takes her seat; does she give me a tiny wink? Of course, at the table all enemies are carefully separated.

We are having shrimp remoulade, filet mignon with squash souffle, alligator pear and Texas grapefruit salad—because I am in charge of the menu we also have tiny creamed onions and a choice of sherbet or chocolate mousse.

Oscar introduces the first of the speakers during the shrimp. By the time the last of the mousse has disappeared, all of us are ready to go to work immediately and produce, produce, produce. Then Oscar winds up the speeches by quoting General Sherman: "Sherman said, 'War is hell.'" There is a twinkle in his eye and everyone waits expectantly for the renegade Sherman to be contradicted. "I say—begging the ladies' pardon, 'Hell, war is *business*.'" The applause is like the roar of a tableful of cannon and the Washington contingent stands and claps to be noticed above the patriotism of Houston.

We break up right after dinner because the men (and Oveta and Eleanor) have been meeting all day and will again tomorrow. Benjie offers to take Cad and me to Jakie's for a nightcap (he is not a member of the Tejas Club because he is Jewish) but Cad feels too patriotic to gamble. Johnny enlisted the day after Pearl Harbor and Cad thinks she should go home and write him a letter—we have been persuaded that letters win the war too.

"Well, *I* will buy *you* a drink." I am holding Benjie's arm and now squeeze it. I have a knot in my stomach as if we are mobilizing against Hitler with our right hand and supporting him with our left, as if my buying Benjie a drink will drown anti-Semitism. As soon as our drinks are set before us the waiter presents Benjie with the check to sign. He hands it to me. The waiter produces the manager just as I have finished signing Oscar's name with a flourish.

"I'm sorry madam, but ladies are not permitted in the Tejas

Club except when escorted by a member," our martinet explains politely.

"I am not allowed to buy these drinks?"

He shakes his head sadly. Benjie starts to rise; I get up too and take the arm I just squeezed.

"Well, thank you very much," I say. The Tejas Club would make a wonderful dancing club but the tables take up all the floor space except for rare parties. I begin dancing in a pathway and singing since we have no music. "Don't be a baby, Baby . . ." I arrange Benjie's arms in a foxtrot position. "The drinks are on the house, Benjie. We have to show our appreciation." He won't smile but he won't abandon me either. "Baby me," I sing. "Come on and humhumhum and baby me . . ." I am looking up at his deep, sad, overhung eyes; his touch is hesitant. "Cuddle up and don't be blue," I sing, disregarding lyric and tune with baby pride. He is getting ready to laugh. I see the manager shrug and sit at a distant table. I know the waiter doesn't care; I know him from when he was at the Country Club.

Benjie grabs my dress at the waist; he begins to tango. He sings with a roar: "Oh, the lady in pink. The fellows are crazy 'bout the lady in pink." The dance is taking all his breath so I do the next line: "She's a bit naughty but lawdy . . ." I point a perfect leg ostentatiously out to the side. "What a personality."

The war has become a musical comedy. I am Betty Grable offering my legs to bolster OPA morale. I wish I had thrown the drinks in the manager's face instead.

"Oh, the lady's in pink, and this fella's crazy 'bout the lady in pink . . . let her be naughty 'cause lawdy . . ." He's running out of wind but he repeats it all gasping, holding my hand in a damp vise. When he stops he steadies his diaphragm and bows frugally.

Our drinks are still on our table. I do not want even a swallow of mine. I address the manager crouched over a table near the far door. "I just want you to know that neither Mr. Falk nor I will ever set foot in this club again and I intend to tell my brother that there's something too peculiar about the heads of a democracy meeting at a place as snobbish as this one is. It certainly won't happen again!" As I wait for the elevator on Benjie's arm, I even believe I have the power to prevent it. "I'll personally see that it doesn't."

When I am alone, ready for bed, I place the First Lady's kiss on the shelf where the company china stays; I store the sentence that got it for me—honoring motherhood—among the everyday pots and pans.

I am thinking of Oveta. I think she does not look down on me. I think she does not feel superior to me because I am nothing but a housewife. I think—of course I could be wrong—that she meant to tell me, by the wink I *think* she sent my way, that she is not deceived. We will never speak of it but I think she is extraordinary and wonderful. I hope she gets her army of women.

PART II

1942–1948

I THINK I have fallen in love. I have all the symptoms: breath darts in and out of my lungs like a hummingbird, my spine is as visible as an amaryllis stalk, my feet dance past grocery shelves, cans of coffee. My ears pick up every sound and turn it to harmony. I am a spring chicken. My blood is a juvenile athlete jitterbugging in my veins—when it reaches my little self, I panic. I don't want to explode right here in Jamail's. I've always worn girdles instead of panty girdles—believing that the whole point of skirts is the ventilation. I decide to go downtown and buy a panty girdle. My barometer has dropped to my crotch. My sky is around my ears. We are in for it.

It embarrasses me to say "I am in love" even to Cad, although I am not one of those women who is afraid a man will leave her. No man ever has. I think I just don't want to be *watched*.

My feelings for Hyke must be obvious anyway. My cheeks are stretched around excess blood, I can't stop smiling.

Cad and I are on the train on our way to San Antonio. To go with my repetitious smiling I say, "You look just like you did in Venice among the pigeons."

We both do. We've been going to Mrs. Bartlett's for a month now, standing in the rollers which fit like a tight girdle and knead away fat from knees to bust. We are inches trimmer in the middle. We have on suits and gloves and hats for the train but I have a fitted long-waisted dress for tonight with a peplum: for the first time in years my hips are svelte enough for a peplum. The dress is a copy of a Nettie Rosenstein and *pink*. I *love* it. It's a wonderful dusty shocking pink, if that's possible. The saleslady tried to talk me into buying rose-colored sandals to wear with it but I can't use all my coupons on such a thing when I have a perfectly good pair of patent leather pumps. Then I went back the next day and bought the sandals. I don't mind saying this out loud: I've never been as happy in my life as I have since the war started.

Cad is talking about Annie Beth, a pitiful creature who works near us at the OPA. She's been wanting to join us for lunch ever since we made friends with her last Christmas; Thursday, though, was the first day we had free since then—the first day we couldn't find a man to take us out. Cad says we ought to fix her up with Dutch Nathan.

"I think we ought to feed her," I say. Her skin is the color of margarine before you mix in the orange.

Cad thinks the soldier Annie Beth writes to is probably married. He sounds married, I agree. His holiday leaves are always suddenly canceled.

"So you think she doesn't eat enough to handle anything but a paper soldier?" Cad's eyes are twinkling. "Or do you think she's starving herself to avoid having a real soldier?"

"Is that Freud again?" We are passing through rolling hills which are a soft brown now set off by the subtle dull green of live oaks at winter's sunny end. But you can still see for miles. I think Texas is as beautiful as any ocean. I am too lucky today to mind Cad's sometimes faddish intellectualism. "Feed a cold; feed a sex problem." I add a smile onto my smiling.

"Of course, if we fatten her up she might be too cute for Dutch. What will we do then?"

"Maybe we could introduce her to Oscar." That strikes both of us as hilarious and we are laughing so hard the other passengers stare. Oscar has a weakness for willowy pale women who can hardly lift a pencil. The Duchess was just such a girl—although she was at least thirty when they married. As soon as she got Oscar she added fifty pounds, began ordering everyone about, and now speaks in a voice so aggressive I have to hold the receiver two feet away from my ear. Cad loves to imitate her: "Somebody's on this line. Julia and Betty, are you on this line?" The Duchess's voice can carry from the bedroom to the kitchen in a mansion. "Betty, Julia, Robert . . ." (William quit) ". . . come here." She shouts to the side of the telephone; she has an intercom connecting every room, which she insists on leaving open. The servants have to whisper. "I hear that whispering. What are you whispering about? Betty, check the phones to see who's on this line." I feel like telling her that the whole Houston OPA is on at my end.

Now we both feel bad because Annie Beth is much too nice to make fun of. We agree that what she needs is to get out of herself; she thinks about herself all the time and is probably just bored.

San Antonio is a magic city partly because of the Alamo. It is early March now; the spring flowers which San Antonio claims reach true beauty only here are, sure enough, beautifully in bloom. Every city needs a persuasive and rich family with taste to help it dress; San Antonio has Maury Maverick, whose very name symbolizes Texas to those of us who love the state. Of course, as Cad points out, the sobriquet "maverick" works equally well for those who hate Texas.

Maury Maverick is responsible for the downtown river project: the branch of the San Antonio river running through downtown, where sewage used to be deposited, is now a filtered water-controlled stream with wide brick walks along both sides, shops, cafes, and hotels, and lush tropical planting. We are staying nearby and plan to meet Hyke and his friend at a cafe on Paseo del Rio. The story is that Maury Maverick pestered Roosevelt and Stimpson so assiduously that finally Franklin said to Henry: "Give that *Texan* his *rivah* so he'll get off my *back*."

Hyke's friend is from Connecticut too, but married. I suspect Cad is disappointed. I don't know that she wants a romance while Johnny is away being soldier but I would if I were she. I want Cad to have a war adventure too.

Hyke has a thousand friends and all of them seem to be passing our stretch of the river walk. Everyone is very respectful to the soldiers here because of the Alamo; of course, the Alamo makes the soldiers behave better too.

I love the way Hyke looks. Until the war we never had faces like his in Texas. He has a tall narrow head with dark hair, dark eyes which only appear close together, a long, convex upper lip, and a short, turned-up nose (the kind I've always wanted). He laughs often. Sitting beside him, I feel myself coming uncurled.

Our nickelodeon is playing "Remember Pearl Harbor and Remember the Alamo" alternately with "As Time Goes By"— which Hyke knows by heart. He does a silent imitation of Hoagy Carmichael, actually kissing me right here on the Paseo del Rio when the line "a kiss is still a kiss" comes up. I guess it will be "our song" (as Mary Cowan says)—we are identical to fifty million other couples. I should object but instead I am diving straight down into ordinariness and won't come up.

I see Oscar first. He is walking toward us talking to a man who looks rich and important. Oscar's company built the army base here and of course Oscar has an interest in several San Antonio hotels; I'm not ever surprised when he turns up.

Hyke has only met Oscar once. As soon as Oscar approaches our table Hyke covers my hand with his as if it were a rare butterfly and Oscar a rival collector. My hands *are* choice: tapered and perfectly manicured and their veins speak up.

Oscar introduces us to Maury Maverick himself and I tell him how much we are enjoying his river, how beautiful he has made San Antonio. Of course, Mr. Maverick says that it is the people of San Antonio who have made the city and made it beautiful, but he is proud to be one among them. He is a darling man with alert, twinkling eyes but I am glad when they don't join us. I could not stand any more calls upon my heart. Like a twitching sponge it is now reaching out open pockets to soak up Hyke's attention and alternately engorged with surplus red of its own.

We do, of course—although there are no spare hotel rooms. Cad and Hyke's friend stay out an extra hour. Cad tells me later that her soldier did bring out pictures of the wife and children and that next time . . .

Hyke is only thirty-five and has skin like frozen silk. He is very earnest. He wanted me to take off my clothes and get in bed. I undressed in the bathroom, wishing girdles did not leave so many marks, but when I came out in just my nightgown he had turned off the lights. There is only a ceiling glow from the open transom and from the street below. I am almost as tall as he is; we thoroughly cover one twin bed.

He is not laughing now. His tiny turned-up nose leaves plenty of room for kissing and we do, for hours it seems. Even my toes are throbbing.

"I love you. I want to marry you," he says hoarsely.

Now I laugh. "What a thing to say at a time like this!"

"At a . . .?"

"I don't want to have to think about wedding invitations right now."

His laugh is a machine gun in my ear; like that of two other men I've met from Connecticut, it really sounds like ha-ha-ha. "You're a Texan, that's for sure. Well, we could elope."

"Or how I'm going to get the shoe stamps for my trousseau."

"Oh, Baby." He nips my earlobe.

"Or where on earth we're going to find French champagne. I don't even like champagne. Couldn't we have bourbon in hollow-stemmed glasses?" I notice that the erection he started with and then lost has returned. I feel twinkly myself. "Do you like the idea of bourbon?"

"I like the hollow stems."

"That's not a dirty joke, is it?"

"Not a joke at all!"

I sit up on one elbow. "You know, I decided you'd never be allowed in my house again after you told that mink story the first time I met you."

"I knew as soon as I saw your face . . ."

"How could you see my face? You were guffawing with your eyes closed." I take one leg and wrap it over his hips. His little hard place gets pushed upward against his stomach. He shudders; I get a wave of echoes. "I guessed you yankees just didn't know any better and I forgave you—later."

"Wisenheimer. I knew the minute I saw you that I'd never have a chance so I blew it fast to get it over with. I hate to be a loseroo." He rubs my neck with emerging bristles.

"You're going to lose something now." I move to straddle him.

Suddenly he throws his weight up and flips us both over. Lying above me, resting on my right leg, his nearly hairless chest arched out like a sail, his darling long-lipped mouth grinning down at me, he rolls my little self around and around with his thumb, his forefinger being up inside me. I feel like I am flying out over the river held up by the scent of the spring flowers. I am already convulsing when he mates me so vehemently that the bed is pounding against the night table and jars the Gideon loose. It crashes to the floor.

"Hubba, hubba, go for broke!" Hyke shouts.

I am dripping with sweat and so is he. I like it that he sweats but I insist he take a shower before he goes back to the barracks. I don't want parts of myself carried off to that place. Fortunately we are completely dressed and having a nightcap when Cad and Hyke's friend come back.

The next morning we learn that the cruiser *Houston* was sunk by the Japanese—off the Java Coast.

I HAVE MY new house. I actually got to buy this one and it is definitely inside River Oaks. If Oscar has said it once he's said it a hundred times: "Baby, you don't want to go tying up your money in a house; it's a terrible investment. Unless you just want a *home*." That from a man who's made a fortune building them. Then all of a sudden last spring he said he thought I ought to buy a house; he said he would arrange the financing.

Sis got it for me. I know because I heard the servants talking at a party she gave for the D.R.'s sixty-ninth birthday. They were all there—Julia and Betty and Charles (Robert quit) and Catherine and Fred. I always go back in the kitchen during a party to see what's going on; I was just pushing open the door when I heard them.

"And then she said, 'I'm *telling* you, Brother!' and she *told* him," Catherine was saying.

"Ain't nobody can stand up to Miss Hortense when she got her fur up," Fred said.

"Well, Miss Baby!" Catherine stood up; Fred and Betty were already standing so I sat down at the kitchen table. Julia was old enough to keep on sitting there where she was.

Sister's kitchen is a square about fifteen by fifteen and right in the middle is a square wooden table with two odd rush-bottom chairs drawn up. Charles perched on the step stool near the pantry. He was not working at this party; he was waiting to take the Yanceys home. Fred was serving drinks and darted out as soon as I came in. Since Catherine, Julia, and Betty did all the work, I told them how delicious everything was.

"What's going on? Everybody having fun?" I said. I love talking to the women in the kitchen; I would have felt uncomfortable squeezed in with Charles and Fred if we had not outnumbered them two to one.

"Oh, yes, ma'am," Catherine said.

"We're just having our little drink before we leave," Julia said.

"Well, I believe I'll just have one with you. *What* was Mrs. Jett telling Mr. Yancey?"

Nobody spoke for a minute; everyone was looking at Catherine. Then Catherine laughed. "Well, Miss Baby, it was like this. One morning about two weeks ago—I think it was a Saturday morning—Mrs. Jett was having Mr. Yancey over for breakfast. Course she'd already eaten and she was moving around her living room like a bumblebee after all the flowers wilt and he *wouldn't* come. I hear her in there: 'Nuisance! You better hide! You better run for your life because if I catch you . . .' I knew she was thinking about Mr. Yancey and sure enough the minute he finished his breakfast she starts in on him. She was wearing her apricot velvet with the lace sleeves but you wouldn't know it from her voice. She say, 'Brother, I want to talk to you about Daddy's will . . .'" Catherine stopped; she was examining my face to see if she should go on.

"Now what secrets do you think we can keep from the kitchen?" I said. I'm sure I was a little tight.

Catherine grinned. "She said, 'I'm not getting my share of Daddy's money and neither is the Baby.' She said, 'I want my full one-third of Mother's half of the business.' And Mr. Yancey said, 'Do you want to run it?' and Mrs. Jett she say, 'There won't be anything to run when my lawyer gets through.'"

Catherine's eyes were glistening—everybody's were. I could feel my heart pounding.

Julia said, "She's something."

I said, "She said what?"

Catherine said, "That's what she said. 'There won't be *anything* to run when my lawyer gets through.'"

"And what did Oscar say then?"

"He said, 'Oh.' He didn't say much. She went right on and said, 'Brother, you can't pull the wool over my eyes. Everytime wool gets near me I just itch.'"

Everybody laughed and laughed. I know Catherine edited that; Sis probably said, You can pull the wool over *the Baby's* eyes but every time . . .

"She *had* him," Catherine said. "Then she said, 'Daddy left you the business with the understanding that you would take care of your sisters and I don't mean with these dribbles. No baby brother is going to dribble me. Go on and pay the taxes,' she said. 'I intend to see my rightful inheritance before I die.' And then Miss

Hortense got to coughing and wheezing like she always does when she gets all het up and I ran in there with a glass of water but she didn't hardly notice. She said, 'And get the Baby a decent house.'" Catherine darted another look at me. "She said, 'It's a disgrace the way she lives while *you* . . .' and then she coughed some more."

Fred was back. He said, "Mrs. Davis, can I fix you a little drink?" I handed him my dregs with a smile for yes.

Fred has worked off and on for Sis and the D.R. for years—he was the one who taught Hallie to drive. I know Fred much better than I do Charles. Charles was still sitting on the step stool silent. He's only been with the Duchess a year.

Still I feel less uncomfortable around Charles than I do around Oscar's private man. He is Walter Stevenson, almost as old as Oscar and more dignified. His wife is an important woman in the Negro world and active in politics; Cad often works with her. Perhaps because they are both unusually good-looking people or maybe because I feel they look down on us, I have trouble talking to Walter when his wife isn't around. I think Walter knows more about Oscar's business than anyone, even Flora or Miss Hugh. Oscar can say anything to Walter because they could never compete—Walter can't use any tips or inside information he might pick up from Oscar and his friends; he is automatically excluded from being in on any of their deals so Oscar trusts him the way he would a large dog. Walter knows where his indispensability lies; he extracts a handsome salary for his role as dog and works only on his own terms—which exclude serving the Duchess in any capacity or even being around her. I don't know what happened between the Duchess and Walter but I can guess the tone: the Duchess is very insulting to all colored people. Of course Walter wasn't at Sis's party and we couldn't have had this conversation if he'd been in the room.

They were all waiting for me to say something. I said, "So that's why he brought up buying me a house."

"Oh, I don't think that's the reason, Miss Baby," Julia said. "I know he been thinking about your house for a long time now."

"And I'm sure he has," Charles said but he was just tired of not getting to talk.

"She didn't make no bones about it, Mrs. Jett didn't," Catherine said.

"She know how to get her way all right," Julia said.

"Thank you, Fred." I took a sip and the new bourbon went hot to my brain. "Well, so do *I*. I've already gotten three houses without Sister helping at all. They may not have been any great shakes as houses . . ."

"Oh, they were fine houses, Miss Baby," Julia said.

"No one ever has as good a time as they do at a party in Miss Baby's house, I know *that,*" Catherine said. "Isn't that right?"

"That's right," Betty said. "Why, I hear everybody talking . . ." She'd never been at a party in my house and Catherine interrupted: "Well, I see and I *know.*"

"And just *wait* until I give a party in my new house. I want you all to be there." I knew I couldn't afford it but I could *see* it so clear. "We'll be thrown out of the neighborhood!" I started laughing and everybody laughed.

"I want to be there," Betty said. "I won't even charge."

"That's gonna be some party. I *know,*" Fred said.

"Just let me know when you want me, Miss Baby," Catherine said.

"I want you right now!"

Catherine was patting my shoulder with one hand and hugging me with the other. "Po' Miss Baby."

I squeezed the hand that was nearest, hard, then dropped it and smiled. There were too many black faces watching. "Is that the end of the story?" I said. We all knew it wasn't.

"Well, first thing I see Monday morning is that Bentley, like it just drove itself up. Sitting out there in the driveway like it *belonged.*" Catherine laughed a deep whiskey kind of chuckle and kept on laughing until Julia asked, "And then what happened?"

"What'd she do then?" Betty asked. We were all leaning toward Catherine, not taking our eyes off her. Catherine threw her head back and waited several seconds before she went on with *her* story.

"So I went in to Mrs. Jett—she was getting dressed and sitting at her dressing table fixing her hair. I said, 'Mrs. Jett, do you know there's a Bentley out in the driveway?' She said, 'Who's in it, Catherine?' And I said, 'Nobody at all. It looks like it might be for you.' I didn't let on I'd heard the whole thing the Saturday before. 'For me?' she said and she got up. She had that look she gets on her face when she thinks she's going to be pleased."

"I wish I could have seen her face when she saw it," Betty said.

"What did she do when she saw it?" Julia said.

"Well, she just stood there looking at it for the longest. She walked all around it and opened the door and she looked inside, and then when she was all through looking she put her hands on her hips and she said, 'Now what in the world was Oscar thinking of. I can't stand navy blue.'"

Betty shrieked. Ever since she saw *Gone with the Wind* she puts on a Butterfly McQueen act whenever she can. "Lawsy, Miss Catherine, I 'spect I'se just gwine to faint if'n I hasta look at a Bentley Mark IV what's *navy blue!*"

Charles shook his head. "I can just see Mrs. Jett now, standing there with her hands on her hips saying, 'Now what in the world was Mr. Oscar thinking of. I can't stand navy blue.'"

"I can just hear her," I said to Catherine. "I really can hear her say those very words."

"So what did she do then?" Julia asked.

Catherine took a big swallow of her drink and tried to stop laughing. "Well, she called Mr. Yancey and thanked him just as sweet as you please and as soon as she found out where he got it she called up that man and asked didn't he have one that was beige."

We were all laughing so hard I knew Sister would come in any minute.

"She always did favor beige," Julia said.

"It goes with her complexion." Betty grinned. "Wonder what color Bentley do go with mine?" The D.R. came in then to pay everyone and the laughter vanished without a trace.

I *am* happy with my house. It has the same number of rooms as all the others but there is space in their arrangement. My bedroom upstairs is the size of the living room. The living room itself is larger and there is a tile-floored porch extending it—a big porch with doors to it off a tiny den as well as the living room. The main difference is the entrance hall with two steps up and a stairway that takes the long way around to reach the second floor. We have a new version of green-flowered curtains, a new print on the sofa, a new rug, with the old one going to my bedroom and my bedroom's blue Oriental going into Mary Cowan's room. We also have two Chinese prints on the living room walls and of course Mother's remaining green-painted china urn (Hallie broke its mate) on the mantel.

I am paying off the bank for the furniture from my OPA salary. I love writing that check and watching the balance diminish—like when you're on a diet and see the pounds drop off week by week. And I have Carrie who comes in three days a week but she leaves at five; I never even see her most weeks. I certainly don't know her but

I think she is a snob and I'm not sure I even like her.

———————

"You're coming in for a drink at least, aren't you?" Cad drove me home—I'm the last stop on the OPA car pool route and this is her day. She sold her magnificent house on the original side of town last year; the neighborhood was becoming Negro. Cad stayed longer than I would have. She said it was very convenient for her work in the Negro hospital—we are both on the board but Cad is the secretary. I'm glad she moved; for the first time in our lives we live only a few blocks from each other.

My new house has practically no yard; Cad parks behind the D.R.'s car and as we walk up to the porch we can see and hear him and Hallie. Today is Hallie's eighteenth birthday.

They are sitting in the living room; we hear Uncle Doctor say, "Have you been a bad girl?" He's been saying the same thing since she was born, while reaching into his pocket. He always carries a roll of bills and peels some off, pushing them into Hallie's hand. "A bad girl always needs money."

Hallie says, "I've been a good girl"; no doubt *bad* struck too close to what she has been to be joked about.

He says that in that case she wouldn't be needing the money and reaches for the bills. Halfway to the money his hand swoops for her thigh, digging into it with a tickle. We hear her cry, "Don't!"

"Oh, I know you've been bad—so bad you're plumb tuckered out now just from badness. Yessir, I swear you were born bad and kept on going bad every step of the way, just like you was bent on being the baddest girl from your holler to your yes ma'am . . ."

He looks up squinting through gold-rimmed bifocals as we come in. His face is deeply pitted from childhood smallpox; when he stands now he is no taller than Hallie. His hands are plump and square, milk-white with freckles and spots; he wears a white-gold ring with a diamond in it; he never touches any of us with his hands except Hallie—as if he were afraid we would nick them. He has beautiful, thick, snow white, wavy hair. Like all of us, I am devoted to him but find him difficult to talk to. Cad is speaking to him in forced English—the words distinct and spaced like children's teeth—as if he were a native emperor. Fondness is palpable in her face tilted down at him.

"I tell you she is all right with me just like she is," Uncle Doctor says. "I'll tell anyone I never seen a girl that is as near perfect in all my life."

I feel a frozen smile on my face and say I'm going to fix us all a drink. When I return, I hear Hallie ask, "Uncle Doctor, why do you call yourself Thomas A. Jett? What does 'A' stand for?"

He pulls back his hand and takes a noisy slurp of his bourbon, a habit that Sis hates more than anything. "Well, now, honey, I was just a country boy entering Tulane Medical School and the dean was asking me what my name was. I said, 'Tom Jett.' 'Tom Jett? Now what kind of a name is that for a doctor? You'll be Thomas A. Jett.' And he wrote that down. So when anyone asks me what the 'A' stands for, I say, A doctor." From his round middle a deep country chuckle begins. "*A* doctor. Ain't that right?"

In a few minutes his store of conversation shrivels up; he says he has to leave. Hallie's years at boarding school effectively ended her horse-show career for them both.

He has his arm around Hallie and is walking her to the door. "You're the apple of your Auntie's eye and you ought to make your Auntie take you out and buy you an outfit. A girl needs a heap of clothes when she's . . . are you eighteen? Now you're telling a fib. I don't believe you're eighteen. Well, now, if you're eighteen you're going to be needing more money than that . . ." He pulls out his wad again.

Hallie says, "No, Uncle Doctor, you've given me enough. Really." Did she say that because I was listening?

"No, no, a girl can't have too much money when she's eighteen. She might be figuring on cutting loose and she'll want to make a good showing." He lowers his voice to a stage whisper; they're standing right on the porch. "Now you mustn't tell your mother I give you this, she'll take it away from you. Yessirree, you're just about the most perfect thing I ever did see for a girl. Now you keep this hidden away, you hear?"

Cad has followed Hallie into the kitchen. Since June, when Hallie came home from school for the last time, Cad has been saying Hallie has an interesting mind. Of course, she doesn't have to cope with it.

You might as *well* think about your daughters as minds; there are certainly no men around. We all have time to be minds, even me.

After I wrap Hallie's dress I push open the kitchen door to fix myself a drink; Cad is sitting at the table with Hallie.

My daughter looks like a devious mouse but she holds her head cocked as if she were one of those innocent cartoon mice. "I'm majoring in money," she is saying. *I* thought it was math.

Cad is nodding like a good cat in cahoots with the mouse so they can share the cheese. "I know just how you feel. I was playing bridge in your uncle Oscar's apartment in the Rice Hotel—you didn't know he keeps a place downtown? They call it Ten Penny because it's suite 10D and the stakes coincidentally are ten cents a point. Of course, I haven't *lost* yet. In fact, last week Oscar and I set the Judge and the Governor at three no-trump. I also held five trumps against the head of the largest insurance company in the state . . ." She throws her head back and lets her sentences rise triumphantly toward their ends. "I snatched the bid away from the president of the First Houston Bank and made it. I played the owner of the Rice Hotel himself for a singleton king and dropped it. You know, Hallie, I am absolutely delighted to be dealt the same number of cards as the most powerful men in Texas."

The word *powerful* has a drumbeat sound and sends blood shivering across the back of my skull. My square white kitchen takes on an air of cabal.

"Although I know money in Texas doesn't mean much," Hallie is saying. "It's just a stepping-stone to getting rich."

"And rich is merely one possible path to victory," Cad says.

"A copper wire." Hallie's eyes are shining green like a frolicking Walt Disney ocean; the sly mouse has vanished. "A conduit which *can* be used but unless it is, it just lies there shining but inert."

"*What* are you talking about?" I ask although I know. The men who play bridge at Ten Penny act as a team—the term has been made patriotic by our war. By supporting each other and parceling out government contracts (one of their wires goes from Houston to Congress) they have turned the marshes between Houston and the Gulf into an industrial bonanza like elves making shoes overnight.

"It is very simple," Cad says. "They set the table neatly and completely. No diner will grab another's fork if he has his own conveniently at the left. And so the bankers make money from the deposits and loans, the oilmen from their product, the tool men, the insurers, the land speculators, the concrete companies, the shipbuilders—everyone has his area, his designated place. Cooperation makes the meal go smoothly. Although they will gladly squeeze together for the right table hopper, they agree that a crowd would be unseemly. The only competition between them now is who can outdo whom for philanthropy."

Hallie is not actually laughing out loud but the way her mouth and cheek muscles are moving with noiseless laughter just beats the band. "I don't know why you said the table was set neatly.

It's a hodgepodge of dishes and utensils thrown on any whichway. They're having a gluttony game so childlike your eyes look for bibs around their necks. Nobody cares what's soup and what's dessert. They each have their own *chair* but after that it's grab and laugh and stuff your mouth. There's *plenty*—that's why they're having such a good time."

"Plenty at *their* table."

I feel a snap of rage like a rubber band in my skull. I am standing at the sink with my back turned, pouring bourbon over my ice.

"But they practice competing—with each other—just to keep their hand in. That's why they love that bridge game so."

"They don't ask me to play," I say, hearing my own voice flat as a warning.

Cad is too caught up with her "theory" to notice. "Baby, you'd hate it. They all talk in code and you know how literal-minded you are."

"What code?" Hallie says. I am certain Hallie is trying to hold Cad as long as she can. She knows what she's doing: Cad can't leave if she has a chance to do an imitation.

Cad puts on Oscar's soft-hearty Southern voice: "'I certainly do appreciate that.' *That* was an end squeeze play when Oscar forced the Governor to discard into his hand. 'I consider it a personal favor, Governor. Every bobcat has a pet spot he likes to have scratched.' Then the Governor says . . ." Cad switches into a country Texas twang: "'You caught the old possum.' Then Oscar chuckles and says, 'Well, it takes an old fox.'" Cad stands by the icebox for Oscar, by the stove for the governor. At the stove she says, "'Well, sir, Judge'—you're the judge, Baby—'Yes, sir, Judge, I'd say we're giving three laying hens for a short-tailed rooster.'"

My hand is frozen to my glass. I feel like the Judge. Cad goes merrily on, impaled on Hallie's glitter of appreciation. She moves to the icebox to speak for Oscar: "'I never saw a man go broke by taking a profit,'" Oscar says pompously.

I have to move as Cad comes to the sink to speak for the Judge: "'Got to keep your eye on where the sidewalks are going.' The Judge," Cad explains to Hallie, "is buying real estate going south and the Governor is positive Houston is going to grow west. Houston is supposed to grow west but darned if it doesn't just insist on moving south. So the Governor says, very testily," Cad moves to the stove, "'If Cad here will deal me a little frontage I'll put down my own sidewalks.' And then your uncle the icebox says,

'Yes sir, Governor, it's a pleasure to play with you. I can't stand a man who likes to lose. Never did understand those people who claim that—what is that saying, Cad?' I quote it for him. 'Now why in the world would anybody not want to win? And if you did lose what on earth would you have to smile about?'"

I can tell Cad is through by the way her ears cock for the applause but I say, "Are you through?"

"I heard Uncle Oscar say once that he thought it was immoral to be in business and not make money at it," Hallie says and then she hears me.

Now both of them are looking at my fury. "I happen to be sitting at the table you all think is so funny."

"Baby, they *want* you to believe that," Cad says. There is love—compassion—in her look but my goodness, my sweetness, my pink, juicy optimism has been clamped off.

"I think you have both lost your minds." Both? When did they become a pair? "The war is benefiting and Houston is benefiting and if those fine men also make some money then that's their just reward. And I'm here to tell you that they *are* fine men, every one of them."

"Of course they are." Cad gets up to leave.

"Uncle Oscar is like a refrigerator, though," Hallie says. "Frost-free." She doesn't see the warning look Cad gives her.

"That's enough." I see Cad is trying to tell me good-bye. "I don't think you should encourage Hallie in her adolescent iconoclasm." I am excited by the sudden white in Hallie's face. How dare they think I have no power?

Cad is leaving. "Oh, I wish you could stay." Hallie's face and voice show disappointment far in excess of what's called for here—is she practicing being a Southerner?

"It's possible you'll get to see Cad some other time."

"I *hope* so."

I can't slap her although I want to. They are the children—giddy, united; I am the balancer. I take a deep breath and drain my drink. Straight bourbon and the arrival into the kitchen of Mary Cowan and Brute restore equilibrium.

By CHRISTMAS 1945 all the men have returned, including Hyke.

"Don't worry about the girls not liking him," Cad says. "If you are firm in your choice they'll come around."

I guess I haven't admitted that they actually dislike Hyke—instead of just being skittish at having a mother in love. "Oh, I'm sure they *will* like him. He wants them to so much. It's just when he feels shy he overdoes the jokes . . ."

"I didn't know he was shy at all."

It's my turn to have the Christmas dinner. I take Hyke with me through the morning milk punch circuit so by the time we arrive home he is too relaxed. Everyone made such a fuss over him—it's just my friends' way but it can go to your head if you're not used to it. Now Hyke has added liquor confidence to his nervousness; his laugh rat-a-tat-tats through the whole downstairs.

As soon as we come in Uncle Doctor steps up politely and offers his hand; Hyke, not understanding what those hands mean to their owner, grips. When the D.R. gets his hand back he asks Hyke what he'd done in the war; Hyke answers that he was a handkerchief-head in the Japanazi theaterama. "Well, what are you planning on doing now that you've been discharged?" Hyke takes the drink I offer him. "I'm just fitzing around, Doctor, but I have a feeler out for the yellow-sheet factory downtown." The D.R., mistaking Hyke's laughter for evidence that all these are jokes, says, "I don't think there's anything more important to a young man in life than a sense of humor," and Hyke says before I can stop him, "You can say that again."

"But I don't want to." The D.R. leaves the floor to Sister.

She is now fifty-six—as she puts it, past sixty—and wears her beauty like a still-wet painting destined for the Louvre. Hyke grips her hand, squeezing her settings into her fingers, puts his arm across her precious silk ruffles, tells her he admires her beauty "hubba hubba" and that if she wasn't in the family department he'd insinuendo the extracurricular activity at the drop of a haterooni. Fortunately Sis doesn't have the slightest idea what he's talking about; she is too appalled at having her perfect surfaces smeared. I turn Hyke toward Oscar. Since they have already met I leave them together, although I stay within earshot.

Oscar asks Hyke what business he was in before the war. I know Oscar knows that I am serious about Hyke, that I hope Hyke can establish himself and become a contributor to Houston—Oscar knows he is talking to a possible brother-in-law.

Hyke knows too and starts backing in. "Mr. Yancey, I can't tell you what an honor and a privilege it is to have a gentleman like yourself to help me get a foothold in a city like Houston, which I know will really be on the map one day. And I know you yourself will be one of the ones who put it there." Hyke squares his shoulders, spreads his legs, holds out his hand. "Put her there, partner."

"Well," Oscar says, "we certainly do want to do everything we can to welcome home you men who gave up your jobs to win this war. I can't tell you how much I think this country owes you a debt. You call me and we'll have lunch next week. I think I might be able to advise you about your future and you don't want to be too careful to get started out on the right foot . . ."

Hyke roars with laughter. "Oscar, you're the best by test, the California kiss-off. You mean either 'I can't be *too* careful' or 'I do want to be careful.' 'I don't want to be too careful' is like saying I'll take the bow-wow chow and be glad to get it, and just between you and me and the gatepost I've had enough army leather to last me a month of Sundays . . ."

Oscar shakes his glass vigorously, rattling his ice. There is no one to serve drinks at my Christmas dinner but I hear the signal and come instantly. I put one arm through Oscar's elbow and the other through Hyke's, happily separating them. "What is more fun than fun?" I say, bending my knees so I can look up at them both. "Who is happier than a happy Baby?"

Hyke loosens his arm and circles my back, placing half his hand on my breast—the breast next to Oscar. Oscar jumps. "Well, now, Baby, I was just fixing to pay my respects to the kitchen while I'm sweetening my drink. As I was explaining to this young man here"—he pauses for emphasis—"you don't want to get on the wrong side of the cook." Oscar detaches himself. He says to Hyke, "You'll call me"—with a sad little droop to the *me*.

Hyke spies Mary Cowan and Hallie trying to get from the stairs to the den where Uncle Doctor is sitting alone. Hyke catches them in the entrance hall. "Is she going to snarl?" he says standing with legs spread in front of Mary Cowan. "First time she laid eyes on me she looked up from the couch: Grrrrr!" He laughs with delight. "Grrr grrrrr!" He steps back in mock terror. "But Baby Hallie here pressed my pants for me!" Oscar, still within earshot, quickly pushes open the kitchen door. Hyke puts his arm around Hallie's shoulders, squeezing her into what she calls his pit. "Yet, your sister gave me the cold shoulder, the old heave-ho. And now she's standing there like butter wouldn't melt in her mouth. Tell you what, Mary Cowan, let's make a deal. I'll bet my ruptured duck that if you give me a chance I can make you like me. Fair enough?" He releases Hallie and my daughters sidle toward the den. "Grrrr grrrr!" Hyke calls after them.

The Duchess is alone in the entrance hall—out of sight but of course we can all hear. Does she expect every entrance hall to be as big as hers? I turn to see if my slip is hanging below my hemline (to see if the cloth has torn away from the safety pin yet) and catch her at a glance. Her pose is the old familiar one for camera (now for Mother's gilt-framed mirror)—head back, chin up, Renaissance eyes dead center; each hand cups half of her enormous bosom partly covered in red velvet. The little lace triangle that used to hide the bottom of her cleavage has been abandoned this year; the v of her dress at the neckline leads the eye to the top of her midriff. I wonder where she got her confidence; she grew up in a small town just like I did and ten years earlier. I back up until I am at the opening to my entrance hall but still hidden. Her hands lifting her breasts, she lilts out the words, "What is more beautiful than a full-blown rose?"

Hyke materializes in front of her, gives her a kiss and throws an arm around her red velvet. She is oblivious of smears. "And if this isn't the prettiest rose that ever walked down a country lane . . ." Does he know how much he sounds like Oscar when Oscar is on parade?

The Duchess thinks he is wonderful. She understands exactly what he means when he says "hubba hubba" to her charms and raises her enormous bosoms in appreciation. She keeps her arms crossed under them in case the gesture is needed again. She tells him that if she wasn't so in love with her darling Oscar, so much in love that her heart still goes pitter-pat (she touches a spot on her bosom bared by the low-cut velvet)—why, he wouldn't believe the number of men who've tried to sweeten her up and he can count on one thing, that it is only her grand passion for Oscar that holds her back because . . . "I am *hot*" . . . she looks straight into Hyke's eyes. "I am so hot that one kiss is all it takes to set me off."

Oscar is just ducking onto the porch. "All right, everybody, let's eat." I clap my hands and go to round them up. I hear the Duchess: "You know what they say about us Texas gals—we mature early and ripen late." Hyke guffaws and assures her that he is no capon himself.

The Duchess moves into the living room and announces coyly, "The first kiss is like the first olive."

"To the table now!" I say.

"It takes a long time to get that one out of the jar but then they all come tumbling fast."

I am just passing the den when I hear Uncle Doctor mutter to Hallie, "I wish her first olive was still stuck in her mouth."

The Duchess insisted on lending me James (Charles quit); she is trying to teach him how to serve and decided to practice on me, I guess. The D.R. carves, heaping everyone's plate with two helpings because he says he doesn't want anyone coming back for seconds just as he is settling down to eating. He always gives the Duchess a huge mound of stuffing, piling up spoonful after spoonful, telling her he knows she likes it the best. Then he gives her slice after slice of dark meat, which, he announces, everybody else has too much sense to like. The Duchess accepts it all like a favored child being shown special attention. Oscar has his lips pursed and his eyes on his napkin.

The Duchess asks Sis how she likes the fire screen and andirons she gave me. Cad suggested it. Sis says they are fine. "I know if I can please you I've really done something," the Duchess says. "I know there's no one harder to please when it comes to good taste—you've got us all hopping we're so afraid of making a mistake. So I feel I've really hit the jackpot now that I finally picked out something that even you think is fine."

The screen, hung on brass plate like a curtain, is atrociously tacky; I know Sis wouldn't have it in her sister's house if she could help it. Now she swallows her food and says, "Next time you might try the Shabby Shoppe. Miss Hattie or Miss Gussie May will be glad to help you find just the right thing."

"Oh, we all know how you feel about your precious Shabby Shoppe. Why, the prices there, Hyke, would pop the buttons right off your drawers. Well, they're not getting this gal's hard-earned money. I can find everything I need right down at Foley's for one-tenth what you have to give at an antique store. Nosirreebobtail, not me. I haven't lived this long without learning a thing or two."

"Wonder how long that is," the D.R. says in a half-whisper to Hallie.

Oscar clears his throat and says in a loud voice, "Baby, I declare, this is about the best turkey I've eaten in a coon's age. What in the world did you put in this stuffing?"

"Chestnuts. Since Hyke is here and he's from the East . . ."

"Why, Popsy," the Duchess interrupts, looking at Oscar. "You always said you couldn't stand chestnuts. You told me they repeated on you from both ends."

"He eats chestnuts at *my* house," Sis says.

I reach for the crystal bell and shake it noisily. James appears through a crack in the door. "James, would you pass the rolls, please?"

"Who's a bad girl!" the D.R. says to Hallie, sitting on his right. He reaches under the table for her thigh. "Are you still my bad girl?"

"Mother, can I have some more wine?" Mary Cowan asks.

Oscar reaches for the bottle and pours it for her. "It's always a pleasure to fill the glass of a lovely lady."

"Hear, hear." Hyke stands up, knocking his chair backward to the floor. As he picks it up, the wine he is holding aloft spills on the rug.

The dark curls that my fingers remember are cascading like a bunch of grapes over his high, shining forehead. "Now I was going to say that I wanted to be the opener-upper in the toast department before I get too boozed up . . ." He laughs. "But as the drunk says to the lamppost, 'I think you've had tee many martoonis, you're out like a light.'" He holds up his hand to quiet the laughter that doesn't come. "I want to make a toast to this distinguished family from a visiting fireman—I want to express my deep appreciation for the opportunity to be here with you today and to say how very grateful I am that you have opened up your arms to a stranger and made me feel right at home . . ."

I have to remember that to tell Cad.

". . . and I hope it isn't presumptuous of me to add that I feel about all of you as I would about my own family and I sincerely look forward to many many more times around this very table with all of you. Merry Christmas!" Hyke raises his glass high and out, tapping mine first with a moist look in his eyes and then leaning across the table to touch the glasses of each person in turn. "And I don't mean maybe!" Hyke adds. "Doctor Tommy?"

The candles sputter with Sis's gasp. "Oh!" she says.

"He's a doctor, not a department store," Mary Cowan says. Hyke cocks an unfocused eye in her direction. "He doesn't have a toast department," she adds with a scowl.

"Hahaha!" Hyke pulls himself to attention and gives her a stiff military salute. "I get it. Like the farmer and the gator, plant you now, dig you later. Hahaha."

I ring the crystal bell although I haven't decided what to ask James for when he appears. He walks through the door and begins removing plates. "I think we're through, James," I say in a weak voice.

The Duchess looks startled but puts down her fork.

It takes James over ten minutes to clear the variety of tiny dishes spread over the table and to remove the plates to the kitchen one by one. The D.R. leans toward Hallie. "Too much shifting of the dishes for the amount of the vittles, ain't that right?" He winks at Sis. "If you ask me, this is a mighty fancy way to fill a belly. But your Auntie likes it and that's all right with me."

Sister is fussing with her napkin; I know she wishes she could let her fingers fuss with Mary Cowan who sits beside her. Mary Cowan looks perfect: a beautiful young woman dressed so exactly in style, including the latest makeup, that she appears to be waxed.

Finally James brings in the dessert; he drops it just inside the door. "That's all right, James." I am down helping him scoop it off the floor. "Just take this one back and bring out the other one."

"Yes'm," James says, looking bewildered.

"That's an old Memphis joke," I say. "One night we were having important guests to dinner and Chanchy—our cook then—dropped the steak on the floor. The platter was heavy, she said . . . that means 'hot,'" I explain to Hyke. "And I said, 'Just bring out the other one.' It was during the Depression and that was our week's grocery bill. Chanchy, cool as a cucumber, picked it up, took it out to the kitchen, dusted it off and brought it back." I excuse myself to go help James put the dessert back together; I see chocolate blanc mange in a lumpy ring. "Now anyone who doesn't mind the floor can have some."

Hyke says, "As long as it's your floor, it's hunky-dory with me. Dirt-schmirt. Since I would gladly kiss your footeroo . . ."

Mary Cowan closes her eyes. "Mother *hates* feet."

The Duchess reaches for the first plate. "The one that doesn't need it always eats it!"

Oscar says, "I have had an elegant sufficiency. And more

would be superfluous redundancy."

Sis says, "I'll just have a taste."

The D.R. says, "Honey, you can't eat that sugar. You'll have a reaction."

Hallie says, "Mother, may I have some more wine?"

The D.R. slips his hand under the table to her thigh. "Who's a bad girl? Huh?"

They are getting ready to leave when Brute drives up with her new beau in hand. Sis and the D.R. leave; the Duchess takes one look at the new man and joins the children in the den. I see Oscar slipping past the open door of the den to hide himself in the living room and Hallie determinedly following him. Oscar turns and sees her; he scatters himself like mercury over the living room rug just as the voices raise up in song:

> The army was scheduled to go to Talagy
> But General MacArthur said, *No* . . .

I see that Hallie wants to seize the moment to talk seriously to Oscar; I follow to warn her that it is no use now.

"Uncle Oscar," she says, "I'm very serious about my life and I want to talk to you about going into one of your businesses . . ."

> This isn't the season and then there's the reason
> Talagy has no U.S.O.!

Oscar stands, drinkless and iceless, staring at Hallie with an astonishing blend of sadness and malice in his Welsh-black eyes, and recites, "Greater fleas have lesser fleas upon their backs to bite them, and lesser fleas have lesser fleas and so on ad infinitum." His laugh is a gust of glee directed at the den.

I enclose Oscar with one arm and give him a kiss. "Isn't everybody happy? Having fun?" I rattle my ice in imitation of his most characteristic gesture as if my glass were a castanet and then loop that arm around Hallie. "Isn't she the darlingest daughter there ever was?"

"Hold the telephone! Hold the telephono!" Hyke shouts from the den.

Hallie's eyes are like a piece of green glass bottle clouded by years under the sand. I feel her shoulders fall an inch; I have never seen them slump before. I am pushing them up a little with my arm when Brute calls, "We need Baby in here!" and Hyke comes for me. "Get the Baby!" he says, throwing an imaginary lasso toward me. "They say, Get the Baby!" I am scuttled off to the den in his arms.

ONE SATURDAY IN March the mail brings two envelopes as if they are twins each insisting on being born first: one from Hyke, one from Harriet Tennant, who lives in Dallas. My fingers open Harriet's first, drawn to it as if her stationery were the ominous yellow of a telegram. A clipping falls out, an item circled; a note in her handwriting in the margin: "Isn't this a friend of yours?" In the marriage license column is the legal information that Haskell Havers Lauderdale was issued a marriage license to . . . the name blurs: Margaret or Martha or Marian, it is not Eudora.

I am standing stock-still in the hall as if I have been dumped into that awful stillness where everything is dead. The sunlight is colorless brilliance, the living room where I sit down retreats and grows dim, I feel deaf from shock. I am paralyzed. I am staring at the envelope from *him* in disbelief. It could not be from him. What could he possibly have to say to me?

The body relies on fingers to get it moving again; mine push themselves into the unsealed corners of the envelope, push and lift and push and lift until they have the flap raised; they remove the letter, nudging my eyes with it.

Darling Baby, I don't know how to explain . . .

What?

. . . only hope that you will understand and forgive . . . love only you always . . . can only hope that you will give me another chance . . .

He is not married. He was married and unmarried over a weekend while I was playing bridge. He can't explain how it happened, it just did—an impulse (he was tight), a sense of hopelessness that I would ever have him, that he could ever be worthy of . . . and when he realized what he'd done he was horrified, wanted to kill himself, only the thought of me . . . annulled Monday morning.

"Annulled?" I am speaking to Mother's green china urn. "Well, you can tell a church and you can tell a judge that a marriage between two adults who thought of it and were drinking wasn't consummated but you sure can't tell that to a woman."

Mary Cowan and Hallie are standing in the doorway like twins. I close my eyes. When I open them Brute is beside them. A second ago I think I heard Mary Cowan ask if there was any mail for her and Hallie ask if anything was the matter. I think I am staring at them; I see alarm in six eyes. "Hyke got married."

"Oh, Mother, how awful!" Hallie cries. Mary Cowan and Brute are hugging me. To prevent tears I disentangle myself and thrust the newspaper clipping at them.

They are a loyal chorus of damnation to Hyke. Their wrath converges on his name stopping just short of making him so awful that I must have been a fool to have ever looked at him. But I can hear an unsaid thread in there that Hyke is showing his true colors and they are flimsy dime store sequins.

"That's enough," I say. Instantly they are quiet, staring at me with such humble recognition of how dangerous real life, adult life is that I kiss them each one. "I'll be all right," I say. "I can bear anything with you all on my side." I take my letter and go upstairs to shut myself in my room.

But how am I going to bear it? No one has ever done this to me in my life. I feel myself turning into a wild mare, ripping off his curls with my teeth, pawing at his skin-like-frozen-silk until it is in slivers, pounding him into raw earth with four hooves at once and then knocking him over the fence with a square hind-leg kick smack into a cactus plot. I become a boa constrictor, slither after his mangled body, and treat him to a Texas-size hug around his rib cage. I am a longhorn cow for the time it takes to gore him in the groin. I am a queen bee until I have stung every inch of the soles of his feet. I am a black widow spider giving him sickening and slowly fatal kisses. I am a swarm of mosquitoes nipping at his blood. I am a herd of cockroaches smothering him with a blanket of my selves.

I have only his letter, which I crumple and hurl toward the wastebasket, smooth out and read, crumple and hurl again. I try beating the bed with my fists. All the rich nervous liquid in my body, from crotch to clavicle, is in a boil; I will die from it; no heart can bear this pressure. But my heart is thundering as if it claims credit for the turmoil, will stir another ocean of blood, whip up a hurricane, never subside. I lie quivering in my bed. I have to cry but there is no slack even then; fever is in my eyes.

I gave him my entire darling self: my concentration (I knew instantly what he needed), my subterranean knowledge (I put the highest interpretation on his every breath), and worst of all, my responses—I let my love for him create an extraordinary me surpassing my ordinary selves. The privilege of bringing me to fruition is repaid by Hyke the fig picker.

My finger rapes the telephone dial. Cad will help me kill him.

I don't wait to say hello to Edwina and ask immediately for Mrs. Mounce. "She's not there? What do you mean she's not there?"

"Miss Baby, is that you?" Edwina says.

"I've got to speak to her."

"She left me a number where she could be reached." I recognize Ten Penny's unlisted number and hang up.

A second rape of the telephone dial and I get the Fascinator's daughter; *she* is at the beauty parlor and will be home . . .

Nanpan, Drukie, Bitsy, Dodie, even Lily the sometime wife of the Tennessee Walking Horse are all out grocery shopping or visiting the hospital or at the dentist or giving a benefit for the library or having a fitting. "Well, I'm having a fit!" I scream to my bathtub.

I call Sis. She's just come in from her garden and wants to tell me . . . I can't stand any more metaphysical weeds and interrupt her. I tell her the whole thing. She doesn't say a word until I'm through—I hear her draw in her breath three times but not a word. Silence. Then she says, "I always knew he had a weak face." Then she says, "Eudora, you're well rid of a man like that." And then, "It's a good thing it happened while you're still so young and have your whole life ahead of you."

I knew she would tell Oscar. He came by that afternoon with a '41 Packard convertible, wearing his funeral face but looking, underneath—inside the coffin, as it were—too peaceful to be other than relieved. The Packard was navy blue too but I didn't say a word. Oscar half-intended it for the girls, he said, probably to explain why it wasn't a Bentley Mark IV. Or maybe because he means for me to behave like a girl—since I appeared to like younger men—and find another quick before I forgive Hyke.

Cad too seemed to expect me to forgive him but I know I never never will so help me God. It will be a while before I forgive

Cad. "What did you expect?" was her comment when I finally caught up with her and showed her Hyke's letter. "A Christmas dinner at your house is enough to send any man flying out of there so fast we could roll the dice on his coattails."

PARTIES AT MY house seem to erupt on their own schedule—as if the house suddenly becomes a magnet drawing all interested drinkers to my porch. Cars turn and head right to our corner on the middle-class edge of River Oaks, where they line up hanging out the driveway like horses waiting to be watered.

I almost always like my parties but today I wish my friends had stayed home. I am feeling unaccountably sad.

Part of it is my role as chief of a rejected nest. I got my first letter from Mary Cowan since she moved to New York; for the first time I am in the audience watching the play I created unfold, out of my hands now, uninfluenceable, and from this new point of view, startling in power. Mary Cowan got a job at the Museum of Modern Art—how did she get such a job so fast? She has three roommates who all Lux their undies; the bathroom flaps with soggy nylon; she is spending her first paycheck on duplicates for everyone to free the bathroom half the time. She has met no men and so must date Wallace Andrews, the too-long-nurtured son of Sister's friend Aileen. I smile because I understand her "must" so well. The past year was one long scene where she accused me of wanting to marry her off. I argued, "Listen to me, darling, *I'm* the one who wants to get married." Or I did. My friends' marriages are not inspiring. Cad and Johnny hardly ever spend a weekend together. Cad is with me and Johnny off doing whatever is in season for he-men. I find myself wondering if Cad and I will end up together in adjacent apartments at the Warwick, lavender old ladies watching the bridge players die off and having to scrounge for a game like Mother and Ida May.

But Hallie has not rejected her nest at all. She has moved right into its center, although today I feel sad about her too; I know she will leave very soon. This is her last home dance, her dress rehearsal, preview of what I know already will be a troubled life.

She beats me to the porch to greet the Mogul; her Southern

vowels lilt when she is glad to see someone and surely dart straight to the heart of the visitor—I know I usually feel picked off the floor by her soft contagious delight even when it is not me she is greeting. Just to hear her when she is happy makes me want to laugh. I want to laugh now beside my sadness. I would say by laughing that I am right and people are good and happiness is our sunshine and we are blooming—the things I can only say through a laugh now; I used to say them in words but everyone derides such simplicity, my Pollyanna, my Shirley Temple, my hopelessly simple coddled-egg of a heart.

The Mogul is already twinkling by the time I reach the porch; he kisses me with the extra warmth of a homosexual man who has just been moved to a fantasy longing by a darling daughter (I now understand that the Mogul is not asexual as I once thought). He has no more money than I have but between us we have raised thousands for my Negro hospital and his beloved ballet.

Two years have passed since the clipping came announcing Hyke's abortive marriage and I have more than healed; I no longer remember my pain. Other pains have taken its place. Hallie is iridescent, arguing with the Mogul over our future with the atom—which she knows more about than any of us because she wrote an article on Rice's new cyclotron for *The Thresher;* she is wearing my favorite, a clear-blue cotton dress which fights with but cannot overcome the greenness of her eyes, making their green seem interior as if chlorophyll were contained in her irises—today the deep emerald-blue of Kentucky. The Mogul is charmed by her; slipping with my glider in delight I know there is nothing to fear from his delight.

I examine the interior mixture of sadness and delight; it is curiously heightening. It is like my martini, which is bitter and gracious together so that every taste bud is touched. I hear the new cars arriving but I am holding on to this moment as if I were newly in love.

The atom talk has ceased. Hallie says, "How's the bookstore?"

"Oh, darling, everyone is waiting for a war novel," the Mogul says. "It's like the country was on a bad drunk. Now with an ice-pack on its head it is pleading, 'Tell me, what happened? Was I awful?'" He crosses his legs pitifully. "'Did I *do* it? I know I've been deflowered and there's no turning back. Oh God. I'll have to get *married.*'"

Hallie's laugh ripples with the astonishment of (to her) a new sexual candor; I keep pace with my glide.

It is the Fascinator (followed by a patient Boots and Jasper) shrieking for us to look at her New Look by Christian Dior. The Fascinator, five feet tall, has on an immense skirt reaching to her ankles; she looks like an overcurtained dressing table. She whirls flirtatiously for the Mogul, for Jasper; she is a fluffy long-dressed baby which one should gather up and crumple into your lap. Hallie says it is marvelous. It is. I know why the Fascinator is saying, "I have to do something because my nose is out of style." Her nose is tiny and pug, pulling her upper lip to it. Raggedy William has been seeing too much of a plain down-to-earth woman who thinks *he* is marvelous.

The Fascinator does not even resent Hallie's glow today—we had a run-in last month, about Hallie always being at our parties; unfair competition, the Fascinator called it but Cad insisted that was nonsense. She feels the Fascinator has been the centerpiece long enough and it is high time she steps off our lazy susan.

Oscar is muttering his way up the back walk toward our porch. Of course he twirls the Fascinator and speaks his line about walking down the garden path with a beautiful girl and kisses Boots and me and shakes hands seriously with our two men but I can tell something is on his mind. Hallie disappears to fetch everyone a drink from the kitchen. Oscar follows her just as Cad appears with the Tennessee Walking Horse (*sans* wife) in tow.

Hallie brings ice and glasses and more liquor to the table on the porch and is gone. The others come; soon the porch is packed with the noises of Friday evening and I cannot get back to my glider. Oscar leaves abruptly, walking from the kitchen to his new car with barely a pause. Since Hallie does not reappear, in a few minutes I go look for her.

Last year I put our conversation about money in my pantry, on that shelf for things you keep but don't expect to use for a long time and almost forget are there. I reach for it instinctively now as Hallie faces me with her humiliation.

Empathy sends me into a panic of alarm. But I am afraid to touch her. I saw her once before like this—the day the milkman kissed her; he apologized so sincerely to me that I advised her to forget it happened and she gave me this same look of excessive defeat.

The word *excessive* helps me remember that I am the mother. "What's wrong?" I say.

She waits to answer as if she knows her energy is required to fight off crumbling. In a minute she will explain it to me: Oscar gave her (or intends to give her) two thousand dollars a year now that she is twenty-one. She can expect, he says, two thousand each year from him. An income.

"I know there is something wrong with it, darling, or you wouldn't look like that," I say into her silence. "But I need you to explain to me what it is." Oscar *should* do something for the children; it was their grandfather who got him where he is. And . . . well, I feel I've earned every penny he ever gave me. Hallie has accepted nothing for four years, even working after classes to pay her college expenses (although that's only forty-six dollars in fees plus books); of course I pay for her to live here and will continue to. She is *my* daughter.

"He wants to give me an income and then I'm supposed to pay you room and board . . ."

"What?" Now my dander is up. I can feel all my arm and head hairs stiffen. "He what? How dare he suggest such a thing—the very idea that I would take money from my own daughter for room and *board*. Turn our home into a boardinghouse? My own . . ."

"Mother, that's not the main thing. The point is that I feel so insulted and I don't even know *why*. I don't *know* what's wrong with it but I know . . . I feel like I'm being paid to buy clothes and catch a husband, that he's saying if I don't decorate myself I can't even do that and if I don't do that I'll be pitiful. I feel like he's throwing a net over me and he *says* it's to keep the mosquitoes off—like I'm too weak to swat my own mosquitoes. He makes me feel so helpless . . ."

I never thought of Hallie as at all helpless and tell her so.

"What makes him think I can't get a job and earn my *own* two thousand a year? Doesn't he even want me to *try*? Goddamn him! He's . . ."

"Hallie!"

". . . calling me an imbecile!"

And it's working, I see with an explosion of pity; her face has turned back into moronic pudge. We hug. We always hug at times like these, hug and pat and hug and drop our tears. I am reassured to feel her back as rigid as ever. "Do you think he's afraid of the competition?"

She looks at me with respect and I nod. Geometry slowly returns to her face. I am never one to let a good thing stand alone; I follow my inspired comment with four others just like it.

Hallie says then, "Does he think he can buy me off for two

thousand?"

"Probably. Human nature is not his long suit."

"Well, unfortunately it's not mine either."

"After all that history?" I get my first smile after what seems now a lifetime, an abyss of despair. Of course I know three minutes passed. "Well, let's think of something. What about asking him for a job for the same two thousand?"

"I already did. He said he could use me as a receptionist. They don't hire girls for anything else, it distracts the men. Besides, I intend to take the money."

"You do?"

"I just won't let it control me, that's all."

Since I have never been able to control her, I assure her that the mere dollar hasn't a chance. But I wonder if a dollar is ever mere.

We have been absent from our party too long. I promise her we will discuss it in the morning, we will huddle on the studio couch and think of something.

"There's nothing to discuss," she says. She splashes water on her face but it has not revived when she turns to me and hugs me again. "I love you," she says simply.

"I love you too. I love you more than anything in the world. You know that." I feel a tiny shudder in her spine and I hope that my daughter, like a dog getting rid of unpleasant water, is instinctively drying herself. "Come on, mugwumps, let's get back to our admirers."

———————

Our party goes far into the night. I know I am too tired, even too tight, to move all those glasses toward the kitchen sink. I turn off the lights and go straight to bed.

I almost never wake up once I am down for the night so I am more startled to find myself sitting upright at two A.M. than I am concerned about what could have woken me. But since we never bother to lock our doors, I listen dutifully, both ears pointed toward downstairs. I think I hear footsteps going into Hallie's bathroom; I relax and refocus my ears. The toilet flushes; the footsteps go back into her bedroom. The footsteps come out to the bathroom again.

My cigarette lights itself; my concentration is fixed on the vanished end of our party: who was left that Hallie might . . . ? I am not stuck on the requirement that my daughters be virgins but since the Heman Sweatt episode, all year I have been expecting

Hallie to pair up with a Negro or Mexican to prove that neither one of us minds if our daughter/self marries one.

Now I know something is going on in my house. I can feel current moving across two A.M. when the air in my only major possession should be sleeping. I open my door a crack. It is possible that the other person was the first set of footsteps and I will only see Hallie's nightgown when the bathroom opens a second time; I am certain it is not possible that both sets of footsteps are Hallie, although in some other air that could happen.

My hand is gripping my doorknob with the tension of self-disgust but I do not throw open the door and step honestly into my own hall. Self-disgust makes me lower my eyes; I hear the bathroom door open; I am just in time to see Cad's round dimpled bottom scurry out of sight.

I almost laugh out loud from the shock of seeing stark dead white when I was expecting dark brown. I almost laugh. My mind prevents me. I am arguing with what I see. Cad had too much to drink and didn't want to drive home—especially since Johnny is likely not even to be there. At least she came upstairs to bed instead of occupying the couch with all her clothes on right in the middle of downstairs. With all her clothes off? Hallie couldn't find a nightgown?—although when Cad is tight . . .

In an hour I have the house spotlessly clean downstairs and still the dawn hasn't come.

I am feeling grainy behind the eyes when I finally go to sleep impatient for morning. Since Cad will sleep late (she hides in bed the morning after she's had too much to drink, especially if she can't even get herself home) I'll have a chance to talk to Hallie alone.

It's not yet nine o'clock when I am back in my spotless kitchen with coffee made and orange juice squeezed.

"How nice of you." Hallie's voice is mechanical but she is slow in the mornings, preoccupied with dreams still. I wait while she drinks half a cup of coffee. She is so compact in her body that I know I am glad there wasn't a Negro boy with her last night. I don't have to say anything but I am glad. Her face is loose and flows sideways every time I try to catch her eye. She knows I want to talk but she picks up the funny papers as if this were any other morning. "Hallie."

"Yes, Mother?" The words slide out like the guts of a crushed caterpillar.

I've been robbed.

"I'm going to Jamail's and Coronet and by Mr. Wade's, I'll be back about one if anyone calls. Do you want anything special from the store?"

She shakes her head still looking at me. Her eyes are rimmed by pale flesh below their eyelashes but between is the piece of glass from the five-and-ten scratched like a dollar bill.

I am staring at her lips pursed to receive fresh scalding coffee made by me. She has burned her tongue; a quick spray of tears is blinked away. She offers to run my errands for me in a voice like the icing used on gaudy store-bought cakes.

Suddenly I know that it is urgent that I leave before Cad wakes up.

I call Hyke from a public booth on Shepherd, putting change into a pay phone like a prostitute. If he is free tonight, I say, I thought it would be fun to drive to Dallas. He will get free, he says, with his machine-gun laughter. I will pick up my pink dress at Coronet and be there by martini time. It is one of our anniversaries, I lilt into the phone and then hang up before he can insist on knowing which one. I will think of that on the highway.

I have been robbed in my own home in my own hometown by my best friend. By the time I am on the highway I am void inside, sucked empty of memory. By the time I reach Dallas and maneuver its strangeness to Hyke's apartment, I know it could not have happened.

Nevertheless I decide to marry Hyke. He will move to Houston as soon as he can. We set an early date.

There is one bad moment: we are in bed, my pink dress with the peplum carefully hung on a chair; I am burying my hand in Hyke's hair, which is coarse, curly, longer now, and crackling clean . . . when my fingers feel his hair as the paper straw that lines an Easter basket. I yank a green curl; the hand which was caressing mashes my breast. I sit up into another room lit by a street lamp and apologize but my chest is tight and gasps. He gets up to fetch himself a cigarette. I am calm when he returns.

PART III

1950–1954

I AM DISTRACTED by a buzzing of my own impatience; my hands would slap it like a mosquito if they could. Being fifty is a very different thing. Who could have foreseen that I would change so radically just by ceasing to bleed? Who would have thought that all those eggs were really money that suddenly ran out: no more dollars, my body says, and no more credit; get out and make some francs or marks or pesos or gulden or print some script but do it now this body is finished, spent; depend on that old currency and you will be as poor as a Confederate banker. My skin is soft like gold and my mind is rejecting all solutions the body proposes; I am ordered by that mind to eliminate everything counterfeit, inked, flimsy, nickel, base, temporary; all values by face, all promises to pay, all chits and charges and buffaloes and Indians. These must be your golden years, mind says.

Hyke is improving. He is changing from a thin, laughing youth into a man of substance (and perhaps too much weight) because I have fashioned myself to fit. I wear pink and dip my knees; I say often, "You know I can't be responsible for my behavior when I'm wearing pink." I say, "Hyke always says he doesn't know what to expect when I walk out in my pink hat." Soon Hyke began to say this. When I spy him floundering at a party I rush to his side singing "Here comes the Baby all in pink"—giving him his clue that he should take on a more charcoal-gray demeanor.

Cad too is fifty and laughs at my feeling that it is a major change: "Those of us who have been changing right along don't have to make complete reversals according to a date," she says. I do not change "right along"; I stay put until I have exhausted every possibility *there* and then I jump over to a new square. I am not a lizard; I am a geological stratum.

When Hallie returned after almost two years in New York she was not covered with any honors that I could see. In fact, she was coated with bus. She arrived at dawn; when I came downstairs to investigate her noises, I saw a thing both puffy and thin at the same time, pasty and flushed, eyes dull with only sudden points of fury breaking through. Her hair was too short everywhere except over her eye where it hung in jagged arrows. With heroic self-control for so early in the morning I hugged her and said how glad I was to see her. I could not control my nose and gasped at the smell. The child I often remembered in absence as a fat blond baby looked like nothing more than a grim bony adult.

"I know I look terrible," Hallie said. "I've been on the bus for three nights."

"The bus?" I was on a bus once in the Mexican mountains; it rattled and swerved up to the edge of sheer unwalled drops into death with its cargo of chickens, babies, women, old men, vegetables, household goods, and me; at each curve we were all thrown toward the abyss, unbalancing the already teetering bus . . . one trip on such a bus convinced me that in redemption the first step is physical order. That's one thing I can handle like nobody's business: bath, beauty parlor, clothes, sunshine, food, rest. I drank my coffee with averted eyes and minimum breathing. In my mind Hallie was already Pygmalionized.

Hallie came home to tell me she was getting married, I guess— to Selwyn Jones whose family has been in Houston for ages. He is darling and looks like his mother's people rather than the Welsh Joneses; he is tall but not too tall, blond, Germanic in the neck, with a darling face that is also clean and healthy-looking. He had met Hallie at the Shamrock pool during one of the infrequent home visits and had seen her again in New York at one of those expatriate Texan parties.

Every mother is delighted when a daughter settles into her life and Hyke was like a kid at Christmas: presents arrived, photographers came, a clean and shining Hallie modeled her trousseau, relatives gave parties to which Selwyn was always late, and Hyke got to give Hallie away.

Sister and the D.R. wanted to have the wedding in their hills but Sis is so sick the D.R. is already insisting she move to the Lamar, that another year in that house will kill her.

After the wedding and honeymoon, I spontaneously suggested they stay with us until Selwyn got himself some money.

But ever since Hallie turned up smelling of bus Hyke had stepped up his campaign; he told me, seizing an off-evening early in the week, the soft times when we didn't drink after dinner, that he wanted above all things to have a home of his own, of our own; that he had never had a real home because his mother died when he was so young and besides . . . I know it is my friends.

They swarm over all my houses as if they were Texas ants. I even understand why he instituted the rule that everyone has to call first, especially Cad. Husbands always resent their wife's best friend; Daddy made fun of Ida May until the day he died. I believe that if the wife is patient, husbands come around.

Cad says Hyke acts like the walls of my house are vaginal and every old pal in the vicinity wants to barge right in. She says, How can anyone *call* when they're in traffic on their way home and feel a signal through the floorboards that a party at Baby's is getting started? My parties have become planned; my house has calmed down now.

But it is still *mine;* Hallie proved it by returning one morning and sitting in the kitchen before we were up so that when Hyke came down to breakfast there was a daughter there.

I began to see my darling house through his eyes. I saw it as a fought-over bone beginning to shred. I saw its ragged threads, its cracks, its uninteresting calcified structure. When Uncle Doctor told me again that he meant it, he was moving Sister to the Lamar as soon as possible, my brain clamped right down and I called Oscar. Since everything was in the family, he arranged for me to pay Sis and the D.R. whatever cash I got for my old house and Oscar would hold the note and pay them interest on the remainder. And since Hallie and Mary Cowan were the heirs in all our wills, everyone was happy.

Hallie must have gotten pregnant on her honeymoon—but why wait, in my opinion; if you know you want children you might as well go on and have them and Hallie is already twenty-three.

She found an apartment two blocks from Main Street near downtown—the entire upper story of a ramshackle old house. We are sitting in the room at the top of the steps, which we call the living room. On the floor she has a galvanized washtub holding a cake of ice; behind it an electric fan is blowing in our direction. Outside the temperature is ninety-eight. I am thankful that I am not pregnant.

Hallie's ankles are the size of her calves and her feet won't fit into any shoes. She is describing the colors she plans to use to paint the apartment for Dora. Neither of us has the slightest doubt that it will be Dora.

She looks so misshapen and miserable that I send my mind back to the day a few months ago when I was buying her trousseau. We were in Semaan's looking for the bridal nightgown and robe set. Semaan's dressing room is huge with gilt chairs and two walls of mirrors, and the scent of something like Chanel No. 5 is filling the store.

I almost could not bear the beauty of Hallie's body. Her skin had the luster of pink pearls, particularly over her high plump breasts (which are now huge and rest on an equally protruding belly). My throat was dry but I smoked several Chesterfields anyway to quiet an intense nervousness: I felt that I had been dumped into the myth of Ceres: I was Ceres and this perfect golden grain of prime wheat was my Persephone about to be seized and dragged off to the underworld.

Through the Chanel No. 5 I could smell Hallie's insistent personal scent, which was like fresh spring air in a wheat field, a smell she has carried in her pores since babyhood, through horse sweat and adolescent glands and young adult experiments with lemon soap, a smell that has only become more definite with age just as her eyes have decided to be finally green.

She had a beautiful bust like the marble of Aphrodite—I remembered Cad telling me that if I can say breast of chicken I can say breast of girl, and smiled.

"What?" Hallie said.

"Nothing," I said. "I was just thinking what a beautiful figure you have."

I didn't remember that her body was so finished before; she had filled out in the two years she'd been away—she looked womanly, ripe and mature as a luscious camellia. I was sorry I was staring and searched for another cigarette, took out my comb instead. I wanted to comb her hair.

She said, "This is just the most beautiful thing I have ever seen in my whole life." It was a silk nightgown in the indescribably vibrant cream-white of a magnolia blossom with fine lace along the neckline and armholes; the matching pegnoir had a round collar and tied at the throat and made her look like a fairytale princess for the first time in her life that I could remember. "I don't deserve anything anywhere near this royal. It's magical. I just . . ." Her eyes were profoundly grateful—not, I thought, because I was ready to buy it for her but primarily because I announced that she deserved it by bringing her here. "I feel like you in it," she said.

"Can I refill your iced tea?"

Her voice shakes me out of my heat trance and I get up. "Let me get it. I hate to see you walking on those poor feet." I wonder if Hallie will survive until the first of November. Because she is normally so small she looks enormous already; tall women don't appear to get as big.

"Maybe Dora will come early."

I hand her a refilled glass of iced tea in which the ice is already melting. "I wish she'd be born on my birthday. I can't think of a more exciting present for my half-century day."

Hallie laughs. "Now you heard that, Dora," she says to her belly. "Mother wants a birthday present."

"Are you sure you want to name her Dora?" I am immensely pleased, of course; I just want to hear it again. She already said she wouldn't name her Eudora, just Dora—so no one could give her a nickname.

"She's already named."

"Well, I'm going to get her grandmother's house ready for her."

As soon as Hallie got pregnant I began to imagine my granddaughter and I was certain my old house was not a grandmother's house. It is too close to the street for one thing, and on the street all the time, except on rare bad-weather days, there are teenagers and children asserting their youth. It is time for me to live in a stately neighborhood where children only visit—in fact, I am tired of hearing half-grown noises altogether. I want to be surrounded by the cheeps of birds and the gurgles of my baby granddaughter.

"Sister's is the only house in Houston beautiful enough for Dora," I say. "My old house is just a party house which people don't look at. But a baby would look. I certainly don't want a house that could twist her esthetic sense all out of kilter, now do I? Isn't it true that taste is set forever while their eyes still have cornea color spilling over into the whites?"

"Maybe even earlier. Maybe if I start painting the apartment now she'll grow up to be a house painter."

"An artist."

"An interior decorator."

"I hope she never grows up at all!" I've got to go. I'm meeting Sis at Semaan's to pick out Dora's christening dress. I stand up.

"Will you be in Auntie's—your new house by your birthday?"

"We'll be in the streets. We have to be out of the Overbrook in a month and Sis won't leave her house until her roses have stopped blooming. She thinks I'll let them all die." I want to leave quickly—

it hurts me to see her standing on those feet. Although her ankles and feet are enormous they look more like jellyfish than supports.

"Well, take your choice," Hallie says, her voice so happy it is clearly unaware of her lower limbs. "What's it to be: a birthday present or a house-warming present? You can't have both."

"Mugwumps." I kiss her forehead, careful not to throw her off balance. "You let her take her time. We want her to be perfect."

"She'll be perfect."

But I am talking to lizards I realize. In Sister's house I am becoming Sis. I sweep the terrace and apologize to the caladium for stepping on its leaf, I reassure the watching lizards that I am their friend and they needn't bother to hide from me. I can hear Sis's voice coming out of my mouth, high and soft and definite: "Now you stop that," she/I admonish the wind. The sun is as warm as a sister on my hair. I love her house and I wish she could have kept it; I feel both thoughts together and ignore the contradiction.

The house is perfect for me. I called Hallie earlier and told her to bring Dora out tonight; Hallie was a long time answering the telephone and I know she is up to something—her voice was coated with sensuality. She said she would try. *Try* to bring me my granddaughter?

At five-thirty I hear Hallie's tires crunch the shell driveway. Hyke's new album from *South Pacific* is filling air formerly satisfied with the tinkle of crystal rubbing against each other. Since Sis left behind most of her furniture (I have added only Mother's urn and gold mirror and bluebonnet painting, which nestles into one wall) the room still belongs to Sis. It is a perfect setting for Dora.

"You look marvelous, darling!" I say to Hallie. She is dressed in her going-away suit, which had very little wear after the wedding and her skin is glowing. There is a visible red spot on her jaw which I pretend not to notice. "And there's that angelbaby Dora!" Dora gives me her perfect gurgle and coo. "Hyke, look who's here!"

Vivid in orange and yellow, Hyke calls as he walks too close for calling, "Baby Mother and Baby Baby! Shake it up but don't break it, wrap it up and I'll take it." He swoops down for a kiss from both, making Dora cry in alarm. "Looks like you've got a cold fish in that basket," he laughs but Dora, swept up by me, instantly stops crying to reach for my pearls. Hyke goes to the record player and in a few seconds "Ain't she sweet" booms into the cathedral ceiling; Hyke, oversinging the lyrics, grabs Hallie's arm and cake-walks her down his imaginary street, grinning hugely. I have to sit down. I am dizzy with the feel of Dora against my chest, the smell of her baby puppy powder in my mouth.

As part of our move into Sis's house, Hyke agreed that we should split our finances, me buying the food and Hyke the whiskey. Hyke buys good scotch since he drinks that, and bourbon and gin on special—whatever he can get at the best price from his friend Mr. Thompson at Cobbs. "Mr. Thompson says you can't tell the difference between this and Old Grand-Dad"—or Beefeater's or Smirnoff or Courvoisier, he always says as he hands out the glasses. Tonight he fixes Hallie a gin on the rocks and says, "Old man Thompson says you can't tell the difference between this and House of Lords."

"Indeed you can't," Hallie says with a sweet smile, "unless you taste it."

Hyke explodes into a paroxysm of laughter. "Hold the telephono!" he says, rushing to his own telephone to call Mr. Thompson and tell him.

When he returns he stares at the red spot on Hallie's cheek just off her chin. "Where's Selwyn? A little trouble in the marriage department?"

"He had to go to Mexico on business."

I'll have to remember to tell Hallie that she should just say he went to a ball game with his brother. Hyke says, as I knew he would, "Now Baby Mother, I never heard of a man who repossesses cars for a finance company having to go to Mexico on business." He chants, accompanying himself with a short two-step. "Just a little baby sister of a little señorita couldn't speak a word of English but her name was Margarita."

"Hyke, come look at Dora; she's smiling just like she knows me." I lean my face into Dora's, who reaches again for my pearls.

Hyke leans over and rubs Dora's pale cap of hair. "The most amazing baby ever born. Or so they tell me," he says, straightening up.

"Hallie, tell Jewell Dora's here."

I am trying very hard to like Jewell. After Hyke bailed him out of jail the second time he offered Jewell a permanent job if he would only drink after work. He was an itinerant grass cutter around our old neighborhood but he had been in the army and was a chauffeur for the officers. Hyke made it very clear that he was saving Jewell's life; Jewell got a room to live in, a pair of uniforms (black coat for driving, white jacket for serving), and a salary that would keep him dependent. Hyke likes to tell Jewell jokes. I hate coming into the kitchen accidentally and having them both fall silent the minute they hear me, but I can't make Hyke understand that I feel disrespected in my own house when he does that. But I won't let Jewell come into my bedroom unless I'm out of the house; I clean up my bathroom before he gets there with the Lysol. I can't logically explain my feeling that Jewell was hired to side with Hyke against me.

Jewell is learning how to cook. He is in the broiled steak, frozen french fries, frozen snap bean stage. He has finally learned how to make meat rare but hasn't yet gotten the knack of keeping the beans crisp. He has a new set of teeth and says he can't taste just yet but even before the teeth he had all the earmarks of someone who uses food as a safety net to break the descent of the bourbon. Hyke is the one who wants him to cook; I would prefer to do it myself. If it weren't for Dora riveting my mind to her face I might wonder how come I always lose control of the food in my house.

I begin feeding Dora. Hallie hovers right by my arm with her bottle. I don't think I approve of Hallie's way of feeding: she scoops a dab of carrots onto the nipple and pops it in Dora's mouth, removing the nipple for more carrots until the carrots are all gone.

"She looks so surprised," I say, softly I hope.

Dora watches first my face then Hallie's as if she were graciously studying our language since we refuse to speak hers.

Hyke is playing "When the Darkies Beat Their Feet on the Mississippi Mud," pantomiming it as if he were the vocalist. It is one of his favorite acts but because the lyrics don't seem to bother Jewell I have almost stopped hearing them. Since Dora's birth I am trying very hard to take them both seriously.

While Dora is being bedded down on my bed I see Hallie examining the room. With its huge bay windows looking out on the pines and small hills rolling to the creek, the bedroom of my sister's house is as beautiful in its way as the living room. Sis left her English Regency bedroom suite but it has been relegated to the guest room; the master bedroom is newly furnished in ivory and black Chinese Victorian: a his dresser, a hers dresser, accompanying mirrors, twin beds, between-bed table, and a large black plastic recliner in front of a new television set. These furnishings just came out of storage; they belonged to Hyke's mother (except the recliner and tv) and he was saving them until he had a house of his own. He also just bought a real oil painting of a snow scene, which takes up the wall over the beds. I didn't want to hurt his feelings so I put the old living room curtains in here—their splashy green flowers draw the eye away from the furniture—and let the old rug guard the floor. Hallie spies a photograph on Hyke's dresser which she has never seen before; when we return to the living room she asks Hyke about it.

He immediately goes and gets it. "That's *my* Hallie," he says, holding aloft a dark-haired young woman with too much makeup. Her expression is a flirtatious smirk—an odd choice to have framed. There are no clothes evident in the photograph at all and the first rounding of the breasts is visible.

"Is she a model?" Hallie asks.

Hyke throws his arm like a whip around her shoulders and roars. "No, but she's pretty enough to be one, that's for sure. Isn't she a killer-diller? That's my family, and you know?—I just discovered her."

"Hyke found her when he went to his cousin's wedding." I am ready to forgive the other Hallie for not knowing how to dress for a picture because she had foster parents all these years, but I wish the frame of the copy she gave Hyke were just a quarter inch higher. "She's the daughter of Hyke's oldest brother, Edward." I don't need to tell Hallie what I think of *him:* he was convicted of selling phony securities from a brokerage house in which he was a partner and spent ten years in prison. "I told you. She came back with Hyke to visit us for two days but you were too busy painting to come meet her."

"I wish I had."

I wish she had too, so much that I may be imagining I hear loyalty to me in Hallie's phrase.

"She was going to stay longer," Hyke says. "then something came up. I don't know what. She's a pianist; she either is or thinks she ought to be temperamental. But let me tell you, Hallie baby, it was one great day for me when I discovered her. Neither one of us has ever had a real family and we just fell into each other's arms like long lost orphans."

"It was so lucky for both of you," I say, giving Hyke's waist a squeeze. "Poor little Hallie's had such a hard life." My own Hallie darts me a glance that tells me I have not managed to keep disbelief out of my voice.

"Well, actually we were all damn lucky she had such a good home," Hyke says. "The Sterns are wonderful people. They loved Hallie like she was their own daughter, educated her, and encouraged her music. She'd never have turned out so well if her father had stayed out of jail and she'd lived with him."

"Is she a pianist?" Hallie asks. She is no longer looking at the photograph; no one is but Hyke. "Concert?"

"Not actually right now." Hyke puts the picture on the table where he can still see it. "She's trying to decide just what she wants to do. She's twenty-seven and that's a little old to become a concert pianist. She'll probably end up teaching—she's very fond of children."

I can't stop my eyebrows; they shoot up unasked. "She is?"

"Oh, yes. She told me how much she wanted a large family of her very own."

"I think it's wonderful that you found her and I hope I get to meet her someday." Hallie speaks the words like a curtain she's pulling down on this scene and sits back down.

"Never you fear, it's right here in the cards that you will," Hyke says with a guilty laugh. "I invited her to spend Christmas with us! Surprised?" His arm whips me around. "I knew you'd want her here with us."

"I hope you told her to bring her battle gear. Just a peaceful little family Christmas dinner . . ." It is all I can think of to say. I am stunned.

But Hyke's eyes are damp and he pulls me close. "I don't know what I'd do without you. I'm so lucky to have *you* and poor little Hallie doesn't have anyone . . ."

I should feel ashamed but I feel confused; happily, the doorbell rings. "Oh, that's probably Cad." I can't keep the pleasure out of my voice.

Hyke grabs my elbow. "Cad? Did you invite her? I've told you before that I don't want her barging in here unannounced. Tell her we're at dinner."

Of course I invited her; I wanted her to see Dora and I decided Hyke had had long enough. I stand frozen, elbow still out.

Hallie goes toward the door. "I'll do it."

"No, let her in." Hyke stomps off to the bedroom and I am afraid he will wake Dora. I go to move Dora into the guest room while Hallie lets Cad in. My mind is in a moil; my hands are stiff under Dora's sleeping bottom.

I see Cad peering around the slowly opening door as if she were expecting a snowball, grinning because she thinks it is a joke.

I know Hyke will turn on the charm as if he'd been awaiting Cad for a lifetime. In fact he rushes to his car and comes back

wearing a button that says: HYKE LYKES YKE. We are all compli-
menting him on his ingenuity in getting them made up, I am bat-
tling hurt feelings because he doesn't consider me special enough
to be the button's first audience, Cad is ruminating over a comment. "It has a definite Middle English flavor" is all she can come
up with.

There is a move to throw Cad off the school board because she
owns some stock in the bank which is the school district's depository. Her father was an early president of that bank. I am indig-
nant: it is ridiculous to think that just because Cad owns stock in a
bank she has anything to do with bank policy. Hallie gives me a
strange look; Cad says it is an attempt to use conflict of interest
against her.

I have never heard the phrase before. My mind seizes on it as if
it were a brand new flag to wave across my life's dilemmas. I tuck
it away for down days. I will bring it out to assert my only-
humanness next time I am tugged by Hyke versus Cad; I will un-
furl my flag and abdicate. However I have never thought of myself
as only human.

I hug Cad, glad that no conflict of interest arose over that
night when she was too tight to drive home and inexplicably slept
in Hallie's room. Although I disbelieve in Freud as heartily as it is
possible to disbelieve in something you know nothing about, I do
think I imagined some crisis that night in order to force myself to
make up my mind to marry Hyke. I obviously intended to do that
all along. It was my pride that almost prevented me.

Hyke has just returned with a drink for Cad. "Mr. Thompson
says you can't tell the difference between this and Canadian Club.
And you certainly can't—unless you taste it. Hahaha."

"My taste buds have long since bloomed and dropped to the
garden floor," Cad says, smiling winningly at Hyke.

I hug Hyke and kiss his ear.

"You are such a funny man," I tell him.

Finally Hyke goes to bed—although I know he will reappear from
time to time, and call from the bedroom that our voices are coming right through the heating register and are we going to talk all
night. But finally we can begin on the real conversation.

Hallie knows; right away she asks me about this other Hallie.

"Well, this child—but that's just it, she isn't a child—hung on
Hyke the whole time and I just ignored it, treating it as an orphan's
excess, until suddenly when we were all in bed and practically

asleep this Hallie came into our bedroom with her comforter and pillow and asked if she could sleep on the floor between our beds. Have you ever heard of such a thing?"

My own Hallie's eyes are as brimming with loyalty as I can wish. "A grown woman wanting to sleep on the floor between a married couple? If she hadn't had that babypie look on her face I'd have thought she was joking. And Hyke thought it was sweet that she wanted to be near us. I just had to put my foot down. I said, 'Now don't be ridiculous, Hallie'—I hate calling her that, I'll never get used to it—'you go right back into your own room and stay there. Don't you come back in here one more time.' She'd already been in to tell us goodnight heaven knows how many times as if she were a spoiled three-year-old—coming in in her shorty night-gown on one pretext or another for the umpteenth goodnight kiss. If you ask me she's got her chickens all lined up, I don't care *how* sweet she looks."

"She doesn't look sweet at all. She looks like a tart."

The residual turmoil in my brain vanishes with a pop but I say, "Oh, I wouldn't go that far." I lean closer to my own Hallie and feel my frown lines loosen. My own Hallie, at this moment, has the face of an intellectual saint. I get up to fix us both a drink.

"I can't deny Hyke a family member after he's been so patient with all of mine . . . I don't mean *you*, darling. He thinks you're adorable. Just a small one?"

Hallie is standing beside me helping me fix our drinks and I love her for not sitting and waiting.

"You make him feel good about himself—you talk to him, laugh at his jokes. But every time Cad comes over she manages to say something that makes Hyke feel he's read the wrong book. Cad does that to me too all the time but I'm used to it."

Hyke appears in the doorway rumpled from sleep. "Are you two going to talk all night?" he says plaintively, heavy-eyed; he pours himself a glass of milk. I pat him, turn him around, slowly lead him back to bed. On my way back to the kitchen I stop for a look at Dora, a little hump of sheet in the moonlight. I promise her—with the gross exaggeration of emotion that midnight brings—that I will provide for her forever.

Hallie is standing by the window when I come through the kitchen door, her back at rest in the Chippendale curve, her body graceful, as fine, as supple and minimal as a dancer's. I am shocked to see that she is so small.

"I am too happy to have you and Dora here to want to talk

about the other Hallie at *all*." I just want to sit here in my own kitchen with my own Hallie and drink till dawn. "Just a small one?"

While we speak of Selwyn and his inability to make money, while we anticipate Dora's brilliant future, my mind explains to her mind what I cannot speak: I ran after your bus and you mocked me. I tried to dissuade you: argued with you when you took the luscious clothes you bought with Oscar's gift and gave them all to Carrie, when you put on the golf dress Cad was going to throw out and packed your everyday horse clothes, cut your hair, and took only what would fit in your old camp dufflebag as if you were eleven. "Chicago?" I said. "What do you think is in Chicago?" I knew: dead animals and a lake inhumanly huge. You were going by riverboat up the Mississippi as if you were safe inside the pages of Mark Twain. You were planning to sit at the feet of Great Books and learn the meaning of life. You were in love with a charming intellectual who found your scaled-down athlete's body close enough to a boy's to give him hope. You were leaving me because I brought a husband into the house.

You hardly talked that last month but I saw the arrogance in your eyes. I felt your brain beg for a sign, scan the skies like anti-aircraft lights for truth as if truth weren't right in the room—but you wouldn't look at me. You were making plans. You couldn't just make the plan and leave, you wouldn't run away on impulse one prebreakfast dawn—you made me watch the cooking, the thickening until I was nervous enough to seize the spoon myself and take a turn, participate, stir—"I want to drive you to the bus," I said. "I *want* to." "In case I change my mind?" Your face challenging mine was like marshmallow. You were carrying your shoulders up around your ears.

You didn't understand that I had to send you away then. I had to get rid of the child to acquire the husband (who is now the child?).

When I turned to Hyke, our love reaped all the rewards.

Although we don't drink until dawn, it is close to it when I am hugging and patting them both too many times before they finally leave.

But after she has gone I see the future held smack up against my eyes like a *Life* photograph: Hallie selling apples in the street with frostbitten toes and a dead doll under her cloak who looks like Dora. I am flooded with adrenalin although I am lying in my bed all set to go to sleep: I will need to run through all the streets, all the cities, to reach her and pull her into a hot, steaming restaurant and watch her expand and grow rosy from baking-bread smells. I am a rescuer who hasn't been called yet. Tomorrow I will start hoarding everything they will need, Hallie and Dora.

I already have the house, the fairytale grandmother's house, which I will snatch them from their hovel to bring them to, lay it before their feet; I will have velvet dresses for Dora and her own string of pearls, and clean ironed sheets for Hallie and a pink-smelling bathroom. She will convalesce in the sun on her Auntie's terrace watching the squirrels run incessantly up and down the same pine trees. And Dora will know that as long as Grandmother is alive she will have Christmas whenever she wants it.

And Hallie will have no more raw red spots on her face. She says she is painting the woodwork in the strange windowed hall of her apartment, cerise, I think. But that wasn't paint on her cheek. A raw spot like that could have come from an impatient unshaven morning husband . . . but I think it was caused by turpentine rubbing paint off the tender skin of the face. As soon as Dora was born Hallie exuded what I would call vitality (speaking to others) but which I knew privately was lust. She received Oscar himself with a diaper binding her breasts to ease their ache and those swollen breasts rising voluptuously out of her trousseau gown . . . of course all my friends except Cad are too polite to notice such things by name.

She says she is cleaning and painting that old apartment to present immaculate surfaces to her daughter, but whether it is the special fumes of the paint that drive some to drink but in other brains opens up the sensual paths, the overwhelming erotic itches and cravings, or whether it is the hot winter sun on her skin too long covered against the wet icy soot of northern cities, I think that no sooner does Hallie open her pail of cerise and stir until the color is homogenized into its oily glue than the first tiny trumpetings are felt inside her shorts.

Cerise is for the woodwork, the wide old-fashioned baseboard above the dark splintered floor, and for some doors. While Dora sleeps Hallie fights—does she fight?—the increasing urge to stretch out in the rectangle of sun on the window side of her floor and wrap her skin's surfaces in the loving palms of her hands. As the fumes rise and the sun's heat grows toward noon, the impulses magnify until Hallie must smear her body in that telltale red and still bring Dora to my house at five.

She paints for an hour or so, an immaculate swathe down the wide corridor that runs from Dora's room to the bathroom—useless corridor with huge windows down one side, too narrow for a room where activities define themselves. Hallie speaks of it as a play area for Dora; it is also a play area for herself. It is on the back of the house and no one can get to it without being heard; Hallie hung an unframed full-length mirror on a jut-out so Dora can play with her image. So Hallie can try on costume after costume, inventing her sexual playmate.

The cerise reaches the jut-out. Hallie outlines the baseboard's top edge carefully, waiting until it is perfectly done before looking at the twin puffs of flesh, the glistening plump flesh on the inside of her knee pushed into crescents by her bent leg. The skin is so tight there where it is forced out that it has the flawlessness of Dora's own. It is the secret curves like these that most excite her—not the breasts or hips that everyone else emphasizes but the knee's bulge in this position, which she is careful to conceal from all eyes but her own. She turns her leg back and forth in front of the mirror. Thigh and calf are squeezed in perfect symmetry, matching ovals more voluptuous than spheres—her eyes glide up and over each side of the perfect curve which is the form of all things that endure forever.

But those same legs, upright, have a soft mound of fat just above the knee. She told me Selwyn had commented on that, criticized her for having any fat on her at all. I was enraged.

Hallie strokes the perfect bulges of her bent inner leg with her hand, leaving a smear of cerise from the creases which have not dried. The surface of her skin is like new soap, like the core of an onion, as finely grained as the petals of a peony. She sits back on the floor and pretends she is her visitor.

To please this sexual stranger who has only a short interlude to give her, she unbuttons her shirt and arranges the button and buttonhole strips over each nipple. Turned slightly sideways, the under scoop is as visible as anyone could wish. She arches her back slowly, cerise palms on the floor behind her. The first school she went to taught acrobatics for gym and her memory jumps back to the pleasures of those classes where each girl's body was thrust belly up in a smooth hemisphere of benediction. In this preliminary arch, button and buttonhole strips stay balanced over each nipple. Then Hallie stands with her back to the mirror and, bent in a U from the waist, watches her shirt slip well away from her breasts altogether and the breasts themselves puff on the neck side as her arms reach for the floor. Upside down in a tight backbend, her face inches from the mirror, she stares at the stretched upper half of her torso. The breasts are subtly suspended as if gravity has vanished; they are in the gentle slope of islands rising out of the ocean, poised in relief. But her face is a hideous red and she pulls herself back up.

The visitor is in a hurry to get to the lower part of her torso. She takes off her shorts and shows the mirror herself in just her underpants, the sight that brought the inhale of lust to Punchy when they were girls. Hallie's pubic bone does not slope mysteriously into her thighs; it forms a mound of its own, protruding like a cap which can fit in the hollow of a palm. She caps it with her palm; her hand sticks to the nylon with a glob of paint.

But the visitor does not laugh. The visitor's mouth is sticky itself now, saliva as thick and oily as paint. The winter sun is a warm cloak over her skin; suddenly she sneezes; tingles from the sneeze reach from her knees to the erotic inner lining of her face. The visitor's anger at being made to wait so long excites Hallie; she feels rushed, vulnerable, about to be seized.

Suddenly Hallie is absolutely still, totally quiet. Tiny question sounds come from behind Dora's closed door, the puppy-breath vowels of her first waking. With an Indian glide Hallie steals down the hall; a floorboard creak brings a louder "da?" from Dora's room. But only one. Hallie takes her visitor into the bathroom.

It is large, in this old-fashioned piece of a house near downtown Houston, with a large bathrug over its wooden floor—a rug not altogether clean. There Hallie lies with her visitor until the tingles produced by the sneeze are obliterated by the grander electricity produced by her hands which also courses from knee to the raw vibrant inner lining of her face.

It is never enough. The minute the great current ceases, throbbing sets in again. All the needs and passions expressed in Punchy's lustful inhale regroup themselves behind Hallie's eyes and long, as if nothing has happened, for another peek at Hallie in her underpants. Her body yearns for the sun blanket, begs the visitor not to go . . . the visitor has already gone. But possibly another visitor is already climbing the stairs.

The cerise is hardening in the can she left open but it is also dry on her hands. Dora is strangely quiet. Hallie turns the knob very slowly and peeks inside; Dora instantly lets out a laugh and reaches over her crib to be lifted out. The entire crib is smeared with Dora's feces. She sees her mother's face and begins to cry.

Dora, streaked with yellow-brown, and her mother, spotted with cerise, go back to the bathroom and in a few minutes are in the huge tub together. Dora is quickly clean and begins poking and laughing at the funny red decorations all over her mother's body. Her pokes are beguiling and Hallie laughs.

But the crib and mattress are still smeared and the crib is wicker. It is impossible to clean. Hallie decides to put the whole crib outside the next time it rains; she takes the mattress out and shuts the door. The mattress is easily washed, fitted with a clean sheet, and laid in Dora's playpen. Hallie smiles at Dora, who is looking alarmed at the mattress crowding her playpen while she is trying to drink her bottle. "We're just putting something aside for a rainy day, my piglet," Hallie says, circling and poking Dora's balloon belly. With perfect charm, Dora removes her bottle, grins and kicks, and then resumes sucking. "You're so precious I'm going to take you to see your grandmother tonight."

I am touching myself but Sis's comforter is covered with satin, which will disguise movement in case Hyke wakes up. He doesn't wake up, I know from his intermittent snoring.

As soon as my circuits are clear again I concentrate on the second possibility: suppose Hallie doesn't end up selling apples but in fact makes a great deal of money, enough for us all—as she used to promise me she would. I know realistically it is not possible but, sandwiched in ironed percale and satin, I indulge the thought. Suppose I wake up some birthday morning and there is a new Chrysler in rich black parked out front for me? After all, one birthday she gave me mink.

Do we ever forget dreams? Did I feel a mere glint of disappointment when Hyke propelled me outside the morning of my fifty-second birthday and there was a Plymouth Fury in honey brown with "made especially for Baby" in gold script across the dashboard? Of course, I don't introspect about such things. I squealed and shrieked and hugged and patted Hyke with pure delight and we drove around to show all our friends.

Hyke never drove it. A curious thing had happened to him the last time he was in New York: he had been returning to the city through the Lincoln Tunnel after visiting friends in New Jersey and his hand froze. It was totally paralyzed. Just before he reached the end of the tunnel the other hand froze. He was terrified; it felt, he said, like he was steering with his feet. Luckily the other Hallie was with him and she brought the car over to the side where he could stop, then she drove.

This is my firmest birthday. Although I am not superstitious, how can I be casual about the fact that I will be fifty-two for a whole year and that particular number is the count of cards in a deck? I will have all four complete suits in sight.

This year, I am sure, will bring a final change in my life—one which will fit my talents like a hand at bridge which only skill can make. I am delighted too that Dora will be two tomorrow; the half-century's connection/separation can only be magical, profound, fraught with the coincidental significance that life's accidents always provide. Since for me life is its own reward and I have never consciously felt the need to produce, prove, accomplish in the standard (the history book) sense, I welcome these curiosities as pointing up the themes which satisfy a woman's yearning for coherence and design. Today I am convinced my life is to be interrupted by a decorated page announcing the commencement of a new (but not concluding, I hope) part: Part IV.

Then Hyke, as if it were *his* book, inserts in my pages an

obscene and irrelevant passage which somehow I must skip over, just as I skipped over the offensive parts of *From Here to Eternity* while Cad laughed at me. "From here to the back alley," I retorted.

It is just after B-Day when Hallie makes me agree to the night away. I hate dramatics. Whatever it is Hallie has to discuss can be done right here or on the telephone, I say; I have no patience with talks that are set up, staged as if they were to be recorded. Actually, I can't stand the anticipation. I am standing at the passenger window of Hallie's dusty Chevrolet, my eyes as usual upon the unbelievable face of Dora waiting in her car seat. "Just give me a hint," I say.

But Hallie is on the far side of the car; it is her foot on the accelerator, her hand by the starter, her groceries in the back seat, her daughter's lunch time. She smiles the casual smile of power. "I just want to talk—not about anything earth-shattering. Just talk."

I have to accept the surface of this and let go of the car.

Hallie is becoming a recluse. She did the one thing, out of sheer perverseness, guaranteed to make her life in Houston impossible: she turned down her invitation to join the Junior League. Although I argued, explained, begged, demanded, she refused. Without reason and, far worse, without a substitute plan. She just said she thought the Junior League was superficial, immoral, pretentious—all the criticisms everyone has heard for years—but still she intends to live as a wife and mother in a town where women rule either through social position or through hard work and, in Hallie's case, the latter is apparently not being considered. I wish I hadn't thought of it. I am too put out with her to relax now in this August heat with a reckless driver and no martini.

My lungs are filled with the smell of hot tar and country dust, machinery mixed with traces of unseen animals. I take my eyes off the road in the hope of seeing at least chickens, a spotted farm dog, a family horse; I need an inspiration: I will be required to come up with something after she tells me what it is she has to tell me. The landscape is static and empty.

Dora is about to become fretful. I fish in my purse and hand her my gold compact.

"She'll drop it," Hallie says. "She'll drop it so you'll pick it up so she can drop it. *She* can do that forever." Hallie briefly rubs the top of Dora's filmy head. "Can't you, pumpkin?"

"Stubborn as a mule," I say triumphantly.

I have to watch for the turnoff to Ten Penny—a farm drive like any other in the middle of flat land—because Hallie has never been here before. We are silent waiting for the house that is Oscar's (an unassuming builder's bungalow behind a white picket fence) to distinguish itself from all the other similar ones we pass.

Like the other Texans who made a lot of money fast, Oscar now breeds cattle. He was hardly into his second million before he discovered a country past for himself—a man who I *know* spent most of his early life in hotels. He speaks of the succulence of broiled pigs' feet for breakfast, the soul-wrenching beauty of cows' eyes, and the sky over Texas—either so high that you could see clear to next winter or so low that the stars bump up against your cowlick; everyone agrees, however, that the sky over Texas is *wider* than anywhere else. We have a song to prove it: the prairie sky is wide and high . . . deep in the heart of Texas. How deep we are into any heart is uncertain. So I believe him when he says he didn't buy this ranch just for a tax shelter.

As soon as he had it he went to the King Ranch and bought him some Santa Gertrudis, particularly a bull he calls El Capitan. Cad and I were delighted; Christmas and birthdays are solved for years. We plan on giving Oscar rancher hats, boots, shirts, belts, glasses with his brand on them, boxes of branded matches, branded cocktail napkins, branded cup towels. I organized last Christmas myself: six different examples of Santa Gertrudis hand-painted on dinner plates which everyone chipped in for.

The picket fence is not expected to keep out the cattle; there is a ditch around the house with a cattle-guard bridge which Hallie drives noisily across. The inside of the house is furnished simply, like a motel room. Hallie grows suddenly shy as if she were in fact entering an anonymous hotel room with her mother; I take Dora for a walk around outside. Fortunately it is short. "I think all this open land scares her," I say. "Doesn't it, Dora? Too empty . . ." My voice trips on the word *empty;* with a mental wrench I focus on my stomach. "I could eat a horse!"

I am aware of how small Oscar's kitchen is when I bump my hips against a counter corner; nevertheless Hallie and I cook, prepare, find dishes and utensils, and do not once seem to be in each other's way. The harmony soothes me; I am grateful to sit down to dinner with two young and now beautiful faces to look at.

We are using the Santa Gertrudis plates. Dora is no sooner in her chair on telephone books before she cries out, "Hamburger comes from a cow!" and uncharacteristically sweeps her patty off her plate and onto the table top.

Hallie gets her a plain plate and comforts her. "Well, I never liked eating off that Niagara Falls plate and getting my grits all wet."

"And I thought I was the literal-minded one."

Hallie's next remark is totally unwelcome. Although it is a simple query—"How's Hyke and everything?"—I read into it a deliberate attempt to upset my digestion. Does Hallie know what I suspect—know—about the other Hallie? If she does, why does she want to attack me with it when I'm helpless out here in the middle of nowhere?

I just say Hyke is in New Orleans and change the subject. Then Hallie, who has everything, contracts her face into complaint. She says that it must be a definition of rich to be able to walk into a house fifty miles from your home and have it ready for you, that some men can be advised by their doctors to take up a hobby for relaxation and, with an investment of who knew how many hundreds of thousands, set up a breeding ground and play rancher for their health. Oscar's chauffeur can drive him out here for Sunday breakfast and sunshine. He can forget his business worries by standing on the fence and calling his "girls" (the heifers), by discussing feed and offspring with his foreman, by reading cattle magazines. She finishes by saying that although this is a second house (or a fifth, for all I know) it has all the appliances, furniture, freshness of most of the families in America's only house. Her voice is like a rusty wheel.

So she doesn't give a damn about my heartbreak. "Poor little baby Hallie," I say.

"*Okay.*" Hallie concentrates on her plate.

I turn to Dora but I feel the jolt from my daughter and, in a moment, I cover Hallie's hand with mine. "Darling, I'm sorry." The sound of the words releases that emotion inside me. "What's the trouble?"

But the trouble couldn't be said until later, after Dora has gone to sleep; by then I am reabsorbed in my own self-pity. It was my own closeness to Hallie and Dora that acted as my enemy, allowing—*encouraging*—Hyke to grow much too close to his Hallie. A snake in the grass.

"Who's a snake in the grass?" Hallie says and I realize I spoke out loud. We just sat down on Oscar's grass and are looking up at stars too bright to fit either of our moods. I forestall Hallie, who is about to make one of her usual remarks about how unfairly people malign snakes; I tell her.

"The other Hallie seduced Hyke. I don't mean just seduced in the sense of pulling the wool over his eyes, although she did that too. She made him think she is virtue itself. But," and I am even more certain now that I am speaking the words, "the other Hallie literally seduced Hyke—got him to go to bed with her."

"What?" Hallie is up on her knees with her arms around my shoulders.

I nod. "I found a letter from her." Against the background noises of trucks passing across land a mile away and monotonous crickets, I repeat the falsehoods of that letter: the other Hallie was so sorry she'd let her passions, her great love for Hyke run away with her—she respected him so much and hoped this one mistake wouldn't change his respect for her—she had to admit that although she was sorry in one sense she couldn't be totally sorry because she had wanted it so much—she would yield to his deep love for Baby and do her best to prevent anything like this ever happening again—or damaging his marriage.

"Can you imagine?" I am now furious. "Can you imagine writing such a letter and mailing it to him? Didn't she know I would find it?"

"Hyke could have destroyed it," Hallie says after a moment.

I don't want to think about why he didn't. "I guess he meant me to find it. So I would see what a prize I had because other women wanted him. I was supposed to be grateful for his heroic self-discipline during all the years he *didn't* give in to temptation. I was supposed to believe he was Clark Gable." I stop. I didn't know I thought all that.

"When did this happen?"

"Last month. When he was in New York. I *felt* that something was wrong. I said to Cad, 'Cad I feel it in my bones. Something's very wrong today.' And I knew it when Hyke got back—he was acting so sheepish. But of course I didn't really know it until this letter, which I found this afternoon."

I stand up, towering over Hallie; I feel silhouetted against the house lights like a target. Hallie scrambles to her feet. "I intend to ask Hyke about it, of course, but first I have to figure it out."

"You must feel totally betrayed."

"Yes. I meant, figure out what I'm going to do about it. Is that what my car is for? 'Made especially for Baby.' I don't even want to get in it."

"I wondered why you wanted to take my unair-conditioned

rattle trap."

"That's a perfectly nice car for a young couple." Privately I would be delighted if Selwyn could make enough money to buy them something less middle-class. "I'll go get us a drink. *I* need a drink."

Hallie follows me into the house. In the kitchen she says, as if it were a solution for us both, "I've decided to get a divorce."

"Oh." I hear my voice draw the word out like a groan.

Of course, I know that Selwyn gambles. I knew that he bought a barbecue drive-in with Hallie's savings and a loan from Oscar; I didn't know he was allowing gambling there and was closed down by the vice squad. I know he just went into the dog food business and manufactured Elfon ("no flea" spelled backwards) with a secret ingredient—garlic—which kept the fleas off but made the dogs' gas explosions smell so awful no one could stand them.

I also know that they fight: I saw the bruise on Hallie's eye, which she tried to hide with makeup and dark glasses; I can't speak of it until she brings it up. She doesn't, even now. She seems only interested in money.

"Why did you give him your money?"

She doesn't answer. My question isn't worthy of an answer. We all do that; we empty our canteens in the middle of the desert to avoid being told we are depriving our man of his masculinity—although all he will do then is waste our water and fill his hose. "You could cut his water off—as Mother used to say."

"Because I thought if we're married, it's our money. If it isn't ours, we shouldn't be married." She is speaking with this logic because she feels strong now that she has just come from comforting her mother. I cannot bear her lack of emotion. "Of course, the main problem now is money."

"I guess you'll have to get a job."

"I intend to get a job. But as you know there's no job on earth that I've been trained for—no way I can make enough money to support Dora. I thought if I asked Oscar . . ."

"I won't have you asking Oscar for money. He's done more than enough for us as it is."

"A job, Mother. He begged my *husband* to go to work for him and just laughed when I asked him . . . and if he *still* doesn't want to have me distracting the men in his office he can give me the money. Auntie says it's yours anyway. And I've earned it, after all—I had your perfect Dora for you . . ."

"Don't bring that baby into this."

"What do you think the marriage was all about? I only married him because I was preg . . ."

I explode with rage and stand over her. "I won't hear another word. I won't hear one word against Dora. She was premature and we're very lucky she was still perfect." I am afraid I will slap her; I turn and finger the curtain, stare at nothing in the night.

I feel Hallie's hand on my shoulder. She keeps her voice soft but still it rakes my head like jagged fingernails. "Dora wasn't premature, she was three weeks early is all. Just like Peg and Lyle's baby, and the Oates's twins, and Brownie Burton . . ."

I take a deep breath. "Well, so what?" I turn and my face is very close to Hallie's. "What difference does it make now? She's here, that's what counts."

Hallie laughs with relief. "That's what counts."

"I can't imagine what I'd do without her," I say. I am laughing too. It truly seems the least important fact in the world. "But I really thought she was premature. I really didn't know that."

"Really?" That word too was a laugh.

"Really. But I couldn't care less. I just can't imagine what life would be without angelbaby Dora."

"Then you understand," Hallie says after a minute, "that I do need money now."

I am staring at the garnet ring that was my mother's—old stone set in old platinum—as if it stands for the deep dull riches of the earth, of family loyalty, of hard work and sacrifice, if necessary—of blood that is a long time drying.

"I only want what is best for you, you know that. Maybe this is your chance to make something out of yourself . . ." I hear Cad's voice teasing me: "And all things happen for the best?" "Hallie, maybe when you have everything given to you, you just coast—you don't really develop your own . . ."

Hallie says sharply, "Mother, this isn't a question of philosophy. I am facing the reality of supporting a child . . ."

I don't know why I am standing here. I was ready to give Hallie and Dora everything I had, push it into their laps, smother them with gold—until right this minute when she asks me. I hear my voice speaking outside me as if I were playing Oscar to Hallie's me. "That reality is something everyone else faces without an Uncle Oscar."

"But *my* reality includes him." I feel slapped by the violence in her voice; she hates me. "*Look* at those pictures." She walks from one to another of the famous, the rich, propped on tables throughout the room: Oscar with Governor Hobby, Lyndon Johnson, Winthrop Rockefeller, Jesse Jones, George and Herman Brown, Governor Beauford Jester, Governor Shivers.

I am shivering and I sit down.

"The money Oscar started with belonged half to *my* grandmother. I've been an *et ux* long enough now to know exactly how the community property laws work in this state—especially since they're going to work against me in my divorce and I'm going to be responsible for half of Selwyn's gambling debts. Your father didn't *own* Granny's half to give to Oscar; one-third of that is yours and if you don't want it, one-sixth of it is still mine and one-sixth Mary Cowan's. So I . . ."

"If you don't stop harping at me over that damned will, I'm going to cut you out of mine!" I will burst from fury: that the child I gave up my life for turns out to be so ordinary. "Do you so totally lack human feeling that you can be on the point of breaking up a home and your only consideration is to stand there and beg me for money like a common . . ."

Incongruously in her fashionable clothes, Hallie stands over me with fingers stiff, eyes flashing. "I knew it was money all the time! You just admitted it! All that talk about higher values just don't mean crap when the big boss *dollar* comes around, does it? Now everything else about me is washed down the drain and I'm called common because the person you raised me to be can't make a living except as a prostitute. Half the jackasses in this country can make a *living*. It's so common it's called normal."

"But it is *not* normal, in my book, for a daughter to use vile language to her mother."

"You demand that even the beggar have style? Oh, pardon me, mother dear."

"The child that mocks her mother mocks herself," I say coldly. "A normal daughter grows up to be an adult who can also comfort another adult. The current can't go forever in just one direction without emptying itself out altogether."

I have not touched her but her face is jarred loose as if I'd slapped it. "Oh!" she cries, her eyes huge and tearful. "I'm so sorry Hyke has hurt you, I hadn't forgotten, I'm so sorry I was so selfish when you . . . Mother, the money . . ."

It is too late. The current is dry as the Rio Grande in August. "I'm going to bed. Goodnight, Hallie."

But I am going to my room where I can talk to Hallie without her hearing me. You pretend to love me so I will give you money, the silent words form in my mind. You are making me a prostitute in my heart. In my *heart*. It is the worst kind, the unbearable. You have tricked me into believing that there was *one* person in the world who truly loved me, a belief that is blood, is oxygen: without that belief, life—as everyone knows—does not exist. For this reason I have worked very hard at truly loving Oscar—I would not want to put him in the category you just put me in. And I would die before I would let him *feel* what you just made me feel.

I have always known that the love between mother and daughter is different from that between man and wife—since almost *everyone* finds a mate, there is nothing so special about that, it is the order of the world. But a real love between two adult women— as mother and daughter, who need only *say* they love—rises like mist from a chilly earth, grows visible in morning sunlight, freely given. Such a love is outside the natural order: there is no security in it, no corporate rewards, no insurance against a lonely old age, no Saturday night benefits, no tax breaks, no credits toward right- eousness for the hereafter which marriage provides.

When I felt—just yesterday? only this afternoon? a mere twenty minutes ago?—that you loved *me*, my heart, even though broken, was falling all over itself trying to mend, my blood thun- dering like it knew that it could flow forever. And I am trapped in this room with only a bed and a book until morning.

The room has been light for some time: the sun is shining through the window shades. I dread this day. When I sit up my eyes dart to stare at my purse, the ogre of my life. It rests on the chair by the door, gaping. The purse is soft white plastic imitating straw, too white in the colorless light of a hot sunny country morning, open like a mouth of a cartoon fish gasping for breath. Open? I can't believe I left it open in a country ranch house where there is nothing to buy.

There is no shiver on earth like this freezing shudder. My body is seized by instant recognition of yet another betrayal. Auto- matically I go to my purse to look inside. It is unnecessary. I al- ready know that I will find my billfold raped; she has left me the change and the one-dollar bills crumpled in my coin purse. *That* is still snapped shut. She did not even bother to look there. Since I went to the bank yesterday and cashed a check for seventy-five dollars, since I bought only gas and charged the groceries for last night's dinner, I must have had seventy dollars—seven ten-dollar bills. I have not one left. She did not even leave me a single ten-dollar bill. She expects me to return to the bottomless bank this afternoon and silently withdraw seven more?

Now they are up. I just heard the toilet flush twice, I think. I am stuck in my room. I dare not go in search of a cup of coffee to bring back here with me; I would kill her in those brief moments. My mouth is dry, charred, but I light a cigarette nevertheless. I hope it will kill me. I won't even cough.

My daughter is a thief. A common pilferer. A materialistic shell in a pretty dress. Blank made-up face of the gold digger. The toilet flushes yet again because my daughters, though raised in the Depression, quickly adjusted to plenty and think of the water meter as measuring mere pennies. They blot their lipstick and throw the toilet-paper square in the toilet and flush. They finish a cigarette and flush the butt. They pull a strand from their hair brush and flush it away. They live in a world where wastebaskets are kept shining and empty. They would not bend over to pick up a penny lying on the sidewalk; why should they when ten-dollar bills grow like weeds in a mother's billfold?

I have a splitting headache. My skull is a block of wood being hacked by an axe. Axelike rage descends into my arms and legs. I am being prevented from essential morning coffee, from the toilet itself by the dilettantism of my daughter who is *still* in the bathroom flushing. I burst into the hall. My hands are dying to wring a daughter's neck, my arms all set to rip her into bits and flush her down the . . .

The bathroom door is open but Hallie is not inside. A face as sweet as a peach ice cream cone turns and meets my eyes. Dora's hand is just leaving the toilet handle. I see over her toddler shoulder a piece of dull green rectangle swirl round and round on the moving water in the toilet bowl and Alexander Hamilton's face disappearing with a flourish down the open mouth at the bottom.

Dora's face is sudden baby agony. She reaches with one fat hand onto the top of the tank where one ten-dollar bill remains; she holds it out to me, an offering in exchange for her life. I am overwhelmed with shock, with devastation; I think I have gone mad.

Hallie emerges from her room with sleep still padding her eyes. She is saying she is sorry if she is interrupting my toilet (in the Victorian sense, she says with a half-awake laugh) but she heard it flushing and flushing. "It's too early for puns," she says. "All that water made me *have* to pee." She is sitting on the toilet now. I leave the bathroom with my lone ten-dollar bill out of sight in my fist; I am leading Dora, her hand unsure in mine, making Dora-talk to her so she will forgive herself, taking Dora into Hallie's room, finding a pair of underpants for her, settling her in a chair on her telephone book just as Hallie comes into the kitchen and I return to the toilet for myself.

When I walk back into the kitchen I feel that my body is in little lumps with too much liquid in between, like cornmeal before enough heat and stirring has made it cohesive. I see a slumped Hallie dutifully watching Dora eat scrambled eggs. She comes to hug me. "I'm sorry I got off on money last night when you needed me for something else," she says tentatively.

I accept her apology. "*I'm* sorry you got so mad at me," I say. *She* is abject when *I* am the one who just saw murder in myself. I hold her by the shoulders, pushing them back up where they belong. "You look like an angel in that nightgown."

"Am I an angel?"

"Well, of course you're an angel—but if someone put the wrong nightgown on you you might not look like an angel. You might look all surprised and funny."

I am rewarded with a delighted laugh which makes Dora laugh.

"Grandbaby, don't you want scrambled eggs?" Dora's face is cocked into the new excitement of morning.

Halfway through my first cup of coffee I say, "Well, I couldn't help but notice that the towels in that bathroom are those of a man whose secretary simply telephones the store and says, 'Send the best you have.' They are certainly towels which will be thrown out as soon as they lose their fluff."

In fact, nothing in a bathroom of Oscar's will ever disturb the free flow of his thought, the surge of his imagination; he will never have to wrestle the devil to the floor because a darling Dora is playing flush-the-money. There won't even be a decision of whether to mend or replace to clutter or distress his brain. "So I decided, there's nothing in the daily business of living that will ever form an irritant in the brains of men like Oscar, is there? And so I was thinking: poor Oscar! Forever denied the creation of a single pearl."

I am grinning and Hallie is ecstatic; Dora raps a tune on the table. I am not sure what is going on but Cad would be proud of my verbal preciosity, as she would call it. I am proud of myself. I feel like Cad.

A week later Sister is dead. She was dragged screaming into death holding out her elongated nervous hands to me, to the D.R., to Hallie, crying "I'm sinking! Pull me back! Pull!" In terror Hallie grabbed her hands; squeezing the skeletal bones she held on with all her might. But still the head sank beneath the oxygen tent; inside its plastic Sis's black eyes opened once more, fierce and black they stared at us accusing us of failure, of betrayal. Hallie pulled harder; she was the root system defying death to take this real flower as if it were a mimic weed, death determined to yank it free while every nerve in Sis's body cried I will bloom again I am still blooming . . . "Hold me!" Sis hissed and Hallie dug under her birdlike neck with one arm while the other pressed Sis's fingers together so no trowel could get through; as Hallie lifted her arm slightly Sis's head fell back and was still.

The D.R. said, "She's gone," in a voice like a moan and turned toward the window, his own abundant flesh dropping and his eyes blank with what I knew instantly was his own death for all essential purposes. Oscar gave a sharp cry like a snake-bit dog and seized my arm; Hyke placed his arm in comfort across my shoulders. Hallie dropped the hand of her Auntie with a quick shudder as if it were an imposition on the dead to be pawing at them, to touch their flesh as if flesh could comfort.

I was the only one still staring at, still facing my dead sister. There is nothing on earth which can make you feel at once as futile as a single breath and at the same time as big with life as the sun. As if death were our mother.

I AM TAKING Mary Cowan and Ed to dinner at "21." We are assaulted by the dark smell of the old wood in the bar, the darker smell of the wrought iron entrance and speakeasy memory, and the smell darkest yet of the feeling I have here inside where Hyke's name got us a reservation. I am not old enough to head a table, the maître d's face tells me as he moves us from a choice spot to one farther back. Ladies just in their fifties, buttressed by strapping adult children, are too often troublemakers. "21" likes dowagers or escorted women. "21" is as quiet as a charge account.

Ed begins to object to our table but Mary Cowan counter-insists almost frantically that she prefers the one farther back. Anger is rising underneath my mink cape from Oscar or Hallie. Since I only like to give presents which people won't or can't get for themselves, I feel caught in a tradition of my own making: I take the children to the best restaurants where, once I feel intimidated, I know I will misbehave. I always have.

Always? My insides smile. It feels like always but I think I only learned how when I got "the change."

I am at "21" at the head of a rear table. There are waiters ma'aming me, bowing, and waving silver dishes. There are unbelievable smells all around: lobster, Joy, browning butter, Old Spice, martinis, Picayunes. The latter are Mary Cowan's; I try one and cough.

Every time Ed laughs my own throat makes an involuntary chuckle. I met Ed the year Hallie refused to make her debut; since Hyke and I had just married I got us invited to all the parties and we debuted instead. Ed was charming from the first, sweet and dear as I got to know him. I am heady with Mary Cowan's good sense in marrying him.

Mary Cowan looks like a movie star in her new Hattie Carnegie. When I suggested this morning that we go out to dinner, she said we had to go shopping first. She didn't need to say she had nothing to wear; I saw her closet: it is full of clothes, all of them piled on the floor—the door won't shut unless your foot is quick because some of the clothes are slippery like baby pigs. She is the only woman I've ever known who absolutely luxuriated in motherhood. I am not surprised that nothing fits her. She nursed the twins for six months, turning night into day so she could lie in bed while Ed brought her food.

Ed brought her food throughout the night and laughed at her power to make him do it. Appropriately he is a lawyer, specializing in contracts American oil companies make in the Near East. Ed is gifted in interpreting one incomprehensible to another; within himself the same process goes on endlessly. I like him because he wants it all—just like me. He makes other people seem too easily constructed. One can say to others, "Is that all you need? Well, *here*." Ed can be counted on to say, "No, I want this *too*," and laugh with a rolling infectious chuckle at the fact that the two things cancel each other out.

I order caviar for Mary Cowan to celebrate my grandchildren. The twins are adorable, I repeat. They have apples in their cheeks and eyes like baby seals and don't look a thing like apartment-cramped city children.

Our waiter is describing the specials in French. He says, "Et pour madame, les escargots?" Now I don't eat snails because the garlic makes me sick, but the Spanish for snail suddenly flashes across my mind; what can I do? I say, "Por favor, deme camarero, los caracoles." He looks at me as if I were speaking Greek. I understand his French (which has an Italian lilt to it); I give him time to decide he understands my Spanish.

Both my children hate public conspicuousness: when they were in school up here, Oscar once took us all to Billy Rose's Diamond Horseshoe. The Duchess stood up when the orchestra played "The Eyes of Texas." She remained standing in gold sequins, chin high, all through it while the spotlight fixed the image of my daughters' embarrassment forever. I was proud of the Duchess; started to stand too but Mary Cowan pulled my arm, in gruesome pain said, "Mother, *please* don't." Where did I mislead them? I have managed to indoctrinate my daughters into believing that public approval is vital: the sole precondition, I know, for unhappiness. When a mother brands them they stay branded. I feel like a callous cowboy with a red hot iron. And now I want to scrape off the dead, scarred skin and let the hairs grow back.

I am holding my knife and looking at the waiter.

"I'm from Texas," I say in Spanish. "We don't speak French anymore except when we're in New Orleans."

Ed's laugh calls forth my involuntary chuckle.

"You should come to Texas some time." I revert to English for this complexity. "We need good waiters like you. Ours won't get down from their cutting horses to pick up your napkin if you drop it."

Mary Cowan has almost demolished the caviar. "Don't you think we need another order?"

Brute and Little Otis Gouverneer are suddenly standing by our table hugging and kissing me with extravagant surprise and delight. The maître d' sees. His chin drops with disappointment. He had so hoped that I could be ignored; Big Otis has frequent gatherings at "21," renting the entire upstairs. Little Otis has always been one of my favorites. I see that Brute is drinking champagne. "Camarero, quiero un vino blanco . . ." I don't know the word for champagne in Spanish so I point to her glass and improvise. "Vino con burbujas por favor."

We are by far the most handsome table in the room. Ed is tall and thin like a Lehmbruck sculpture with gray eyes from the pages of romantic novels where they are said to crinkle, Mary Cowan looks like a madonna in winter white, Little Otis is even better-looking than his father and Brute has abandoned her blossom-in-the-hair look for a Ceil Chapman sophistication. Of course, I am wearing black; pink is impossible with waiters.

I sense we should expand. There is a forlorn-looking middle-aged man alone at the bar watching us; I ask Ed to invite him over. As I guessed, he is content to laugh at everything anyone says, a perfect sixth: we don't need any more performers.

There is no room now on our table for food but only Mary Cowan cares.

The newcomer, Mr. Pickett, asks what we are celebrating.

"The Alamo," Little Otis says.

"Your arrival," Mary Cowan says, fixing him with a maternal brown stare. Mr. Pickett nearly swoons.

"You must be from Dallas," Mr. Pickett says, proud that he recognized the Alamo, betting now on Neiman-Marcus.

"Dallas?"

"Allow me to reintroduce you," Ed says with an excess of crinkles. "The lady through whose gracious gregariousness you are privileged to share our table is none other than Baby Houston."

Mr. Pickett's eyes widen. "I thought I recognized your face. I'm proud to meet you."

"Indeed you should be," Ed continues. "You are in the presence of the four-way stop sign of the future. She faces east, west, south, even north—simultaneously, of course. Perhaps you've never heard of Houston but you will. It used to be referred to as Houstontexas. It is named for the lady here who has single-heartedly created such excitement over her city that those in the know refer to it familiarly now as—Houston." Ed, who sublimated his talent for acting into law, pronounces "Houston" with throaty reverence, dropping his eyes.

"Houston," Mr. Pickett echoes softly.

"Houston," the other five of us say in chorus. You would think we were conducting a language lesson.

"Never 'How-ston,'" Ed continues. "That 'ow' in the middle of our dear lady's name is onomatopoeic for the excruciating pain in her shell-like ears caused by such pronunciation."

"Furthermore," Mary Cowan says, "Baby Houston is not only the mother of daughters, she is also the mother of mothers as well as, of course, the daughter of mothers."

"Obviously the end and beginning in One," Ed says.

"Your daughters are both very beautiful ladies too," Mr. Pickett says with heartfelt sincerity, looking from Mary Cowan to Brute and back again.

Brute giggles. "Thank you, sir, but I am merely an applicant daughter, a petitioner."

"The other daughter, my illustrious baby sister, is in Houston shooting husbands," Mary Cowan says.

I have to laugh although it was only this morning, when I told Mary Cowan about Hallie shooting Selwyn, that I was so upset about it. When Hallie first told Selwyn she wanted a divorce, he agreed. Then he discovered that she was pregnant—we all discovered that—and intended to have the baby. Selwyn was suddenly possessive about his uterine "son." With curious logic he found a lawyer who agreed to fight the divorce on the grounds that the baby was not his; his countersuit threw the divorce into a jury trial, the projected date of which coincided with Hallie's eighth month of pregnancy. Selwyn figured to embarrass her into withdrawing her suit or to persuade the jury she was deranged not to.

One of the few flaws in my city, which it shares with other cities whose fabric is held together by threads of social behavior, is that most of Hallie's friends withdrew from her life in case the divorce did not go through. They withdrew from Selwyn too: no one wants to get pegged to the wrong side. Only Punchy, pregnant with her fourth, was unshakably loyal. One night Punchy was visiting Hallie. It was about nine o'clock and all the children were in beds or pallets on the floor when Selwyn pushed open the door. He wore his educated politeness like a mantle of tissue paper; in less than ten minutes it crackled and tore.

He accused Punchy of trying to take his place in his own house with his wife and, as he reached to grab Punchy in his rage, Hallie stepped between them and was thrown to the floor. She called the police, who would not interfere unless she had a peace bond out against Selwyn. Then Selwyn, his voice flirtatiously violent, echoing the blend of power and leer that was in the policeman's voice, reached for the cotton housecoat Hallie wore and ripped it open, leaving her full belly and breasts bare while he cursed her with the single distinguishable word: mother. "You mother . . ." he repeated, a curse neither Hallie nor Punchy had ever heard and for a few seconds did not understand. Then Punchy grabbed his arm and threw him back; in the next minute Hallie ran into the other room and returned with her Colt .22. She pointed the gun at Selwyn and told him to leave now. Apparently he stared disbelieving for too long. "Right now," she said, and then pulled the trigger. The bullet went through the top of his left shoulder.

With her own identity just concentrated into motherhood, Mary Cowan was as shaken and enraged when I told her as if she had been present, as if she were Hallie.

"My sister is the keeper of the language," Mary Cowan explains to Mr. Pickett, and to Brute and Little Otis (who have probably already heard). "There are certain words that husbands must not use except with respect—first among them is the word mother. My sister's husband, at his peril, dared to do otherwise, so naturally she shot him. She does not shoot all husbands or even encourage the shooting of all husbands. In my sister's case the police decided she had only meant to scare her husband since her bullet went through his left shoulder.

But I ask you now, Mr. Pickett; you're a man who looks familiar with the educational theories since Dewey: do you believe children are taught to speak because someone scares them? Did you frighten your own toddler into his first 'ma-ma?' I am not saying it is not possible, of course, merely that it is not logical, don't you agree?"

Mr. Pickett, hypnotized with her attention, nods; he would have nodded to anything. "Add to this obvious fact the circumstance that my sister had had no training in shooting husbands—this was in truth the first one she's ever shot; the fact that the Colt .22 has traditionally a slight upkick; and the widespread knowledge that a husband's heart lies, physically speaking, just below his left shoulder . . ." Mary Cowan shrugs her own gently sloping shoulders helplessly.

"I think we are forced to conclude," Ed says with gravity, "that the use of the word *accident* by the police department and the courts may be construed, in this case, as the kindest legal label we can attach to the husband's behavior. In effect what we are saying, through our system of justice, is that a husband is innocent of premeditated misuse of language until it has been proved beyond reasonable doubt that he actively plotted to walk up to his estranged wife and with malice aforethought say that very word in that exact tone. The fact that he damn well did, of course, and got off with only a shoulder wound is the traditional chance democracy takes."

"We are becoming overcivilized in Houston," Little Otis says with a shake of his head.

"With a Colt .22 in her house . . ." Mr. Pickett begins.

Little Otis interrupts. "Exactly. Peggy Taylor, who came from Lubbock and was more in touch with the olden times, used a shotgun."

"I heard that was over money," I say. "Wasn't he claiming she owed him some enormous sum?"

"Money *is* the obscenity of the educated," Little Otis says.

"Filthy lucre." Brute winks at Mr. Pickett.

"I think it is sexual." Mary Cowan throws a hopeful look at me—hoping because of my second marriage and advancing age that I will not play censor.

"I blink not," I say, smiling. "We're paying for this conversation, we might as well enjoy it."

"I'd like a *fine*," Mary Cowan says to the waiter. At home we call it brandy even when we mean cognac; I'm sure a *fine* is five dollars an ounce. For that I admire the French. We say our oil is black gold but we sell it for forty-five cents a quart.

"What is sexual, Mary Cowan?" Ed can no more remember to call her just Cowan than I can.

"Money. If you think about the words we use to describe sex, those that don't come from food refer to money. The question is not which has more words for sex, food or money; the real question is what separates two people who were in love faster—food or money. It's obviously money because the comic strips always use food." She shares my distaste of the funnies, an antipathy vigorously opposed by both Hyke and Hallie: *they* consider the funny papers the mad Cassandra of our culture. " 'I'm getting screwed in this marriage,' a husband might say meaning he was paying the bills and wasn't."

It's always a shock to me to hear adult wit coming out of my own child's mouth.

"When the wife feels like she's had it, she says, 'I've been laid, relayed, and parlayed.' That's a betting term," Mary Cowan explains to me. Does *everyone* else know it? "Selwyn talks that way. If Hallie paid attention to language she'd have left him earlier."

"And to think *my* generation was satisfied with 'When the wolf comes to the door love flies out the window,' " I say.

Rearranging his features to indicate that he is about to talk, Ed says, "Now I have to agree with you, Mary Cowan, that money breaks up more marriages than food does. But the point we should consider is whether the rising incidence of divorce is evidence for or against happier sexual activity."

"It must make for more expensive sexual activity," Mr. Pickett puts in. Of course, I have to start feeling sorry for poor Mr. Pickett since I'm the one who invited him to join our table. I'm just getting ready to say something nice to him—something that will also persuade him not to try for wit but just to be nice—when I see him tugging surreptitiously at his sleeve; I see the reason glinting off his wrist: a Tiffany gold watch. He isn't content to let his fingers glitter but must make sure we see the whole of his wealth. My sympathy halts in confusion; I say senselessly, "There must be a wealth of reasons why marriages fail . . ." Everyone laughs and I hear my words then and join in.

Little Otis says it's time to go and leans over to kiss me again. I express my fondness for him by taking his hand firmly; inside myself the fondness I feel becomes a hard gritting of my teeth as when I see a darling puppy—or any puppy. I am *very* fond of him although Cad says it is only because he is young, rich, handsome, and makes a fuss over me. She says I don't really *know* him. I am content with the four reasons I do know.

"Time is money," Brute says with another wink at Mr. Pickett. I fear for his sanity.

As soon as they have gone the maître d' takes his revenge; he presents me with a check. In dollars. I pretend we are spending pesos and extract a hundred-dollar bill. Mary Cowan wants to check the addition (as if she could add); I seize the damage—as Hyke calls it—and turn it over. It is only fun to spend money when you treat it like dirt. I hold the check and the money gingerly, as if they were distasteful; I am impatient for the waiter to rid me of them. I convince myself for a second that I am sexily rich.

Of course, I expect Mr. Pickett to offer to take us to the Monkey Bar since I bought him four rye and gingers. He says he has an early appointment (tomorrow is Sunday) but asks us all to his place around noon for milk punch. Of course, I refuse. If he were interested in me he would buy me a drink now; I know what milk punch invitations mean: he thinks I am rich because he saw me spending pesos. Tiffany watches are not sexy, I decide.

At one o'clock Sunday I am extricating myself and packages from a cab in front of Mary Cowan's. I have bundles of pastrami, pickles, Italian bread, herring in sour cream, roll mops, quarts of beer, and six chickens for frying.

The man in the delicatessen slapped his joviality so fast in my face that I felt abused. I am feeling forlorn in this city of hard money where no one says good day as they pass you coming in or out of a shop. My daughter's arrangements are too certain of success. Mary Cowan leaves no ragged threads for me to bite off, no drooping slips for me to pin up. There is forethought and neatness far into the future. Twin sons, handsome and quick, inheriting nothing darker than Ed's slight tendency to arrogance—which will only help them succeed. Already Mary Cowan knows more about raising children than Dr. Spock. Hers will go to Montessori schools, then to Exeter, Yale. They will be tall like Ed and soft-eyed like their mother; they will sail and marry debutantes or lively career women . . . I almost drop my bundle of groceries getting through the apartment building's heavy glass door. I have just missed my grandsons' childhood altogether, I have zipped my grandsons through their years so fast I might as well never have had them. I am turning into Grandmother the potential provider—shunning the favored, the fat. Although these perfect twins did nothing to deserve the exalted level at which they will ride through life, I am acting as if I believe Dora single-handedly overcame her father's gambling genes and therefore earned that angelic purity of face.

I am just lonely without Hyke, the only single among units,

here where even the babies arrive as a pair. Loneliness makes people bitter, I know (besides making them talk too much). I stop talking to myself and decide to smile and nod at every single face I see on the slow ten-floor elevator ride to Mary Cowan's.

But after five days (and I am only staying six) a resentment I have been warding off overtakes me. Mary Cowan and Ed are not interested in *me* although they are interested in lots of people: Arthur Miller, Maria Tallchief, James Jones, Florence Chadwick (*I* brought her up because Cad met her once, before she swam her channel), and especially Wendell Willkie. There is no doubt that Mary Cowan and Ed both love me; they beg me to visit, to stay longer; while I'm here I have difficulty even drinking my morning coffee alone. But I sense that my presence is what's wanted as audience—my new ears for old stories, my responding laugh, the nods of my head and the smoothing quality of my words. I rearrange what is already perfectly arranged so it can be visibly perfect. My wrinkles help: I remind them that they have lots of time to gain everything. Already they feel they are way ahead of where I was at their age and they are—out front in money, Montessori, and . . . I search for another *m* word and come up with mold, mothball, mop; with manipulation, mufti, mediocrity. For the life of me I can think of nothing but mean *m* words. Not a single good *m* word raises its sail in my brain. Mildew, mundane, munch. My floor has arrived. Mob, murder, mud, malice. Mentholatum, mullet, migraine.

I push their bell with my elbow and gladly let Ed take the grocery bag, now very heavy.

"Mother!" Mary Cowan calls. "You're just in time for lunch."

"How about a martini first?" Ed says.

"Marvelous!" I hear myself saying. "Then we'll have lunch and start frying this chicken."

It is our extravagance yesterday that started me to thinking fried chicken. Every time I go on a trip I tell myself that whatever money I decide to take I will spend without thinking; as soon as I spend it I forget my resolve and start worrying: Am I encouraging Mary Cowan in her natural extravagance?—her genetic extravagance, I say when she reminds me of Sister. Suppose she is left without money, shouldn't she understand that fried chicken is possible for a party, for a stomach dangerously used to caviar? I want to conduct a lesson in grease for my daughter.

We drift into exchanging fried chicken stories as we cook. I tell Mary Cowan about the morning Hallie and Punchy and their gang were going to Galveston. The night before I gaily promised to fry chicken for them. I was on my way out the door. I regretted the promise by the time I got to bed that night at what A.M. But of course I had to get up early and start frying and wonder whether I will always feel I should feed my children just at the moment when I am about to gallivant. I am conditioning them to salivate at the sight of Mother dressed up and perfumed.

Of course, lots of women have spent a Sunday morning frying chicken in ninety-degree heat, frying chicken after chicken cut up, as Southerners do, into small pieces (the pully bone separate; we even fry the backs)—but most of the women have been Negroes. If the South had not had slaves I doubt if fried chicken would ever have been our characteristic dish. In a South without slaves or Sunday servants, how many women of any color spend the day frying chicken?—as if we all were preserving a myth. Who makes the best fried chicken in the world? *She* makes the best fried chicken in the world. I know the "she" made her reputation in winter or else is a colored woman over a certain age. Although it is winter (from a Southerner's point of view) now in New York, I am wringing wet. My hair is coated with grease spatters and also wet: on this head oil and water are mixed. Even my lungs are slipping around in my chest cavity. My fingertips cannot stand one more coating of egg batter stuck to flour; I start rolling it off even before I have placed the chicken piece in the bubbling grease, carefully so I won't also fry my fingertips. The fingers therefore will get re-battered when I transfer the chicken. All my nerves are poised on those digital whorls. They are ready to scream. I start taking the chicken out when it is golden brown but before it is done; someone will bite into a luscious thigh and see blood coagulated near the bone, raw pink meat clinging there.

Is fried chicken really the best thing in the world to eat?

I tell Mary Cowan about the time I got Hallie a ride on the Carter plane. Genevieve Carter called Hallie and asked her to bring fried chicken for everyone so Hallie arrived with a huge box of fried chicken carefully wrapped in Saran wrap; she was so thrilled to be going to New York free and was polite as pie. At lunchtime Genevieve Carter said to her, "Of course I asked you to bring sandwiches—two other people brought fried chicken and now we don't have any sandwiches at all. But don't worry, dear, it doesn't matter that you made that little mistake." I tell Mary Cowan, "*I* was the one who was mad. I was so mad I swore I'd never fly on one of their private planes again. Next time I don't have the money to buy a ticket I just won't go."

Mary Cowan moves a pile of chicken off grease-soaked paper towels and throws the towels in the garbage; the garbage has a quart of grease caught in paper towels and I think of the war when we used to save everything. "Well, you shouldn't encourage Hallie to withdraw. She should take advantage of Houston. She knows or could know everyone there."

"She says she likes being alone in her apartment."

"But what does she do?"

"She likes being by herself so she can think, she told me."

"Think?"

"Think. That's what she said."

Mary Cowan has decided to leave the last skilletful to me. She perches on the step stool and lights a Picayune. "I think Hallie should move to New York now that she's getting a divorce. Ed could introduce her to some decent men and Dora could grow up with her cousins close."

"There are plenty of decent men in Houston," I say.

"Oh, Mother. You know how Hallie is. She goes out with *any-body*. She's always either hiding or parading."

I catch sight of Ed through the doorway. "Angelbaby Ed, will you fix a martini for the cook? I need something to cut this grease in my throat."

Mary Cowan says, "She's always felt that for you to think she was great she had to be popular with men."

"Why on earth would she think that?" Before Mary Cowan can say, "Oh, mother" again I say, "Well, she is."

"But she just sleeps with them. She isn't going to try to find another husband."

"I've always liked that about Hallie," Ed says, handing me a beaded glass smelling deliciously of gin. "She doesn't use her charms to buy herself a man."

Mary Cowan says, "If she did she might get a good man like I did?"

"Mary Cowan, you know I don't mean that—that you did any such thing. You don't need to; you're every man's fantasy. Now that sounds like I mean Hallie isn't so I'll shut up. I'll only get in deeper." Ed ducks out of the kitchen.

"Well, I know Hallie and Selwyn were happy sexually," I say.

"How on earth do you know that?" Mary Cowan says.

"Because I saw them the morning after their wedding. They invited us up to the Shamrock for champagne and Hallie said to me with that unmistakably happy smile, 'Mother, you didn't tell me he was so sweet.' She couldn't have been referring to anything else."

"You don't honestly think they hadn't had sex before they were married . . ."

How could I think that, since Hallie told me she married Selwyn because she was pregnant with Dora? But I did think that. Now it looks like I still think that. "I guess she wanted me to think that."

"She thought you wanted to think that."

"I guess I did."

"But Mother, that's just a nice thing to say. I know they weren't happy—at least after Selwyn started gambling with everything they had and then getting drunk and . . . I saw him start to hit Hallie and I told him right then and there that if I ever saw him hit my sister I would kill him."

"I said the same thing."

Mary Cowan gives a cynical laugh. "Well, neither one of us killed him. But it doesn't matter whether they were happy or not, the point is that Hallie needs to get out of Houston so that, if she does sleep with men, everybody doesn't immediately know it."

Now I know from my own experience that previously married women are considered fair game for every man; and I know we have our own needs. "I certainly don't expect her to live a cloistered life," I say with a certain haughtiness which I feel has to be injected here. I hate it when the children treat me like I am still wet behind the ears. "But Houston is hardly Main Street, USA."

"It's a lot closer to it than New York."

I take out the last piece of chicken and turn off the fire. My fintertips relax and my brain, defilmed by the gin, understands that Mary Cowan, like all of us, wants Hallie to do the same thing she did. Although both my daughters go to extremes—whatever they are doing they go at it like a thirsty man trying to drink the ocean—I pretend now that only Hallie has this trait. "Maybe you're right. She has always seemed excessive . . ."

"The most excessive thing she's ever done is try to own you," Mary Cowan says. "It's obvious that she won't develop as long as she is tied to mama."

"Tied?" I strip off the cup towel I tucked into my waist to keep off the grease. "I haven't worn an apron if I could avoid it in my life. I certainly do not tie any daughters to it."

"I know you never tried to tie *me*."

"I never tried to tie Hallie either and I resent . . ."

"Well, I resent talking about Hallie the whole time when you come here to visit me. I'd like to be the subject of the conversation sometimes but I know, since I don't have those interesting problems, that I won't be." She lets me see her face smooth as glass, not a fleck of a tremble, before she turns and walks out of the room.

I clean up about half of our frying mess and, leaving the other half for Mary Cowan or Ed, go take a bath.

By the time I have bathed and washed my hair and am ensconced in totally greaseless clothes again, I have programmed my mind not to mention the name Hallie for as long as I am here. I meet Mary Cowan in the hall; she is carrying a twin (Teddy?) and smiling as if nothing happened at all. "I'm going to give the boys their bath now if you want to come help."

She has two bathinettes although the bathroom is so tiny that while we are both bathing our charges we are stuck to the wall. I see that this bathing is one of her delights; I begin to enjoy trying to soap my own wiry wiggling twin—George—thankful that we are so packed in that he can't knock over the bathinette nor is there any room left in here for him to fall out of it. It is a different matter though to hold him still long enough to get him diapered. I distract him with roll-'em-and-stick-'em. No baby can resist my performance at roll-'em-and-stick-'em. I feel as powerful as a grandmother should. Mary Cowan has Teddy diapered; I am doing one more stick-'em toward George's barrel-shaped doll-belly when his toy penis squirts on my chest. "George!" I cry in surprised rage. George was laughing, now is not sure. I have never been squirted before. The bathroom air is tense. Mary Cowan is afraid I will traumatize George, I am afraid I will beat him. I will have to bathe and change again down to my skin layer. I grit my teeth and cover up his squirter while he watches me fearlessly, ready to laugh again the minute he catches my eye. I hold my eye out of reach.

Nevertheless I honor my commitment to feed them. I am tempted to stick the bottle nipple into the little meat jar and the little carrot jar; I try it on George, who screams. I have to put in carrots, scoop carrots off his chin, catch carrots on his lower lip until that spoonful of carrots evaporates from being transferred so often. I hand him his bottle and try the contents of Teddy's little meat jar riding on the nipple; Teddy looks surprised but accepts it. I am so excited with victory that I feed Teddy the whole jar of meat before I remember George hasn't had any yet. I scrape the bottom for George who looks surprised.

"Baby, what are we doing to you?" Ed says. I leave the babies in his care and go to take my third bath of the day.

I should have stayed in a hotel. The bathroom, small to begin with, has been shrunk to a minimum by the bathinettes, diaper pail, rack holding Mary Cowan's laundry, plus containers of baby oil, Phisohex, talcum, cotton. The tub is ringed with toys. The bathroom smells like baby. I'll be leaving tomorrow: we have had no fights but no real closeness either. Although I will enjoy telling my friends about the twins and how well Mary Cowan looks, I do not think my children are an extension of myself and do not feel puffed up over their looks or accomplishments.

So how did it come about that Mary Cowan considers me an extension of herself? She brags about me, parades me—this party tonight, for example: I will be asked to perform so that when I'm gone she can collect her friends' delight in the fact that she has a mother unlike any other. I don't want to perform (I know I will, as soon as I've gotten into clean clothes; I know I may even enjoy my performing but right now among the soap-coated plastic toys I feel like staying right here until the guests have come and gone). I wish she had not been born a beauty. She surrounds herself with men who are married to less lovely women so she has only to dress and *be* while everyone basks in her face. She does not have to try and she doesn't. And I know that she, like Sis, will be a beauty until the day she dies and will never have to try, will never have to be interested in a single other person, will go through life considering all the world an extension of herself. I don't want to criticize her, it is the way she is; it is the world's fault for overvaluing her outside with such persistence that her inside atrophies.

I am dry and powdered and perched on the toilet seat in my bra and girdle putting on my stockings when Mary Cowan knocks and immediately enters.

"I have to talk to you," she says, standing with her back against the door, avoiding looking at me anywhere except my eyes.

"Talk away. I know better than to expect privacy." I smile.

"It's about George. I won't have him growing up feeling anything but natural about his body."

I am puzzled. "I think you're exactly right. I . . . ."

"*You* tried to make him feel ashamed."

"I . . . ?"

"He couldn't help peeing on your blouse but even if he could, even if he did it deliberately, it's perfectly natural for him to want to experiment with his body."

My left stocking stops at mid-calf. I see rage in her face, feel it coming from her body to me in the crowded bathroom. "Darling . . ."

"Don't try to tell me anything about little boys! You never had one!"

I feel strangely accused of having a major fault, "No, but I had a miscarriage after Hallie; that was going to be a boy."

"I remember your letting Hallie and me play on the beach naked and then hitting the ceiling when a little boy no older than Hallie toddled up to us, naked too. You hate penises and that's why you felt like killing George when he squirted your blouse . . ."

"Stop saying he squirted my blouse. *I* was inside it."

"Exactly." Her face is triumphant. "You felt that he deliberately peed on *you*. And you responded on the same level—you wanted to hit him back—just as if you were a baby too. Don't you know he can feel that? Don't you understand that he senses that you think he wanted to hurt you so now *he* thinks maybe he did want to hurt you and so he feels guilty even though he didn't start out doing anything to be mean? He held his penis as if he were trying to protect it when I changed him just now."

"Mary Cowan, don't you think maybe you're making too much of this?"

"That's impossible. Every single thing that happens to him while he's a baby is crucial. I know. And I'm not going to have my sons grow up thinking every woman they meet wants to castrate them. I'm not going to have my children warped because their grandmother doesn't know anything about boys."

"What do you want me to do now?"

"Just stay away from them! You hate penises; you always have. I can feel your hate in the air, it's all over the apartment; even Ed feels it . . ."

She has gone too far. I can't hear anything else although there are more words steaming up an already steamy bathroom. I finish putting my stockings on and stand up. "I'll leave right now."

But now she is crying. "I just don't see how you could have done it, that's all. I know you hate me, you've always hated me but I didn't think you'd take it out on my baby—on a little baby who hasn't done anything to hurt you and who just wants his grandmother to love him . . ."

I am holding her soft, enlarged, maternal body, trying to comfort the tears, my mind frantically sorting, sorting. "What on earth gives you the idea that I . . . ?" I can't say the word. "I love you.

You're my darling daughter and I've always loved you. And I certainly love my darling little grandsons." After a few minutes I ask her, "What's the matter?" I'm hoping that the bare whisper will work.

"Ed's impotent."

I'm not surprised that I am being blamed for that. I feel the surge of mother power return; my mind stops, like an airplane propeller, revealing design. This blame restores me to my rightful place.

"Well, I can certainly see that that would be my fault."

I expected a chuckle, even a laugh; I don't expect the softness I am holding to melt in my arms. Her amusement, when it comes, is the high hysteria of a child suddenly pushed in her swing—a deprived child, I think. My Mary Cowan, I repeat out loud.

She wants to tell me everything—although there is a party coming soon, arrangements waiting. I sit back on the toilet seat and she on the tub rim while she tells me that she only married Ed because I approved of him (I protest that I more than approve, I like him very much). She chose him because he insisted, because he had the right genes to create children—she means he is handsome, intelligent, sensitive, educated. I begin to wonder if both my daughters are fixated on the genetic pool.

I think even she knows Ed's impotence is a temporary thing, anger at being used and discarded. But she can't really help her obsession with her babies any more than she can help her beauty. I listen; I marvel at the cool voice which comes from her melting body—even her anger at me is spoken calmly and meant to educate rather than hurt. I decide that there is an aspect of Mary Cowan's vanity which I often feel myself: she dresses only partly for the artistic effect of her outsides. The larger reason is the pleasure her skin takes in its silks, the feel on her palms as she smoothes on a dress which is money translated into its finest surfaces. She has been oiling herself since I can remember. The present nightgowns, underwear, overwear are experienced by that skin as another layer of oil. I doesn't surprise me when she says she plans to take a course in dressmaking and turn the little room where I am staying into a sewing room.

It runs in the family. We handle someone's anger by getting involved in something else until they get over it. Ed will get over it because he adores Mary Cowan and she at least admires and respects him. I always knew there would never be a grown man whom she could adore. Loyalty is her grand passion.

I begin to revel in Mary Cowan's beauty. I concentrate on her words, her thoughts, but that takes only a single kernel of my mind. Her beauty flows off her like pale fog on a suddenly cold night. Her hair is alive, tiny new hairs in pea-size curls standing up out of the main hair like the series of o's I used to draw as hair on my childhood people.

That inexplicable feeling of happiness scoops me up like a giant hand under my seat as the plane lifts off. My veins are running red with hope. Every smell my nose can seize—high octane gasoline, plastic walls, my neighbor's talcum—sends messages of *now* into my head. My mind is uncrowded, all its past suspended like bubbles in Alka Seltzer waiting to be deliciously rearranged. I order ginger ale out of loyalty; I don't want a martini anyway and besides it has no carbonation.

With great welcome the old torch songs play from memory to my happy ears: he was my man but he done me wrong; when a lovely flame dies; gloomy Sunday; lover come back to me; say good-bye to the Isle of Capri.

Everything was clear as soon as I saw that loyalty is the major artery feeding Mary Cowan's heart—loyalty so necessary that objects which require that trait will be invented in order to assure the flow. Invented as the twins were.

As if the defection of Hyke untied the pink threads holding me still, now I see the people I invented over two decades ago. For the first time in my life I think I can also analyze Hallie as I was unwillingly sprinkled with the analysis of Mary Cowan in her bathroom. Analyze instead of repeating to myself who she is (by which I used to mean me). I can embrace Mary Cowan's mind but I cannot enter it; I can hover; I can be compassionate but not passionate. I hear Mary Cowan adamant: My God, who wants passion from a *mother?*

I enjoy thinking of birthing as an invention. The girls are characters in my novel. At first I was so caught up in the mechanics of plot (my conventional eighth-grade plot) that I scribbled out their years with one eye to the pretty illustrations I imagined someone talented would add for verisimilitude. My darling Mary Cowan made me reconsider.

I order another ginger ale and smile warmly at the woman who is my seat neighbor, and see that she is interested in having a conversation.

She has just moved to Houston and wants to know how I would describe it as a personality. "Oh, in some ways, Houston is a mess," I begin happily.

I AM SITTING here thinking of Hallie. It is natural to be thinking of Hallie and my newest grandchild Emily and angelbaby Dora since Christmas is coming, but I find that I think of Hallie in *m*'s: motherhood, money, and mathematics.

The last might have been expected to save her from the first but in fact it has multiplied her motherhood commitments in the twinkling of an equation—in deference to the middle word, *money*, the meat of our sandwich. She tells me she knows the exact relationship between numbers and fertility and she has even bragged that she feels a sensation the limited hours when ovulation takes place in her uterus (a Scorpio brag: I am a Leo myself and never pay attention to those dark, dank places); nevertheless, she has acquired by twenty-seven two children of her body and seventy-eight from other bodies. The second group, for whom she is arithmetic teacher, are predominantly twelve and thirteen years old, although some of them are fourteen, fifteen, even sixteen.

I have to be proud of her for teaching because she is earning a living but she has taken on a definitely chalky look and I hate thinking of her as a school marm.

M is the big letter in Houston this year: on July 3 our population reached a million. Mr. Million, due to arrive that day, was met at the airport and presented with Houston bucks—million-dollar bills with Sam Houston's picture on them. The fact that he was chosen from those who come by plane soothed the undemocratic fears of our city. They had less control over the first baby born on M-Day: a girl from a poor Negro couple. Since she will be an eldest daughter, I know she will make good use of the gifts they gave her.

Cad picks up one of the matchbooks Hyke had printed up. It says in gold, "Houston: the reason Texas brags." She lights her cigarette without comment. She is talking about McCarthy and his search for supposed communists in our government. Yesterday someone was called a "loyal security risk." Because I am immersed in *m*'s I think about Maury Maverick, who died this year, who will always be associated in my mind with San Antonio and my first real weekend with Hyke, whom everyone else will remember as the man who invented the term "gobbledy-gook."

Cad has been on the school board for two years now. She is responsible for getting Hallie the job teaching math at Cullen Junior High, an old school recently expanded by Quonset huts.

One of her sections is a slow class whose IQs range from 69 to 101. It also has the boys for whom this is their last year of any schooling: the sixteen-year-olds who are held at the seventh-grade level unless they actually do the work and pass. They have to be promoted out of elementary school to protect those younger children from full-blown adolescence; they are never promoted beyond the seventh grade, known to teachers and administrators as the holding pen.

There are only eighteen children in Hallie's slow class and she was told to forget lesson plans and teach them whatever she could. She decided to teach them the numbers of money. She invented a game for them: one student was to be a dishonest storekeeper; each remaining student was to draw a slip of paper stating what he or she was buying, how much it cost, and what bill the student had to pay for it with. The storekeeper was supposed to try to cheat the buyer. The buyer had three minutes to figure out if she or he had been cheated during which time the storekeeper was allowed to interrupt and try to hurry the buyer any way possible.

At first the very shy girl, who knew only how to write her name, refused to be the storekeeper; the sixteen-year-old bad boy refused to be anything else. But last week the shy girl grinned instead of crying when she caught herself being cheated and said in a loud voice: "I get more money than that"—her hand was held out palm down—"six, seven, eight more nickels!" The sixteen-year-old boy pulled out his knife. "I ain't playing this stupid game," he said and retreated to the back radiator by the window by the back fence, holding his knife open in front of him.

The other children stared at the window. Across the back fence, five yards from this Quonset hut, was another section of town entirely, a colored section. I understand that the children are terrified of that land they cannot see and often ask if they are going to be integrated—a word which means to them that over the fence will climb hordes of knife-wielding black students to cut up their books, their hair, their clothes and that as soon as the first hordes start over the fence, parents will come and snatch the white children out of school and they will be home all day, stuck in their IQs.

"Gary, bring me that knife," Hallie said.

"Come get it, teacher."

Without a word Hallie walked over to the window and took the knife out of his hand. As soon as the knife disappeared folded up into her pocket, Gary let out all the words . . . the words he was concentrating on saying to argue with her, while she was walking over, while she was telling him about the rules, about nice boys, about right and wrong; he had all the words ready just behind his tongue and was thinking so hard on them that she surprised him by saying nothing and left him paralyzed behind words as if they were a huge pair of hands holding him down.

Although she only took one boy by surprise one time, I control my own fear for her by pretending she has hit upon a basic truth—and besides I like all stories in which explanation is ridiculed. Hallie said that her fear was that he would ridicule her, like parents of small children do, by holding the knife out of reach, by darting around the room behind desks, forcing her to chase him, never to catch him, to make herself a laughingstock by chasing a man-size boy around desks after a knife always out of reach until the assistant principal came in just as she lunged for him and fell . . .

Cad nods. "My fear exactly."

"Well, hardly mine," I say. But I want to tell her the rest of the story. Hallie, of course, feeling as I would that she had acted from some deep wellspring of intuition, dances up her steps, scooping Dora and little Emily in front of the grocery bags, and prepares for a perfect evening with her daughters.

I *hope* Cad has known such nights: when mothers believe the child can be everything. They begin with exultant half-hours during pregnancy when all ancestors are scanned and all the traits you admire are plucked out and dropped into the very egg you carry. These moments return throughout motherhood, usually when you yourself have done something special. When Hallie was telling me this story I could see Dora and Emily sprinkled with their mother's invincibility, the cerise woodwork holding them cozy.

When the knock on the door came—a banging really—I was more furious than anyone; I wanted to hear more about happiness. It was Selwyn, of course, with a birthday present for Emily (whose birthday isn't until tomorrow). Divorce doesn't stop him; he's even reopened the custody decision and is suing for custody of the girls—although no one believes for a second that he has a chance of getting that. I have felt his charm; I couldn't expect Emily to do otherwise when he called out in response to Hallie's telling him to leave: "I'm not even allowed to bring my own daughter a birthday present except by a timetable? How will she know I love her? Emily, you old goofball, it's Daddy! I love you, goofball. You hear me? I'll just put the present on the doorstep and Mommy can come get it for you. Happy birthday, sweetheart!"

Cad groans and says, "Hallie didn't! Don't tell me she fell for that."

What else can I tell her? Hallie opened the door to get the present and Selwyn pushed inside; Hallie walked over to Main Street to call the police and when she came back Selwyn had locked the door. She was caught outside in rumpled shorts and mismatched shirt without even a cigarette (as one always is) and the police were a long time coming. By the time they got there, she decided that they could only get her inside and ask Selwyn to leave: in other words put the situation back exactly where it had been.

They did this; Selwyn screamed about "his wife" and told them some story about another man and so confused them that they merely escorted him two blocks to Main Street and let him go. But he had pocketed her key (along with her diaphragm) and returned within thirty minutes to make his speech that he loved her, to beat her for not accepting this.

I want to know what we can do. I know I expect instant answers. After a very few seconds I say, "Well?"

Cad chuckles and rattles her ice in imitation of Oscar. "You won't let me think about it?"

"Oh, think if you must." I know what *I* would do: I'd move all three of them in here with me. But even Cad, although she has been ousted herself in favor of the rightful husband (I mean Hyke) would cry out in horror if I went against the twosomeness of marriage by intruding a daughter and two grandchildren.

While she is thinking I tell her about little Emily.

Dora, who at four can sound uncannily like a sorely tried mother of dozens, asked if Daddy and the policeman had gone and Hallie answered yes; then Emily threw a fit. As if Emily at not quite one understood nothing of the fight except that she had been a pawn in Daddy's vendettic love for Mommy, therefore she possessed no more identity than a towel torn in two by angry sisters. The feeling was a wordless knowledge imprinted in her pudge. Safety rested with Mommy and violence with Daddy but Daddy also brought the surprises, the after-bedtime adventures in the living room with real policemen.

Her screams grew wild. She had been brought to the pitch of excitement and suddenly expected to follow that by quiet sleep, so Hallie picked her up and walked, danced her around the apartment, nudging her sparsely haired head, patting her round diapered bottom, humming nonsense ditties which Hallie invents from time to time, snatches of song describing whatever moment was happening . . . thus Hallie reinforces Emily's expectation that violence is the best adventure because it is followed by the most precious special attention from Mother.

"I wonder," I say, "if nightmares will be the most treasured part of Emily's childhood."

"They were of mine," Cad says.

At one Emily is still so closely wrapped in her body that she never questions its tyranny; unlike Dora she has not started to look around at adults and see that the little bodies are considered merely cute by the larger folk. Emily assumes that she and her body will be friends forever, twins, in fact, who will always love each other, talk to each other, be on the same side. She is her wrappings. She feels loving and her legs grab around a waist; she touches a cut on your arm and her forehead frowns in pain; she opens her square meter of flesh to every bath, splash of sunshine, sudden rain/hailstorm/early morning dew; mud puddle, strange dog; stranger. "Don't!" we all shout constantly, knowing how meager a meter is.

Cad is Emily's godmother and listens attentively; I think she has forgotten she is supposed to be thinking.

Emily's body expects her mind to follow and the mind supposes the same but recently the mind wanders very far afield. After quieting Emily down, Hallie was in the bathroom; Emily stood in the window a tall floor above the sidewalk and imagined how it would feel to be a bird. Hallie was just coming out of the bathroom when she heard Dora's voice: "Emily, get down." Hallie, who thought she had had enough for one day, entered the room just as Emily began her descent back into the room from the open window; Hallie had to stand stock-still and let her do it.

The nail had come out of the window. She got the hammer and knocked in another nail which prevented the lower window from being opened more than a foot. "The wood is rotting before her eyes—that's why the first nail fell out," I say firmly.

"I can see that it is impossible to live in a place where you have to watch the wood every minute," Cad says.

Then shouldn't they all come and live here is shouting itself so loud inside my skull I know she can hear it. But she has her brows knitted and fingers entwined to match and I wait for her conclusion.

"You have to get a private detective to sit there every night. Tell Oscar to pay for it. He should be there when Hallie comes home and stay there until she leaves for school in the morning."

We had one during the divorce; I dropped in to see Dora and there was a man, nice enough himself, with a mammoth glistening gun lying right out in front of him on the table where Dora sat to eat her dinner. I begin to protest but there is no other solution. It is settled. Somewhere inside me I feel (but do not know I feel) that it is settled wrong.

"How are things going?" I have avoided the question until Hallie has been offered all possible refreshments and shown or told everything remotely new; now the question is hanging between us like a mildewed towel.

At the first of this week Hallie came out of school to find her car gone. When the principal heard, his cheeks puffed up with delight. He knew exactly who did it. There were several car thieves in the school—he knew them personally from their years in the holding pen; he reached for the telephone as if it were the razor strap he himself could wield. While they waited for the police to trace the car, he told Hallie that she should have locked her car but that it wouldn't have done any good, those thieves could get inside anything. It was the neighborhood. Ever since the Negroes began moving in he's watched it change until now it wasn't safe to leave *any*thing on the street . . . but when the police called back, the principal listened a moment and turned his shaming eyes boldly on Hallie. The car has been repossessed by the finance company.

Selwyn himself once had that job—to locate cars whose owners missed a payment and hot wire them, drive them away in the dead of night, leave the owner asleep or in this case stranded at school ten miles from home. The fact that Selwyn forged Hallie's name on the loan did not soften the finance company's heart; she was married to him at the time the forgery took place, wasn't she?

Hallie didn't even know there was money owed. Too late now, they said. She argued. She begged them to let her pay now. They were stonily silent. Finally she asked if she could go through the car and get out whatever had been left in it. In the dark storage garage, elevated into gloom by ramps of concrete, Hallie fished behind the seats for bits of Crayola, candy wrappers, a sock—crying and angry because they would not let her now pay what was owed, would not let her have this worn, cluttered, dented, filthy car which smelled like sour milk and diapers—even if she paid off the entire note; would not let her buy it back at whatever price they planned to get for it, would not even tell her what used car lot it was headed for.

Of course, Oscar had to buy her another car and she had to accept it. Our lawyer's view is that this is good because it is another black mark against Selwyn.

But Hallie felt as if she'd been stuffed into the dirty clothes basket—like a rank sock jammed to the very bottom. The new car cost almost exactly what her year's salary brought. "I am furious that Oscar can negate a year of my life like that," she screams at me. "Why can't Oscar pay the judge and get this custody case dismissed?"

I heartily agree. I get Oscar on the telephone immediately. "If you don't do something about this, Brother, I will," I tell him. "I went to school with Albert Thomas." I set my mouth like Sister's in a first-born determination. "Call Lyndon. You know perfectly well Selwyn doesn't even want those girls. Lyndon has daughters of his own . . ." I signal to Hallie to get me a cigarette. "And bring me my tea," I mouth. I listen for a minute or two while I light the cigarette and take a large swallow of the coffee-substitute required because of a recent allergy. "All right, Brother. The lives of my daughter and my granddaughters aren't congressional matters—although who they think will vote for them if Selwyn gets his way . . ." I let the sentence lag, knowing the triviality of its predicate. "Well, just buy a judge, for heaven's sake!"

But Oscar and Hallie's lawyer is more far-sighted and insists that the foolproof custody decision, if it involves future inheritance or maintenance trusts that the family might want to make for the children, is the one granted by an opposition judge.

That was five days ago and Hallie looks worse, if possible. Gloom has settled in dents around her mouth, revenge creases her forehead, enforced helplessness coats her eyes with dust. She is as pale as dough, as tense as a wire; she jerks even when she sits and her fingers roll bits of paper constantly. Her birthday has come and gone; the election was barely noticed; our few deciduous trees now have leaves of subtle brick red mixed with their paler green. My yard is honey brown with pine needles. It is a chilly forty-five outside and the air has lost its softness; it is a day when those of us who have fireplaces create roaring fires to celebrate our brief winter. But even the erratic gold of the flames on Hallie's face seems to exaggerate its despair.

I could invite her to a party without hesitation since even the Fascinator would see that Hallie's comparative youth is no longer any competition at all. I notice with dismay that after years of wishing I were my daughter I now feel relieved that I am not. Hallie's life has abruptly lost the qualities of energy, health, possibility that I, a veteran optimist, have been assigning to both my daughters for years. Now I realize that I myself am more attractive, more alive, *younger* than my own daughter.

I draw myself up tall among my sister's brass and tapestry. I will be very careful not to let Hallie see even a hint of where the tendernesss I am determined to express is coming from. I will, I must, inject such a hearty dose of nourishment into the area around Hallie that she will plump up like a dried apricot in soaking but without Hallie herself feeling even the slightest bit wet. I can do it, I say to myself. I alone can create without the created one noticing. It is my special talent, which I have spent years perfecting for just this moment. For just this woman.

I myself feel plump as an oyster, swollen like the orange of the autumn sun: I am here with my powers in their prime working order when the one life which I alone can save is threatened with extinction.

Years ago, when we had just moved to Houston, Hallie was invited to a costume dance; although she was just twelve, two other mothers and I persuaded our daughters to go, rented costumes for them and arranged for their transportation—all of us agreeing that a girl can't get started on her social career too early. Just before Hallie ran out the door I reached for my rouge pot and quickly smeared a bit of rouge on her cheeks, grabbed my powder puff and dusted her nose and shoulders. Her eyes when they met mine were filled with the rage of betrayal. But the car was honking for her and she left.

I simply wanted everyone in Hallie's to-be future life to think she was as adorable as I thought she was and I knew her skin was freckled and sallow, pale in artificial light. I am not naturally given to analysis; I either see my mistake whole on the instant or I never see it. I said to my own fully rouged face in the mirror, "Hell. At the very last minute I told Hallie that she isn't pretty just as she is. I said it plain as mud." All the persuasion, the nice ivory and blue costume, the after-dinner dancing practice were up-ended into a falsehood. I saw that I believed like an idiot that I would be going with Hallie to the dance to watch over her, to entice her out of her shyness—I even knew in that bolt of insight that I expected to dance with her! It was only at the very last minute when I heard the car honk that I understood Hallie would be going alone and snatched at the rouge pot to make her into me.

I finish the memory just as my hand picks up my bottle of Joy, which I was going to dab behind Hallie's ears. I stop and smile. "Would you like a little Joy?"

Hallie's laugh—although it sounds half like a sob—is the first she's allowed for days.

"Oh, Mother!" Hallie laugh-sobs again and works her arms around me in a hug that would not spill the perfume. The sobbing takes hold and, reaching to set down the perfume, I hug and pat and nestle her head into my shoulder—no doubt scratchy from the first wool dress of winter. Although I begin thinking right away that Hallie must not give in to the kind of crying which multiplies tears, which overwhelms the brain with self-pity and so overstimulates the tear ducts that the crying becomes cause for crying and so will never end, I know that a few tears can loosen the blood like taking off a girdle.

My own arms resting lightly on Hallie's shoulders will judge the exact moment when enough tears are shed; my flesh adjacent to Hallie's will sense the same tension and feel the same release; my will will act for us both.

When the moment comes, my right hand begins a slow circle on Hallie's back, a light touch becoming stronger; I whisper and then croon my favorite rhyme: "Roll 'em and stick 'em and mark 'em with B, and put them in the oven for baby and me." I say it again and again until Hallie's consciousness is caught by another time and she rises up out of the tears.

I hold her head and sniff at both ears. "I don't smell any Joy."

"You forgot to put it on me," she says, grinning through the last of the tears.

Lunchtime women can steal without penalty—in the new South at least. Although I certainly remember the first years of my marriagehood when Rusty came home for dinner at noon, now—particularly on Saturday—lunchtime is a middle time considered unimportant in the lives of women and children; Saturday's noon hours can be easily hidden under errands, hobbies, duties, even silence.

Saturday lunch is also the first date a girl ever has. I say, "What about a little lunch at the Bayou Club?"

"I'll ask my mother if I can go." Hallie's voice is that of an eight-year-old but her expression is oddly flirtatious; it takes me a few seconds to get the joke.

"Your mother says you've been a good girl all week and you can go. We're overlooking the mud you tracked into the kitchen and the fact that you tore the hem out of every dress you wore this week." I give her a kiss on the forehead. "Get brushed! I'll tell Jewell to take the girls to the pharmacy for hamburgers."

Hidden off a little-used highway and barely marked, the Bayou Club is supposed to be the most exclusive club in Houston because it is so small the members personally accept each candidate member; it is also, I'll tell anyone, the dullest. "Don't worry, there won't be a soul in the place," I say when Hallie wonders if she is dressed all right.

We will have lunch in the bar, a room with glass doors off the pool, brick floors and walls, dark oak tables, and only one huge Persian horse in tapestry on the wall. All Houston prefers sherbet colors and *House Beautiful* white when near pools; this room at the Bayou Club feels intellectual by contrast.

Hallie slumps into her chair like a failure and smiles wanly. I immediately order us each a bloody mary. I only took my eyes off her while driving and she collapsed.

I lean on the table, my arms firm as stakes: "Do you remember the time you and Punchy brought the gang over here for swimming—climbed over the fence when the club was closed? And broke into the kitchen and ate up poor Mr. Watkin's menu for the week?" Hallie glances up. "Of course, they knew exactly who did it. You left my monogrammed towel right by the icebox!" I laugh and hold my glass up to Hallie's. "To the mugwumps!" But after one sip: "George, put some Tabasco in this. It tastes like tomato juice."

Half a bloody mary later, most of the yellow-white has disappeared from Hallie's face. Halfway through lunch I begin to relax. The food at the Bayou Club is perfect; since nothing is ever prepared in advance—no one believing that anyone will show up— even the vegetables are cooked to order. I have re-created the past so vividly to cheer up Hallie that I myself am swamped with nostalgia. I shake my mind now, noticing that no color has entered

Hallie's skin in the last ten minutes, and address myself straight to what I think is depressing my daughter.

"You can't blame yourself for marrying Selwyn in the first place, you know." I have forgotten—as I do easily—the shotgun aspect of the wedding. "You can't always know how someone will turn out. And Selwyn is from a good family—one of the best. I mean everyone else in his family did something with themselves."

But she claims she knew from the moment she met him: he was only interested in watching ball games on tv and hanging around with people he felt superior to—although his name for it was democracy. "Well, he was attractive."

"I don't mean *that.*" I make a firm break in my roll and bite it for emphasis.

But *that* apparently sends a current of lust through Hallie, making her eyes shine: eyes which have to see me sitting tall, the brown of my eyes straight and strong, my face fixed forever in its particular beauty. Hallie lowers her eyes as the shine grows to a tear, lust to lost: she wants her perky, adorable prebaby body back. The hand in her lap pushes against her soft stomach and it gives easily; Hallie slumps into her flab and stops eating.

"But not as attractive as baby Hallie is." I smile warmly.

"Was."

"You're much more attractive today than you've ever been." I order coffee and speak of the definitive grace, the human experience, the range . . . I mean *tomorrow,* of course, rather than today; I mean hope not fact. "Do you ever see . . ."

"I don't see anybody."

"Oh, darling. You have to see your friends . . ."

Alone in the room as we are, both of us look toward the door the minute we hear someone approaching it. "Paula!" I hold out my hand. "Ben. How's the next Republican governor?"

They are a lanky English-looking couple. Paula takes a chair immediately and turns me toward her with a breathless story. Ben stands hesitantly by Hallie's chair. She was distantly in love with him once because he was kind to her. "I don't know if I should speak to you or not," Ben says with a partial smile.

"Why not?" Hallie smiles fully, opting for it to be a joke.

"The rumor has it that Selwyn is naming every man who ever danced with you in his custody suit and I can't afford the scandal."

"You're joking."

I don't hear Ben's answer. He looks quickly around the empty room. Apparently lacking my faith in its perennial emptiness, he motions to George that they will sit at a table down at the other end; he fumbles in his pocket for a nickel and waves to his wife that he has to make a telephone call. A slight tilt of his head toward their table tells her to be seated at it when he returns. His wife, who once also thought he loved Hallie, will loyally oblige.

Color is rampant in Hallie's face now but it is a splattered motley red. Her lips quiver as she tries to bite them.

All of us are mumbling "excuse me." I follow Hallie who has gone into the women's locker room, passing the turtle chasteness of Ben's back. I find her cupping water in her hands and dipping her face in it over and over.

"You have to see your friends," she mimics. "I don't have any friends. A friend is someone who'll speak to you. No one in this town will do that. Every time someone tries—comes over or takes me out—there's Selwyn at the door sooner or later calling the men adulterers and the women lesbians, accusing the men of sleeping with me and the women of influencing me. He says whatever he wants to right and left regardless of logic and no one ever comes back a second time. *No* one will see me!"

My hand trembles on her shoulder. "Oh, Hallie. How awful."

"I told you."

"But I didn't think . . ."

"You just didn't want to know."

"I . . ."

"I haven't done anything. Not one goddamned thing. Selwyn's made bad debts and insulted and fought with every man in town, he's broken furniture and terrified the children, he hangs out all night with women and drunks and hoods—and everyone in this town treats him like an emperor because they do exactly what he wants."

"No one has any respect for him at all."

"They underwrite him, don't they?" Hallie has stopped washing her face; it is drying by itself in patches. I take a towel and pat her cheeks and forehead. "Ben just now said he couldn't be seen talking to me because he couldn't afford a scandal."

"Hallie, he was joking." But now I rehear his tone and am not sure.

Hallie talks around the towel. "Go ask him."

"I will. I'm going back out there and tell Ben to stop this nonsense . . ."

"They're all confirming Selwyn. They're handing him a scepter. My lawyer talked to a psychiatrist that Selwyn went to once—only once—to see if the doctor would testify that Selwyn was unbalanced or insane or even bad. The psychiatrist threw up his hands and said, 'Not me. Have you seen the size of him?'"

I hear the psychiatrist's words as an echo of Hyke's remark last week. "Sometimes people are scared. Not that that makes it *right*, of course . . ."

"It makes it just right for Selwyn, doesn't it? You might as well defend him as defend everyone who makes him possible. Oscar took Selwyn into his company and gave him three thousand dollars to pay off his back debts because Oscar was so sure that once Selwyn had a clean slate he'd go far. How do you think that makes me feel? You all might as well *adopt* Selwyn!"

I see her hand reaching toward me and pull my own, shaking, out of reach. She has gone too far. I can stand to be reminded that Hyke is scared of Selwyn and Oscar flattered by his youthful charm, but I am *not* going to be criticized for trying to like the husband *she* chose to bring into the family.

"I can't *stand* it. I can't sleep at night over this whole thing and now you're saying it's *my* fault. I *caused* it." I whip my head to the wall and stand with my arms clenched to my sides. My shoulders are shaking.

"Mother. I'm sorry. I'm really . . ."

"Blame Mother. It's Mother's fault."

"I just said . . ."

"That I'm to blame for Selwyn because suddenly he's become *my* child. That's what you said."

"'Might as well be your' . . . but I shouldn't have said that. I just felt so ostracized . . ."

"I have quite enough children with you two and I'll thank you not to assign me any more."

I feel her touch on my shoulder as if there is a smile in the palm of her hand. "That's a wonderful remark."

I turn my face; halfway between anger and love my expression struggles for dignity. Hallie picks up the towel which I used earlier on her face and wets a corner of it. She presses it between my eyebrows smoothing out the frown lines, careful to avoid smearing my eyebrow-pencil marks.

I say I want to go out to Teas's to pick up some tulip bulbs. We seat ourselves in the car enveloped in confusion. How are we going to connect the two women driving slowly beneath private trees with the two who attended to each other's faces with towels a short while ago? Hallie starts to tell me a washing machine story.

The washing machine she made a down payment on with her first month's salary worked two weeks. Then it began to drain and fill constantly through the wash cycle, taking all the Tide with it as it rinsed and rinsed the diapers. The repair man came twice, each time saying the machine was now fixed. Hallie was so furious yesterday, she says, that she called the manager and told him that he could come get all her rinsed wet clothes and take them to the launderette or bring her another machine. Or he could drop off two dozen diapers a day and she'd throw the dirty ones out. Or he could take the children to his house. Or he could come pinch the drain shut with his fingers while the machine got through its wash cycle. I smile encouragingly and ask what he said.

"You know what they say down here." Hallie is pretending the two years she spent away are a lifetime. "They've got degrees in politeness. They read from the book. You tell them you'll sue and they read the paragraph under 'sue': 'I am as sorry as you are that this happened, it hurts me in my heart.' You call them a son-of-a-bitch and they flip the page to 'lady calls you a name, page 23': 'We are dedicated to serving you and want to do everything in our power to satisfy you because a satisfied customer is our business.'"

I laugh and agree that it is maddening but I am thinking about towels: envelope for a just-washed baby, sponge for spills, protection from beach sand, mat to lay over all the wet that sheets are prone to—blood, urine, sex stains, sudden rain from an open window: "get a towel" a common household order like "cut off the light" and "go to sleep." The towel touches our bodies where we don't dare, shields our hands from our children's or mothers' bodies when hands would be too bare and yet my hand on the towel and the towel on your face connect us by a thousand strings.

It has been years since Hallie was bold enough to attack the frown lines on my forehead but the urge to smooth them away remains live on her fingertips just as the same urge lives on mine twenty years after Mother's death. Terrycloth is our book of instruction on what to do if a mother or daughter starts yelling or crying: for tears wrap her up, for anger wet one corner.

I don't know why, right now, I think about towels as a symbol of wealth, that the meager rectangles bought at Penney's and the luscious-colored thickness sold in stores designed especially for them sandwich American incomes. Whenever I think of the advantages of being rich, my mind focuses on the secret, private comforts. For years I longed for folded lusciousness, yearned to snatch down from a huge pile a mere top towel as casually as one would take a cracker from a box—a towel that to my precious clean skin would combine fur and velvet, adoration with immediate satisfaction.

Three inches of satin and lace so expensive it can afford to be cream-colored slip over my nylon knee as my dress slants into my lap. For Hallie, does my body come lace-covered? Lace less polite, less distancing than terrycloth.

"I'm glad we can't get mad at each other," Hallie says. "I know you hate argument but I wouldn't want us to be reading answers out of the book."

If I close my eyes I see my daughter's body barefoot. Hallie's feet are short and broad, almost flat; sturdy not feminine feet. In rebellious college years they were bare on the couch, tables; a denful of bare feet quickly hidden when I came home. In childhood they were bitten, stubbed, split wide open once on a coffee can that older children were successfully jumping over. And in babyhood they were the toys of both mother and baby, tiny plums to be kissed, held, wiggled to nursery rhymes. Hallie's feet were extraordinarily ticklish; I saw her at five learn to cut off all sensation to her ribs and avoid that common torment but her will never could overcome the sensitivity of her feet.

Rising up from my own feet and into my head I feel an ugly, violent urge to break something, smash, explode. I wish I were running behind my car pushing it. Sitting calmly driving this shiftless, power-steered living room on wheels produces the same torture that tickling does with the same need to control, freeze reaction. I cannot allow myself to smash into the rear of the car in front of us; I do not want to do that; something inside of me is doing it. I slam on the brakes and merely bump the bumper of the car stopped at a stop sign.

Although the driver of the bumped car drives on, seeing no damage, I burst into tears. Hugging the curb, I stop the car; I push my fingers against my eyes as if I could shove the tears back inside.

"It's nothing. Really, it's nothing," I say, pushing but failing to force my eyes into containing the tears.

Alarmed, Hallie turns off the ignition and tries to see into my face. As Hallie asks if it is menopause or Hyke or the flu or money, I shake my head at each, but because I continue to insist that it's nothing, I know Hallie thinks that it has to be her then. The tiny monogrammed handkerchief fumbled out of my purse and held to my eyes by Hallie is all we have for a towel—sheer fabric barely preventing Hallie's fingers themselves from touching my face. I am feeling only the sunken sense of failure; far from restoring Hallie, all my own energy and optimism are dribbling away down my cheeks; soon I too will be shriveled into despair and uselessness.

I am helpless to help anyone, I am in need of help myself; this is not what I had in mind early in the day when I congratulated myself upon being the right person here at the ultimate time. I no longer feel that Baby counts; how can I insert into Hallie the knowledge that Hallie counts? I feel that if each blade of grass in that field there were a woman, the entire field would be chosen by one team or the other before either side picked me—for *any* position.

"I feel worthless," I say finally.

I am thrilled with the astonishment in Hallie's voice as she says, "*You?*"

But I repeat, "Worthless. And I can't even remember *ever* feeling like this before in my life." Since all new feelings demand attention, this one too surprises me into stopping crying. "Ever," I repeat emphatically and begin to wonder. "How is that possible?"

"I don't know." Relief causes Hallie's voice to sing strangely. "Except that you are certainly the most valuable person in the whole world and everybody who knows you knows it. Could that be the reason?"

"No, you are."

"*I'm* the reason?"

"Mugwumps." I blow my nose and start the car. "You're the most valuable person in the world because you had Dora and Emily."

"Then you have to be even more valuable because you started it all by having me." Hallie grips my hand and we mutually squeeze—but somehow it isn't exactly enough.

When the man at Teas's tells us that they don't have any bulbs, that the bulbs someone told me they had, this morning, have now all been sold, anger rises as suddenly as tears did and anger too comes up from my feet. I have driven all the way to Bellaire in the Saturday traffic, I have spent the afternoon getting here for my bulbs, which he told me he had this morning. If he had so few that he intended to sell out in four hours, why didn't he warn me, why didn't he suggest I reserve some if I really was coming? He's been in business long enough to know how fast bulbs sell on Saturdays— or he should know. He could at least have told me to call before I come to make sure they still have bulbs. Or he could have ordered enough bulbs in the first place so this wouldn't have happened. But he merely apologizes from the paragraph headed "lady accuses you of being remiss in stocking bulbs."

There is nothing we can do but turn around and drive facing the sun the long way back in worse traffic.

"Let me drive," Hallie says.

"No, I want you to relax and not have to do anything."

"We're not really facing the sun."

"I know. I wanted to make him feel bad. But I'm not mad anymore. It's silly to get mad at something as minor as tulips."

"Let's try Cornelius. Maybe they have some bulbs."

"You don't want to drive all the way over there."

"Yes, I do. I love to drive your car." Hallie gets in and pulls the seat up closer to the pedals. "Where is Cornelius?"

"It's way over on Buffalo Speedway. Honestly, Hallie, I don't have to have tulips . . . you'd be better off turning on Bissonnet, Westheimer is so crowded. Look out for that truck, it's going to pull out."

"I won't hit it, Mother."

I pull down my sun visor and stop looking. "I used to tease Sis about having to have tulips and here I am scrambling all over Houston for them and mad when I can't get them. Honestly, Houston isn't Holland. And they only last a week at most. You have to put them in the icebox for over a month—move all the meat and stuff over—so they'll think they're in the North. If you plant them now they'll just rot. Then after they bloom you have to dig them up and refrigerate them next year."

"They're so pretty though. I think I'll get some."

"Honey, you won't be able to have any ice or ice cream for six weeks!"

Hallie is leaning over the wheel to watch the green light on the right as if she has to know the second it turns yellow and the second hers will turn green—as if she has to show me she is the best driver in the world. "Maybe I could just keep them in the icebox."

"I think they like to be frozen. That's what they're used to. Honey, the light's green," I say after she has already started up. "I'm sorry I said that. You'd already seen it!" I force my eyes away from the road.

Cornelius has tulip bulbs—dozens of them in all the colors I want. I put my purchase happily in the trunk and start toward the driver's side. "I'm driving," Hallie says.

"All right, Miss Stubborn as a Mule."

Hallie drives as if she were singing, as if the road were a bed of tulips and we are skimming over their tops, as if the sun were a magnet pulling us smartly by the forelock, as if our cargo were already the rainbow of spring color it will with luck become. I imagine that her ears have snapped shut and she hears nothing of the traffic noises, her nose opens and she smells my Joy and Chesterfield with its tantalizing just-lit smell, and her brain, swaying free just over the tulips, is roaring with memory. The car is a vial containing the essence of every moment she has ever shared with the one person she has known forever: me.

I too am thinking about tulips and wondering why people —even me—constantly point out how brief the bloom time of flowers is. I can close my eyes and see right now the yard massed with white azaleas at dusk. I don't have to close my eyes; the splendor of last spring, the spring before, of any moment anywhere in my past, I can conjure up fresh on the instant. At least I can if people keep quiet. Any moment anywhere in the past? No, only those in full bloom. At intensity. All others in between soon sift like silt to the bed of my brain and will one day, I believe, stifle me.

Not all moments of full bloom come from my children but very many do. Hallie herself has prevented layers and layers of silt, has produced so many light bodiless floating antisilt images . . . I laugh out loud. I am thinking like Hallie.

"You know the old saying that a daughter takes years off your life? I was just thinking about how many years you've added to mine." I explain my silt idea to her—although I feel strangely that explanation is unnecessary; I feel that our brains are meshed.

"You're the only person I know who can make tulips healthy."

She's right: I cannot simply enjoy my flowers, I have to see them as useful, as vitamins counteracting clog. "You know me. Baby says, 'A happy person is a better person.'" I use my self-mocking voice with pride. I have defeated my culture's puritanism on its own turf: local clay made friable by deft mixing with sand and peat moss.

"I guess that's why I'm so bad." She says it lightly but it comes out crunched.

Move in with me, the words beat like trapped wings against my skull. Bring the girls and live with me where you belong, where I can watch over you, where I can sleep knowing you're there and wake up with the sun breaking through the window and the morning a tickle on my arm and the day—every day—in full bloom. Move in with me!

And before the phrase is complete I enclose the garage and insulate the attic over it and then add a bedroom off the back, finish in a wink the most perfect apartment for Hallie and the girls right there off the kitchen. I know I cannot put them in Hyke's end of the house but who can object to an apartment on the back where they will be private but close . . . Hyke can, and my mother would uphold him. My heart soars into a silent giggle. Then Hyke can move into the apartment and you, Mother, can go uphold him there, and Hallie can sleep with me, and the girls in the guest room. I am speaking in absolute silence and I can say anything I want to.

But since I can hear Hallie's mind I guess that she can hear mine. I hear her hearing me . . . or feeling my thoughts bump through her brain like puffs of corn pinging against the skillet lid and with every ping she clamps the lid down tighter. She sees the apartment made from my garage where the windows are not splintered and will not drop their nails and threaten Emily with death on a sidewalk below. She sees the grass where the children can play while Jewell kills snakes to impress them and Hallie and I mingle our feelings for each other, our thoughts of perfection, through the dappled cocktail hour; she imagines the dinners during the week when Hyke is away on business, evenings so quiet all past blossoms can be recalled at will. And she shudders at my final violent resolve: in the room with me? in Hyke's bed separated only by a nightstand—a clock and an ashtray? Now the cover rattles and skids, jumping like a skittish filly in the April dew, and Hallie's nostrils flare and she gasps. Every reasonable force in her brain pushes down and sits tight; all its circuits lock and hold. Impossible. Clearly impossible. Still she hears her own voice in a whisper of yes say "Baby"—the name and the particularly Southern word for darling.

Now I feel Hallie's shudder deep inside my own skull, which answers with an echoing shudder of its own. It is the moment of shudder that explains to me the irrepressible depth of my longing and leaves my mind as soft and open as it was at origin. It is in that fragile state that I hear Hallie's unmistakable "Baby."

PART IV

1955–1962

THREE YEARS HAVE passed since my presentiment that my life would change absolutely at my fifty-second B-day. I am sitting on the flagstone terrace overlooking Sis's rolling lawn, examining the lines on my palm. My lifeline, which swoops boldly around my thumb to my wrist, gives only one clue: a deep groove, flanked by two lighter, shorter lines, reach out from my thumb to my lifeline like a spear.

I can't budge Hallie. She is stuck in fornication. I know because I dropped by last Saturday morning: the girls were playing in cornflakes and Hallie, quicksilver, slipping rumpled through her bedroom door, tried to hurry me away with the hasty dishonest ruses of a guilty daughter. But I saw the jacket—black cracked leather with an awful soiled gray sweater band at the waist and wrists—hanging off the couch in a living room where no such jacket ever should be welcome.

I sit out sex in the young. I do not care, I tell myself. Hallie is not a good picker—it is better that she not marry again soon and at least I know she will not marry that jacket. I close my ears when Cad tells me everyone in town is talking. Ears are easy. How can I blind my mind's eye to the picture of Dora and Emily's wide-eyed surprise at the brassy parade across the breakfast table?

I am burning with longing for Mother now. Usually I catch sudden glimpses of her through a fall of light or shadow, or an exact duplicate of her voice pricks my brain—memories which last less than a second. But today Mother's presence hovers like summer heat over the entire terrace, thick enough to glide out and cover the hills of the yard and not be diminished. Mother isn't visible nor is she speaking at all; she is felt like pressure or a magnetic force, like tasteless, odorless density. She was here when I came out to the terrace ten minutes ago and she is still here.

Fortunately Hyke is not home yet. I am sure Mother likes Hyke but his chatter like Rice Krispies popping could interfere with her more diffuse messages. Messages?—Mother is stingily giving none at all. She envelopes the terrace with her thereness, activating all my impulses to touch, hold, feel, smell, enwrap her as a physical mother . . . or at least hear her speak.

Of course, I know that when I die I will see Mother again—although that phrase makes no sense because vision can't be a part of such seeing. I will see her in a way that has no this-world words to describe it but which will—must—utterly satisfy that-world needs . . . why am I suddenly ice-cold? My skin is crawling. I feel—I must be wrong—that Mother is urging me to come now. And see what I will "see."

I stare at my palm. I know Mother cannot see me doing this; she would pooh-pooh such things. Life, she always said, goes in a straight line out from whichever direction you're facing.

But if Mother could see, would she like the way her daughter looks at almost fifty-five? I wore my hair shoulder-length and loosely waved until my fiftieth birthday; now it is short and more tightly curled—a style meant to lengthen my neck but which merely bares it. I wear the straight-skirted linen sheaths without sleeves during Houston's eight-month spring and summer season and their darker variations at the other season. These clothes are not only bland, they make my body—which I have to hold upright, tummy in—graceless and stiff. Would Mother, who regarded weight as a metaphor of the older woman's importance, find my slenderness retarded?

"Mother." I am whispering. "Tell me what to do. Tell me." But I will collapse if I have to beg. I no longer whisper, I think: You won't tell me, will you? I see Mother's black eyes flashing with "that's for me to know and you to find out," with "I've led my life, you'll have to lead yours," with "I always let people do what they want to; they will anyway." I hear Mother's imperious laugh, which could reach inside to tickle your heart if you were feeling happy. But if you were feeling bad, it said, "Don't look at *me*!" It said you have no one, no one or no thing, to blame but yourself.

"Nothing to blame?" I remember crying out just after Rusty went into the sanitarium for the final time and my fatherless girls both had a terrible flu. "Nothing to blame? But this awful thing happened to *me*!"

I was born at the wrong time. At the very moment I was ready to enter my own Part IV—my vital fifties wherein all my talents were to culminate—a pall of fearful caution lay over the land. Doubly unjust because it was the second great time this happened to me: just as I emerged from college, in full possession of independence of brain and a strong Texas body, the country fell into the morass of another Red scare, another retrenchment into the swamps of timidity. The two most important decades of my life coincided with a damned vacuum of adventurelessness.

The last time I was absolutely happy was when Cad and I marched down Main Street with our galoshes unbuttoned. The march was for women's suffrage but what I remember is the daring flap-flap of our galoshes, the flap-flap of drumbeat joy, the flap-flap of feet—heard, acknowledged, *marching* feet. Our feet. We wanted to vote, of course, but only in the way a child wants to eat at the big table and not be fed preselected nourishment in the kitchen. I certainly did not want to spend my youth *voting*. I wanted to be free to explore . . .

"Your own backyard." Mother's voice pierces the summer air like off-season woodsmoke obliterating the smell of flowers.

"My own backyard, then." Because *my* backyards have held pigs, chickens, horses, mules, babies, children, friends, roses, honeysuckle, peonies, bulldogs, snakes, trees, swings, creeks, fish, frogs, love, sex, hate, murder, mutilation, candidates, art, argument . . . don't you dare name coward, Mother; don't you call me a hostess.

I see Hyke's car nose over our rattling bridge. "Please let's not argue in front of Hyke, Mother." I am adding my thank-yous for the visit she paid me just as Hyke toot-toots announcing his arrival and that of the cocktail hour.

"Do you think I betrayed Hallie?" I whisper quickly but Mother has gone, leaving only the echoing "don't blame me" brushing at the trees. Hallie had not acted betrayed; she seemed calm, acquiescent—but she must have felt betrayed or where did the word come from just now?

This is the first time ever that my backyard has been the bone of contention. I have owned Southern land, and through an investment of Brother's, Western land; none has caused such trouble as this neither/nor Houston land. It is my backyard across the creek that is in question—the unused land where Uncle Doctor had his barn and horses.

A month ago Hyke gave the stables to a neighbor in return for moving the structure off the property. Hallie was tactless enough to comment that the wood alone was worth a couple of thousand dollars; Hyke, furious, withdrew into an icy calm. "What use would it have been to you?" he asked Hallie, who at least knew better than to say more. But she told me once that her dream was to remodel the stables into a house and live there—one much later day, one day so far in the future that her language grew gauzy and I, because I know my granddaughters do not belong in horse stalls however remodeled, forgot about it until Hyke asked his bitter question.

Hyke immediately began searching for possible buyers—for four acres without road frontage, hemmed in by old man Vito's home and store on San Felipe and by commercial stuff on Post Oak. Hyke was elated when he did get an offer; apparently there was a deeded roadway from the end of the property through to Post Oak and a builder offered him forty thousand dollars for the whole lot.

Oscar was delighted. "Take it, honey," he told me. "I never saw anything like the prices people are paying for land in Houston. Why I remember the D.R. bought that whole piece for twenty-five hundred and you know a man never goes broke by taking a profit. I can't imagine that land ever being worth much more than forty thousand—the way they're going to have a freeway going down Post Oak and nobody's going to want to live near such as that. I'd say Hyke did a smart bit of scouting . . ."

Since Hyke and I were married when I sold my other house and bought the property from Sis and the D.R., naturally the deed is in our joint names; Hyke's share will be twenty thousand, which he appears to need—after half a dozen years in Houston he feels like the only man here who is as poor as when he came.

And it has nothing to do with Hallie, Hyke pointed out to me twice. I am trying to see the land as a flat, treeless rectangle, as clay and weeds, as a dead piece of past. Hallie and Mary Cowan will inherit when I die the rolling hills and house, the gorgeous half of the land . . . but I can't seem to shake a strong feeling that the sale in fact has nothing much to do with money. Cad believes land should devolve with blood, but that is her Southernness asserting its claim to gloom and lace. Oscar believes that land is an investment that pays no dividends and charges you taxes; he says that a man who won't sell a piece of dirt for cash isn't in business to make money. No one but me sees that those two traditions are humping up the earth right here where they run into each other, head-on, in my backyard—and I wish I didn't see that. Because, of course, I chose Hyke and agreed to sell the land.

All our telephone numbers were changed yesterday; they are now five digits. I search for the piece of paper I wrote Hallie's down on. There is no answer.

I go back to the terrace with the drink Hyke fixed me. I can be alone here for another few minutes; it must have been over ninety today and, although dusk, it is too hot for Hyke. My upper lip beads immediately but I love breathing the moist shadows into my lungs, which can coat and fur my linings with velvet.

We are just finishing dinner—Hyke is telling me that Houston is tops in Texas in dope traffic ("Another first for Houston —hahaha")—when Hallie walks in. One look from her tears through my linings like a pad of steel wool ripping all sense of velvet. Hallie hands Hyke a piece of paper. She sits next to him. She stares at him while he reads it through, twice more than necessary.

Hallie does not look at me; my heart hurts and anger rises to comfort as it can. "What is that?" I demand. Hyke hands it to me. I read that it was always the intention and still is the intention of the undersigned that the land which belonged to the undersigned and his wife go to Mary Cowan and Hallie on his death. It is signed with the D.R.'s shaky, cramped, but still recognizable signature.

"Well, now, baby Hallie," Hyke says with a smile and a dipping kind of chuckle. "You know the Doctor sold the land to your mother and me. It isn't his any longer."

Hallie is obviously fresh from her Uncle Doctor's tiny apartment in the Lamar where he sits surrounded by the things Sis moved in, the pictures of Sis, her hats, perfumes—moving nothing; we all know vividly that he simply died when Sis did. Mind and memory ceased the day of her funeral. He abruptly stopped operating, closed his practice as soon as possible; although he still made periodic trips to his old hospital, reports from the nurses who had loved and admired him made us all wish he wouldn't.

"He didn't know what he was doing. He thought he was giving you permission to live here until he died. I think a court would have him declared incompetent if . . ."

"Hallie!" I hit the table with both palms flat, spilling water, sloshing coffee. "You wouldn't . . . *can't* do that to a fine man's memory like that!"

"*I'm* the only one who ever loved Uncle Doctor! I'm the one who refused to let you all put him in a home just because he walks around downtown with soup on his tie as you put it—meaning with the crotch of his pants wet!" Hallie grabs back her piece of paper as if it were her only hope. "You can have the house and Auntie's part of the property but the land on the other side of the creek belongs to Uncle Doctor and me. It always has. We're the ones who worked on it, we're the ones who took care of it, and the stables—the barn—belong to us too. I told Uncle Doctor you'd given it away laughing about the good deal you made . . ." Hallie's face is above Hyke's and her hand is up as if she would hit him. "He said he'd always known you were a fool but he didn't know anybody could be that big of a fool."

I grab Hallie by the shoulders. "Now you leave this house. This minute. I won't *have* you . . ."

Hallie ducks free and runs into the living room part of the room, separating herself by Sis's Louis XV sofa. "It's my land and you can't sell it!"

Hyke's face trembles but he maintains a small crooked smile. "Is that why you've been paying the taxes on it?"

"Uncle Doctor gave me the money to pay the taxes." Hallie fishes in her purse and pulls out a crump of five-dollar bills; her eyes begin to water. "He reached in his pocket for the roll of cash he always carries and peeled off five fives. He thought they were hundreds, or he thought taxes were still figured in fives, or . . . I don't know what he thought but he meant to give me all the money he had. He peeled off those bills as if they would still buy everything. Then just as I was leaving he went back in his pocket and peeled off another five. He said, 'Here, you better take this too. Taxes might of gone up since I was there.' I hugged him—he smelled like ether just like he always did—and he tried to say, Don't let your mother know you've got it, but he couldn't even remember that that's what he always says! So he just patted me and started to reach in his pocket again . . ."

I am standing halfway between Hyke and Hallie, frozen by betrayal. Both of them are forcing me to choose and I want neither: neither the fool nor the one who dared name fool. If two children can't teach Hallie what motherhood is, where loyalty comes from . . . Hallie flaunts her excess here in the middle of Sis's crystal as if she would shatter all decoration, smash the flowers that keep me from being smothered with silt, *kill* me. How dare Uncle Doctor go against me? I created him. I gave him Hallie. I gave them all everything they have: life, not once but daily; *I* insisted that Uncle Doctor's country crudeness be elevated into salt, that Hallie's refusal to rise and puff and grow golden brown be rescued from failure like the first upside-down cake; *I* served them both up to the world proudly as imagination, creation, genius, the frontier itself.

"I had no idea you were so upset, Hallie." My voice finds the words like neatly folded linen on top of a heap of holey underwear. "When we told you this yesterday you didn't say a word. Hyke, why don't we sit down all together and talk about what we're going to do."

Hyke's smile slips but does not quite vanish. "Of course, Baby. That's a very good idea as the cow said when she . . ." He catches my eye and stops.

My chest is boiling incoherently. If Hallie persists in showing up Hyke, in goading him to reveal foolishness, she is no daughter of mine.

But Hallie is sitting down on the edge of loss. She had merely borrowed gumption, ashamed to be herself gumptionless—the D.R. once said, after repeatedly announcing that she was just right for a girl, that if she'd been a boy she'd have needed more gumption but she was just perfect for a girl. Houston fails only when it tries to be New York. Hallie is gumptionless; to make this lack work for her she has only to be passive, refrain from acting, be as still as a copperhead lying across the path, quiet as a mottled snake.

"What did you plan to do with the land—build a house on it?" Hyke does not need to smile when he has a direct hit: Hallie already put Selwyn in jail once (to the disgust of everyone I know, even Cad—though she tried to hide it). The payment he made to get out (two month's back child support) went to the lawyer and there have been none since. Her teacher's salary, just raised, is five thousand a year. We can help her—we will help her if she will stretch quietly across daughterhood and wait, exhibiting the beauty of her redbrown back, her smooth, harmonious scales, her golden shadows each like a uterus carrying twins, her slender needs. Now she has struck and I must protect Hyke.

"You must understand," Hyke said, "that your mother can't afford to give up forty thousand dollars just so you can build a house on your . . . *childhood*."

"Jewell, leave the dishes for now," I call over the back of the couch. "Give the girls some ice cream or something." I am squeezing the fingers of one hand with the other to prevent my granddaughters from wandering into the abrasions of money and being scratched and scarred. It is money I hate. Unlike the rich earth of the South or the grassy space of the West, Houston land was nothing, no one wanted this flat, treeless plat until we invented Houston. What is the value of a piece of paper except the words written on it? Now we have written and our land enters the

marketplace, our love shines waiting to be grabbed up at the ba-
zaar. There was no forty thousand dollars last week. Hyke's debts
command my help but my share—the other twenty—might be
turned back into land again. After Jewell is safely back in the
kitchen I say, "Maybe we can sell half the land only . . ."

"I've already signed the sales agreement," Hyke says. "But of
course, Baby, whatever you want."

"What I *want* . . ." My eyes will not drop, they are looking
straight out smoldering with insult. "I want none of this to have
happened. I don't want any part of it!" I see Hallie frowning at the
floor when I wheel to face her. "How could you do this to me?
How the hell could you?"

Emily has slipped free; she has reached the back of her
mother's chair. She comes around front now and stands boldly by
Hallie's knees.

"Emily, go on back to the kitchen with Jewell," I say. Emily
doesn't budge. "He's got some ice cream for you." Emily inches
closer to her mother. She is facing Hyke and me, pale round eyes
fixed like a cannon, unblinking.

Hyke has had enough of all of it. He gets up quickly and
reaches down for Emily. One hand on her shoulder twists her away
as he says, "Mind your grandmother now. Git."

Emily slips free of the hand just as her mother did earlier from
my hand; she ducks and reappears standing by Hallie as before
only slightly to one side. Her mouth quivers, her chin is up, her
eyes are aimed.

Hyke's face is red with rage but he doesn't dare touch her
again. "I said go to the kitchen. I mean it."

Emily is still as bronze except for one tremble at her mouth's
corner.

For three of four minutes Hyke threatens, pink and sputtering
and clenched, and Emily stands. She is pure baby skin dotted by a
nose-to-be and capped with hair so pale and thin it barely reaches
over the tops of her ears; her knees are locked and her arms loose
and ready by her side. Her eyes are her only weapon and she keeps
them glued to Hyke's, preventing him from touching either her or
her mother. Water gathers now from staring but she will not blink.
Finally Hyke turns heavily and leaves the room.

Hallie takes Emily into her lap; I see a single huge heave of
Emily's chest, a shudder.

"I'm sorry, Mother . . ." Hallie begins but my own face is
hiding in a window.

HALLIE CHOSE MONEY over me.

Cad and I are sitting at the long table shaped like a dollar bill which serves as lapboard for the Houston Literary Society. We are going over the budget. This morning we were at the board meeting of the Houston Negro Hospital going over their budget. It is money day in April.

Hallie is in full violent pursuit of money now. Ever since Hyke (as I knew he would) apologized to her and told the buyers that there was an unresolved claim on the land—and then the buyers immediately upped their offer to fifty thousand, and of course Hyke felt it was only fair to offer Hallie the extra ten, and Hallie accepted more quickly than one would have thought, considering the territorial emotions that she bombarded us with—ever since that month almost two years ago Hallie has been in full violent pursuit of cash. When I listen to her I think I am hearing a foreign language. And she smells different.

Cad is telling us about the Minute Women's new forbidden book list. "They are forbidding books that no one has thought of for years," Cad says. She names a few.

"*Black Beauty?*" several women shriek.

"Well, it presents property owners as sadists," Cad explains as if it were obvious. "That's communism, you know."

Hallie herself sadistically scratched out the eyes of every man in the *Black Beauty* illustrations before she could read the text.

"I always thought literature was sex," Betty Jane Rayzor says, ducking her head. "The lust to read a nymphomania of the mind— you want to open a book's cover and peek inside at society's private parts."

I am shocked but Cad chuckles and someone guffaws.

"That explains why Houston doesn't read," Cad says. "We are a boy scout culture."

"Well, at least they respect literature," I say. "I had no idea so many people thought books could win enemies and influence people."

"But they are a menace . . ." our president begins.

"Well, they're scared of books and that thrills me," Cad says. I am unaccountably thrilled to have her back me up.

For a year Hallie ignored me. She talked to me about literature while she thought only of money.

Cad says, "Texas art won't be treated with respect until the Smithsonian sends someone down here to research indigenous Americana."

"Nothing is treated with respect while it is alive and growing," I say. I am surprised at my cynicism. Of course I don't mean it; I'm just matching wits with Cad. To mean it I would also be implying that I did not respect Hallie, my own indigenous Texiana. I do respect her but I wince at her smell.

Our president suggests establishing a prize for a young Houston writer, having an annual contest. "Call it Discovery," I hear.

"Or why not Exploration?" I say. "In case we hit a bunch of dry poets."

Cad projects her voice; mine died at her shoulder.

"Exploration," Cad says. "Then we get a tax write-off if we hit a dry poet, a depletion allowance if the poet sells, and we've managed to drape the flag of Texas over our sedition."

Delighted laughing drapes the mantle of wit over Cad's shoulders—Cad, not me. Is it the way I'm dressed? The roundness of my face?

It is the odor of competition—acrid result of glands stepped up for wartime production. Money itself does not smell at all although it is supposed to—figuratively speaking. I have sniffed the dollar: Hyke's carries the leather whiff of his billfold, the D.R.'s wad somehow reeks of ether, my own is tinged with a touch of Joy . . . but the average passed-on dollar of our nation has no smell at all beyond the faintest cinnamon. Hallie in pursuit of the dollar, however, smells as metallic as nickel. The sweet-smelling, slow-gurgling blood of early wife- and motherhood has vanished.

She discusses her orgies with Cad. As soon as she got her money from the sale of the property, she deposited it in a savings account: a poor way to become rich, as she had succeeded in teaching even her slowest students. Only gambling could turn a dollar bill into a chip which might then attract other chips.

"Of course," Cad reported to me, "the first thing she thought of was Hetty Green. What Hallie has in common with Hetty . . ."

"Besides arrogance."

". . . is capital—never mind the size of it. Hetty said that it is simple to make money: you buy cheap and sell dear."

"Of course!" My voice is sarcastic to muffle the feeling I have that I am "dear."

She subscribed to the *Wall Street Journal* and for a month watched the big board's ups and downs, concentrating on companies whose products she knew as a consumer. She had a negative and a positive page of lists: she did not intend to invest in the company responsible for her washing machine, ever. She checked the performance of General Electric daily and noted that its general direction was up, although she felt certain women who washed were not buying the stock or the machine. This was a lesson as important as any Hetty ever taught. She did not automatically buy—when she finally bought—the food company whose products she herself reached for first, whose good was in the can not on the tickertape. She bought Frito instead. Corn chips greased and salted (Texas tortillas), Fritos were tastier and crunchier than potato chips but sold for a nickel a bag and could not be considered food. At the first sign of a depression they would gather dust on supermarket shelves. But only, she stated gleefully, if housewives had a vote that counted; since they didn't, Fritos must be regarded as a mathematical entity only. The numbers beside its name in the *Wall Street Journal,* after a month of watching, were heading generally up. They were not going up any faster than those beside the name of General Electric but Hallie chose Frito because it cost much less a share. Just as she could get twenty packages of the product itself for a dollar whereas she had had to pay a hundred dollars for only one washing machine, she could get many more shares of Frito for her ten thousand than most other stocks. It was her first purchase and she wanted as many shares as possible—an unreasonable, possibly a feminine, certainly, Cad commented, a greedy approach.

Betty Jane Rayzor's nervous cocked leg swings against my shinbone again. She apologizes profusely. I think she is doing her ankle-slimming exercises underneath the table. She has one of the prettiest faces in Houston—the prettiest anywhere—that no one seems to like. A pale rosebud of a face. When she tilts it into mine I feel like she's begging to be watered. She is married to a Rice beau of mine who is very rich. At Rice he was a country boy from Beeville, awkward as a cornstalk, hands like hooves, and a blue-eyed patina of worship for every girl he dated. Of course, Betty Jane guided him into money; but that's nothing for a wife. If she really wants to.

At five dollars a share Hallie bought sixteen hundred shares. She called it a nickel a bag. She had sixteen hundred bags of Fritos. In two months each bag was selling for a dime—not because more and more people were eating Fritos but because Frito expanded into the dietetic food market, producing a line of food with even less nutritive value than the corn chips. It was her second lesson: the less real value the product has the more money is spent on it.

"I would not have thought," I said, shivering to my toenails at this whole recital, "that Hallie would stoop to lessons that are developed from the stomach."

She sold half her Fritos and bought into a company that dealt in business real estate—on the advice (Cad names our mutual friend) of a man who wears the finest tuxedos and exposes himself to all our daughters in every pantry hall.

I miss the next sentence or two. I am stuck between two images: the frayed leather jacket, the rotting tuxedo. My daughter is bent on breaking my heart.

Is this all to pay me back for one indiscretion with Ben Falk on the porch off Shepherd Drive? Ever since the terrible outbreak of staph at Jeff Davis last year, Benjie has been dedicated to reforming our hospitals. Partly because he moved into the hospital and personally examined the halls and rooms for cleanliness, but mainly I think because when he went on television to explain to Houston how he felt and what he was doing, Houston saw a man with a face so ugly, so totally without any quality that would make him appear on television for vanity, that everyone immediately believed him. Personal ugliness has not yet been fully credited as a way to political power.

From his first appearance, letters to the papers referred to him as that man who spoke on our hospital and, very soon, simply as Mr. Hospital.

Benjie was in love with Hallie, Cad once told me. (It was after I married Hyke, of course.) Since she already has her children, I thought she could do worse than marry him—but at the time I said, "Don't be silly, Cad. Benjie and *I* will end up together—in a hospital named for him."

Our budget today is resolved without my help. Both of them were. I am ready to face the sun on a drive to Cad's if I concentrate on the martini there.

Hallie's real estate stock doubled that fall. She was just getting ready to sell it when she saw, in discreet *Wall Street Journal* type, that the boy-genius who caused the stock to soar choked to death on a piece of meat. Her stock was already down to what she paid for it—those present at the dinner party sold before breakfast. By the time she could sell she had lost two thousand dollars. It happened, Cad said, at Thanksgiving—"turkey" an apt nickname for a genius who wouldn't chew.

How come this never happened to Hetty Green? Cad has an irritating habit of making other people's anger into a joke. "A portent that women should buy food on the shelves, not that on the financial pages," Cad chuckled.

"She lost two thousand dollars?" I feel that pain in my ribs.

"Just on paper. All told, she had—when she sold everything—eighteen thousand dollars and change. That's when she bought stock in Oscar's company. She wants a house." Cad didn't need to spell it out for me; Oscar would help her get a mortgage in return for putting her money where his mouth is.

Since I have lost her, I want her to have a house. I want to think of her safely nestled inside walls which arrange themselves in my mental picture surprisingly like the interior of a garage apartment I once planned.

"He already has," Cad says now.

I'm the last to know.

I⊤ HAS TAKEN me a year to sort out that terrible November and December.

Catastrophe's beginning coincided with a series in the *Post* on the fat cats of Texas. In it Oscar's name was mentioned as a junior member of the in-group, sort of a plump kitten. The company he begat out of Daddy's now included more other companies than I could remember and had just been accepted to be traded on the New York Stock Exchange instead of over the counter. Oscar was enormously pleased with his kitten status: he thinks public name-shouting is typical of crude oil–money but an occasional whisper is surely good for business—and the ego.

Both the whisper and the New York acceptance came at the right moment for him. Years ago he had, from the goodness of his heart, let an old friend in on a profitable business scheme: Ernest Nye, a man whose good nature was as winning as his money sense was a disaster, was told confidentially by Oscar to borrow some money and come on in on a project Oscar and the others were sure would make a lot of money. Ernest had, and made a big profit.

But because Ernest was a social equal of the others, it was a mere hop for him to think of himself as an intellectual equal also. He wanted to join the planning for the future. He talked to the others as if his advice were important. The Colonel and the Judge were furious. They told Oscar to get rid of Ernest. Oscar tried to explain to Ernest (without using the words) that if he would remain humble he would be allowed to get rich too, that it was Ernest's trying to take credit for his money that reflected badly on all their money.

The Duchess saw her chance and adopted Ernest as her best friend. She had him and his family over to the house on every traditional celebration. Oscar warned Ernest again, stooping finally to the words themselves. But words are the Duchess's only weapon; Ernest believed her. He believed in the personal charm that had given him a smooth ride since babyhood. He believed that his good friend Oscar, husband of his best friend the Duchess, was merely under temporary tension. He didn't know that Oscar maintains the kind of self-control which never allows a word out unless it is permanent.

Ernest entered the next scheme proposed by Oscar with more borrowed money, and in less than a season lost fifty thousand dollars. In addition, the district attorney prosecuted him for fraud. His was the only name legally responsible. The Judge and the Colonel—as one could expect—thought it was the perfect joke. Each time they met they had a story about Ernest's pickle. Oscar himself, of course, was obsessed with the dread that there is no simple path possible ever again. He was dreadfully sorry about Ernest's misfortune, he told me sincerely, shaking his head and saying he doesn't understand now how it all could possibly have happened.

Then Ernest shot himself, sprayed his brains over the ceiling and walls of their bedroom while his wife was downstairs watching tv, and Oscar had a heart attack.

Coronary occlusion, it was called; he was recovering in Methodist Hospital, now scared to death, knowing he wanted to live, trying to work out through me the philosophy which would make that possible. No one who has not stood at the bedside of her dying brother can tell me what *I* should have said. Of course, I reassured him that he was honest. And who alive can be *utterly* honest—certainly no man in business who has women and children to support; the very concept is unknown to the worldly and only cherished by women like me whose innocence is underwritten by Oscar himself. He didn't die.

He was still in Methodist Hospital when Hyke was admitted to St. Luke's with hepatitis.

The night before, without my knowing I did it, I called out to Hallie—she and the girls were spending a weekend at the bay in the rain (why I don't know). Hallie telephoned me at two A.M.; she said she had heard my voice saying in a dream "Come back soon." By the time she arrived I was frantic about Hyke's sickness. There were no symptoms: there was no fever, no nausea, no yellowing yet, no definable ache or pain, but he was completely *sick*. I was so relieved when he turned yellow by breakfast time and St. Luke's accepted him as a hepatitis patient.

But when the jaundice disappeared on the third day and Hyke was much worse, the doctors told me the truth: Hyke's blood

platelets had ceased to function. The next step was massive transfusions. In four days Hyke, too weak to go into the bathroom
without both me and Hallie or a nurse supporting him, wept like
a child at the pain of the transfusions and used his last pitiful
strength to scramble to the other side of the bed when the nurse
appeared with yet another transfusion ready.

I had become too accustomed to Hyke's poor health. I had
even made bad jokes about marrying a man six years younger than
yourself only to have his body act like it was sixteen years older. At
first, this time too, I'd thought he was just "feeling poorly" and
tried to snap him out of it. Now I felt terrible. I wanted to give him
my blood but his was not type O (for ordinary, I know).

I was going to lose him and I couldn't bear it. I simply didn't
admit it although an emphatic *déjà vu* pestered me and I saw
Rusty's final days, saw him visibly sink below the horizon like a
darkening sun. I read Hyke's palm and called his attention to his
long unbroken lifeline. Together we will turn this blood process
around, if we could just get those damn platelets to take hold . . .
today they were up and I told Hyke we had beaten it.

I sat holding his hand, thinking of his strength. It was his
strength which brought on the affair of the other Hallie, I long ago
decided. When I faced him with his letter, he admitted it all. He
was contrite but within contrition he achieved a dimension which
surprised me: totally lacking in abjectness, in shame—like a born
Southerner he brushed aside the incest factor—he told me he did
it mainly to get back at me, to have a family of his own which
I couldn't share just as I had against him. I felt a new admiration
for him but a decidedly lesser lovingness; for a while I loved him
mentally but inside, my heart said it would hug itself unto itself
for now.

I guess my heart never completely let go again but I promised
God now that if He would just let Hyke get well, I would make it
up to both of them. Hyke in fact never seemed to notice that a part
of my heart held back. Being a yankee he may even have thought he
preferred a more civilized, a less tangled-up-together marriage. Although there were times when I longed to be seized (metaphori-
cally or right out with it) I think I adjusted very well to calm. Better
than Hyke, in fact. He began to drink too much *all* the time.

My fault, darling, I said to his eyelids closed now against the
glare of our winter sun. Just you get well this time, even partly well,
and I'll never abandon you to a civilized marriage again. I'll get
right inside your chest if I have to and thump your heart to make it

get going like it should.

The eerie—the hateful—thing was that just at that moment Hallie came in and we stared into each other's eyes. I saw and she saw that we both had always known he would die before me, known in the dark chamber of the brain where wishes live. It was the briefest of seconds, instantly gone. I said, "Hyke is much better today. We've finally got those damn platelets under control."

By dawn, he was dead.

The night after the morning he died, after the funeral arrangements were made and Hyke's body lay in an open casket in front of the huge French windows overlooking Sis's rolling hills, my living room held two hundred people drinking after the manner of Houston grief. In our city, bereavement visiting is strangely like a cocktail party.

I had lost him because I gave in to his wish to be detached and I was too sad to mourn. I wanted to talk about how much fun he was, how lively and full of entertainment; I wanted everyone to acknowledge that the parties we'd had right here in this room had been something to brag on. I wanted every one of the two hundred people here now to suddenly look up and expect to see Hyke walking through the door ready to do his silent mimic of "When the Darkies Beat Their Feet on the Mississippi Mud" or "Little Albert." He was lying in his coffin by the window and tomorrow he would be gone; this was his last night in the room he loved. "We are all here, we all loved Hyke, he would want us to remember him with joy," I said to everyone. Hallie put on Hyke's favorite *South Pacific* album and everyone's eyes were misty at the memory of the fun we used to have. Soon the casket was avoided and some of the young people, as the evening grew late, began dancing in the far corner. I knew Hyke would have wanted them to.

Suddenly Oscar's voice boomed into the silence left by the abruptly cut-off record player: "All right. It's time for everyone to go home now. That's enough of this."

I did not believe he could hurt me like that. I took his arm placatingly but he said, "This has gone far enough now. The Baby has to get some rest."

I was burning with shame. I could only blame my heart, which betrayed my mind's training in seemly behavior.

Hallie stood before Oscar. "If Mother wants music let her have music. She's the one who suffered the greatest loss . . . "

Oscar rattled his ice and turned away. We watched his shoulders, which are beginning to slope and hump, move toward the door leading the crowd with him.

Hallie stood behind him while the last guest left and said, "One day I will arrange a humiliation for you in front of all your friends." I have never heard a voice so like a scorch as that. Oscar turned slowly.

"I am very disappointed in you. I can't understand what you were thinking about when you sold all your stock in my company yesterday. I was so pleased when I thought you had some protection against disaster, and now . . . you should never spend your capital. And just when I thought you were doing so fine . . ."

In an immaculate black chauffeur's uniform, Walter Stevenson stood like a seeing-eye dog just off the porch light, waiting to take Oscar home.

THE SMELL AND smoke of barbecue and the fresh-cut smell of the clover-grass lawn mix with sawdust and four-legged air. Just as we are walking across the field being used for a parking lot, a bull escapes from its pen. Several cowhands are circling him, laughing; he is standing on his short, ridiculously inadequate legs, fat body motionless, staring at a woman in diamonds and silk alighting from her Cadillac.

"El Diablo wants to ride in a Cadillac!" one of the hands says. "Don't worry, lady. He won't hurt you." The woman is already back inside the car shutting the door. "I think El Diablo's fallen in love," a second hand says. They whisper and guffaw together.

"I think they let him out on purpose," Hallie says to the girls. This is their first time at one of Oscar's cattle sales.

"We're down the list in Cadillacs anyway," I say. "Only sixth in the country." I quote George Fuerman's *Post Card* from the morning paper for my grandgirls: "Though Texas lacks for Cadillacs, it's rolling in petroleum."

"Isn't it dangerous? Emily says. El Diablo is turning and turning and I think sentimentally that he is looking for a way through the parked cars to the plains beyond.

I lean down to Emily. "No, darling. They're very sweet and they can't even run very fast. Look at those tiny legs and that huge body. He's just frightened by all the cars."

"What if he bumped into someone accidentally?" Emily says. She is standing behind Hallie.

"They're not dumb just because they're big," Dora says. Almost nine, Dora has already developed an adult conversational ability and a sure sense of style, wearing only plain cuts and muted colors to offset her cherubic blue-eyed blondness. Hallie has taken to fighting me for her childhood. Whenever Hallie decides Dora should join a play group, the girl scouts, go on a picnic, Dora refuses; she doesn't want to get dirty, she says. I support her: Why should she get mixed up with Baptists who catch bugs? Hallie says that the few friends Dora has, she seems to have chosen for her ability to boss them around; I say: Bossiness is just another name for leadership. And now, when Hallie thinks that Dora has just about missed her childhood altogether, I claim that she can have her childhood later, like me.

It is already clear that Dora will be tall like me. In the strong white noonday sun her eyes are crystal gray, their pupils tiny, their interior faceting revealed like a honeycomb of glass . . . I take her hand and lead her into the crowd of both our admirers.

Emily is sniffing the air like El Diablo testing for adventure. She has the dark crisp face of her great aunt Hortense and has already delivered evidence of Sis's useful temper. Neither of the girls is interested in horses, cattle, dogs or cats; they listen like strangers to stories of Houston twenty years ago. Hallie takes Emily's hand.

We will stand near the drink table. What you can hear on the prairie is wonderful; I pause at tidbits.

"At a place like this, it's mint julep or nothing in my opinion." Punchy holds her drink aloft, grinning at Hallie. "Have you picked out the bull you're buying?"

"Emily doesn't like the way they smell," Hallie says.

"I agree. For twenty thousand you'd think they could throw in a bottle of Joy."

I smell too *much* Joy among the manure and consider changing my perfume.

Punchy has in tow the man who painted El Capitan, Oscar's prize bull. He is the town's foremost portrait artist. "I usually paint from life, you're damned right," he says, now including Hallie and Emily—especially Emily. "But when they wanted me to squat down next to that bull with nothing between me and him but a wire fence and piece of canvas I said, 'Don't you have some pictures of him?' I said, 'It's hay fever season and I can't see in the meadows.' So they brought me out some pictures of him and damn if I didn't get the balls wrong. They *looked* pink but I thought to myself, no, that's Kodacolor. Mr. Yancey didn't want to mention it but the Duchess popped right up and said, 'His balls are supposed to be pink!' I had them almost white with just a little pink shadow. 'Let me fix it, Mr. Yancey,' I said. 'Let me take that thing back and touch up those balls' . . . but the old man started rattling his ice. He was scowling at the Duchess and she saw his face and she said to me, 'If he wants to leave them white then leave them white.

They're *his* balls.'"

The pasture-lawn is now jammed. Lyndon and his wife just drove up; the Duchess, kissing Lyndon on the mouth "where the lipstick belongs," she says, latches on to Lady Bird and takes her over to meet Winthrop Rockefeller's new wife. Oscar heartily shakes hands with Governor Shivers (now retired) and takes him off to examine the herd.

Cad is in a huddle with the Democratic chairwoman, who is trying to persuade her to run for the legislature. Shuts me out like a peddler, always has. Knock knock, Hallie used to say, driving us crazy with the joke fad. Knock knock, I used to try at the portals of Cad's forehead. Not even a speakeasy peephole opened onto a wary eye. "Not *me*," Cad had printed on every pore, as if she alone had seen the idealists, the dancers, the snake charmed, the holy rollers, the Southern carnival of the possessed who become possessionless. "Reason is enough for me."

For life, we lock horns. A person is only as good as the good she produces, she has maintained since our youth. But I'm perfectly happy just to be me, I always insist. Neither of us has budged an inch in these philosophies since our flapper days but although neither of us will admit it, half the time *I* think she is the better woman and want to be more like her; my guess is that she feels the same. She fights her feeling, I try to give into mine. Then I am like a baby sunk into a warm bath. Dry, I want to lock horns again, although I can't believe I really want this. There is a rosy sore at the skull where the horn bases itself that craves a pull and a twist and a bumpbumpbump, a cranial elbow geared up to laugh although the bone feels slightly bruised already. My foot taps when I focus on it—jiggle-jiggle goes the knee, kick-splits say the fingers . . . *say* the fingers? My spine rolls: a ready chord sounds out from beginner piano, *any* tune.

When Cad was on the school board I never saw her; I hope she doesn't run for the legislature.

A cattlewoman is describing the Santa Gertrudis breed and origins to a man who is clearly a stranger; the woman explains that the Santa Gertrudis's loose skin increases their sweat area, enabling them to endure the heat better. Nearby I recognize Brute's voice:

"I hear they're going to have a big cattle sale in the Shamrock Ballroom. Can you feature that? To celebrate the creations of Texas: Santa Gertrudis the only breed of cattle created in this country, the quarter horse developed in Texas, and Texas western painting because it is the historical documentation of these Texas brags." Brute's low melodic laugh has been practiced in New York. "A pretty girl in an evening dress will lead old El Bigballs across the dance floor while the band plays out—Oh you beautiful bull, you great big beautiful bull! Give me one of my cigarettes, would you, Paul?" She smoothes the sleek, close-fitting shantung over her hips. I wish I had not heard her next remark: "Every time I come back to Houston I feel like a dog returning to its vomit!"

"Do you?" the cattlewoman asks.

"Then the sixty-three shades of green make the Shamrock just the right place for you," the man called Paul says, fishing her cigarettes out of his jacket pocket.

"Do you know what I like about Texas?" the cattlewoman says.

"Do I!" Brute throws back her golden hair. I wish I could have stopped her from divorcing Guy and moving to New York; I know she doesn't have to be like this. "You like it because it's so real—those warm friendly folks and all that honest open space. But the only thing Houston *thinks* about is putting up another skyscraper—in the middle of the desert. So we have skyscrapers rising out of the plains like toothpaste tubes."

Paul laughs. "Like the precious part of the bull mounted on the prairie."

From nearby I hear Hallie's voice call over to Brute: "That's the point . . ."

Brute roars with laughter.

Unaccountably I remember Brute the year she lived with us (her mother had joined the WACs); all year Brute wore a blossom over her ear, usually white to emphasize her fair skin and pale hair. She was the daughter I always wanted—charming, well-groomed, blond—she was as unblemished as the girl in the Breck shampoo ad. I remember my outrage when I heard Hallie (who was jealous, of course) say Brute looked like a bleached savage with a two-grunt vocabulary.

". . . Houston didn't grow, we invented it."

"Don't tell me about Houston, I was born and raised here," Brute says. "And learned enough to get out the minute I could."

"You know what Mother always says: a person who denies herself will deny you sooner or later." Hallie doesn't know I can hear it all.

"Oh, Baby! Baby's perfect. She's one in a million." Brute throws up her hands helplessly. "I just love her too much to argue with her—if she says Houston's wonderful then it *is*."

Hallie turns away; I try to close my ears but they are enjoying a luscious pink tingle along their edge and won't shut.

"What're they going to do in that ballroom when the beast shits?" Paul says in that gross New York language to Brute.

"Someone will make a joke: Lower your bid! He sure doesn't weigh any two thousand and ninety now." Brute exhales her smoke in a perfect ring.

"Will they make the pretty girl clean it up?"

"She's not a 'pretty girl,' she's the trainer!" Hallie is back in the fray. "If you're talking about Cissy Benton, she's one of the best cutting-horse trainers in the state."

"Well, good, then she won't be scared. *I* certainly would be."

I turn to hug Julia, telling her the food looks delicious as always (although I won't eat it) when I hear a man say to Cad, "If *Life* still went to parties this is where it would be today." He must be the journalist from New York. "I hope I get to see one of your famous snakes too before I leave."

Cad chuckles. "They'll be here later. They're writing a story about New York journalists."

She is rewarded with a smile from the reporter, who takes out his notebook and pen. "So Houston is the richest city in the country." He moves close to Cad and slumps in a winning way. "Tell me a money story."

"You've probably already noticed that these cattle aren't branded, they're monogrammed."

"Ah." He scribbles.

Cad says, "Won't you have something to drink?"

"Do you think they have soft drinks?"

"How about a Tom Collins?" Cad says.

Now the journalist guffaws and scribbles some more. I could shake Cad. I know she won't explain what she means and he will put in his story that in Houston a Tom Collins is considered soda pop. I spy Dutch Nathan and tell *him*. He's no help at all; he says, "We're moving up in the world. In the old days bourbon and water was our soda pop."

We both hear the journalist say, "When Texas agreed to join the union you made it a condition that you could secede any time you wanted to, right? Is there anybody around here who might want to do that?"

He surveys the crowd. Oscar's pretty secretary, Flora, walks by in a white satin cowgirl skirt and vest with fringes and knee-high white boots. The Duchess is smiling for a photographer in a watercolor silk print that looks like it should be framed. The Santa Gertrudis have been washed and brushed until they shine like new pennies in the sun. The rich are relaxed, perfectly safe (for the moment) from the unexpected.

Cad says, "No, but you never know which way a half-broke steer will run."

I look around for Hallie but she has disappeared.

The auctioneer, in a few flowery words, announces that Mr. Yancey is going to make a speech before the sale begins.

Oscar stands before the microphone in his cowboy khakis and hat. "Well, no, I beg your pardon, Colonel Hutton, but I'm not going to make a speech. We all came here to buy some cattle and that's what we're going to do. I don't know where in the world some people get the idea that a man buys a ranch to lose money"— a murmur of chuckles from the crowd—"but I want to tell you that every time I go into any business I go in aiming to make money at it. So let's get on with the sale. I want to hear those bids!"

Colonel Hutton begins his singsong immediately. The bulls are brought out first and the auctioneer gives the name, weight, and the breeding—which is all in the catalog anyway. I know the buyers have already made up their minds. Even if they consult their foremen, the ranch owners do the choosing, do the bidding themselves—solemnly, touching their hats or nodding their fingers. Only visitors laugh at the auctioneer's occasional jokes.

The first three bulls sell for eight, nine-five, and eleven thousand dollars and then the fourth for twenty-two. That's equal to the highest price a bull has brought this year. We are all excited. I am sitting by Hans Mannheim, who is my age but looks a hundred. During the war a rumor got started that he was a Nazi spy; of course none of *us* believed it but enough extraneous people did— they so hounded poor Hans that he had a complete breakdown.

"I can't tell the difference between *him* and the eight thousand dollar one," I whisper to Hans.

Neither can Hans but he tries. "Maybe two men experience an affinity for the same animal," he says. "I've noticed that these cattlemen, after a while, begin to resemble the beasts they deal in—as if their legs grow shorter, their bodies heavier in the middle, their faces hung lower so their eyes look up and then out instead of out and then down or up." He dips his head and looks at me with lowering brown eyes as if he were begging me to buy him. I laugh and say, "Twenty-three." I see Colonel Hutton's startled look. Fortunately the bidding already closed; I am shaking my head unnecessarily.

Of course Hans's theory is the sort of thing an intellectual would think—that the bidding breaks a record when the same two men bump together within the same bull. But I know that these men buy each other's bulls to repay favors. The rancher who just bought Tarzan Two for twenty-two will be thanked for his excellent judgment in the next advertisement of Ten Penny bulls. They do that for each other. When they don't really want the bull they donate it to A&M.

Everyone leans forward. The next bull is named Mr. Oscar and the auctioneer makes much of his special heritage. He is a direct descendant of the original El Capitan. The governor himself opens the bidding at twenty-two thousand. I explain to Dora that a King Ranch bull sold for twenty-five thousand last year—the highest price ever paid for a bull at auction. We all hope the record will now be broken. Through the singsong I hear twenty-two-five, twenty-three, twenty-three-five, twenty-four. Then the bid jumps to twenty-six thousand and everyone is silent. I can't see who made the bid. "Someone wants Ten Penny to hold the record," I tell Dora. The governor? Winthrop Rockefeller? The auctioneer calls twenty-six once, twenty-six twice, twenty-six three times, *sold;* now everyone is asking and craning to see *who . . .* there is a collective gasp and a distinct *who is that?* and I think I am mis-seeing when Hallie stands up to receive her applause.

"Mommy!" Dora says; our neighbors laugh and clap.

Hallie is standing at the microphone. She says, "Now I'm not really a cattle breeder and I don't have a ranch, but I wanted to make sure that the highest-price bull ever sold in the state of Texas went to the most wonderful woman in it. I bought Mr. Oscar as a present for my mother."

The crowd is laughing and cheering and hollering for me to come up and claim my present. I never heard such noise. I go into the center sawdust, kiss Hallie; Mr. Oscar and I look at each other. I stroke his glossy brown nose and kiss his soft white muzzle. I don't even feel scared when I put my arms loosely around his neck but I lean forward so he won't step on my foot. Flashbulbs are popping. The auctioneer congratulates Mr. Oscar with great gallantry.

Of course Oscar himself has to get in the pictures, join in the smiling and congratulations. "Well, Baby, I can't think of anyone I'd rather see have this namesake of mine than you—but where in the world are you going to put him?" Oscar has had too much practice controlling himself in public for me to get a clue as to what's going on. He only glances at Hallie once—with respect.

Hallie writes out her check and hands it to the auctioneer with a flourish. It is a publicity stunt, I decide; I play my part to the hilt. I am so pleased to be wearing my new Trainer Norell beige silk suit with a burnt-orange scarf and my new hat by Charles (it is natural straw with a brown ribbon and one burnt-orange feather).

We make all the papers—because of the record-breaking price the bull brought and the human interest details of it. Even the *New York Times* carried a picture of Oscar, his namesake, and the young woman who bought a present for her mother.

OH, I CAN'T stand it.

I am watching the ridiculous squirrels endlessly running up and down the same gauzy trees but I am seeing Oscar and Hallie as forms humped together.

They are ensconced in the Houston Club. Their hands have that lean of power, are set on the exact bias for catching an edge of money turning the corner on the street yards below.

Oscar is saying something like "What do you expect me to do?" He isn't surprised that Hallie's check was written on air.

And she says something like "I don't know"—although she doesn't mean she doesn't *know*. She knows perfectly well; this is a game they are playing. "Because I *expect*"—she uses the Western verb that drawls—"Mother is going to want you to buy back that bull. She doesn't want him." (She doesn't *seem* to want him?—with an inside twinkle of a too-bold eye?)

And Oscar will emit from the well-fed paunch the chuckle so quick that anyone would recognize a man whose brain whirs at a word like buy. "You want me to pay your mother twenty-six thousand dollars for a bull I haven't collected the first twenty-six on?" I am "your mother." I have lost even my nickname.

"You won't have to pay a gift tax on it." (Hallie, Oscar's twin.)

"That's true."

"And then you can sell the bull again—after you change his name, of course.

Of course. Why not name him Mr. Baby?

If I had a slingshot I would shoot every squirrel in my yard because they are so dumb they don't know that it is only a bushy tail that saves their lives.

They are congratulating themselves on the trick they pulled on me—never mind that Oscar didn't know at the time; his after-knowledge chortles and the chortle is the ugliest sound in the world.

"I will not take it, Brother." I speak out loud on my way from the window with its idiot squirrels. "I will not accept your twenty-six thousand for a bull Hallie didn't even buy. I will not."

He has already tried to persuade me once; I expect him to try again. "Now, Baby." It's the voice of the nursery. "This is a way I can get some money to you without paying a gift tax on it. You know Daddy left me the business with the proviso . . ."

This is the last sentence on earth I want to hear. "Give it to Hallie!" "The IRS might consider that a wash. You think it over . . ."

What I am thinking about is gift tax. Isn't it unreasonable to be considering handing me twenty-six thousand dollars but to refuse to give me even five if the government has to get *any*?

Money killed Hyke. Because he could not keep up with Houston's demands for success (or because he simply paid his taxes and was always broke), he let his body slip into a giving-up state, into an opinion of itself that Hyke didn't count. It is hard to feel you do count when everyone around you is as focused on the government as a fifth column. Uncle Sam is not watching us; we won't take our eyes off him.

I walk down to get the mail, hoping to spy a neighbor with an infant daughter so I can warn her. But I chose my neighborhood and there are no half-grown noises here. Along with reminders of the money I've spent and enticements to spend some more, I have a letter from Nannie Walker. She at least is white-haired sanity: a slick glistening unbroken egg in a nest of shells; wisely, an eighty-year-old-maid. What? I can't believe it. She has sent me the clipping from the Kingsville paper: a picture of me grinning around the neck of Mr. Oscar and Hallie with chin tilted beside his chopped-off horn. Oscar wasn't in this picture so the Kingsville editor ran a formal portrait of him captioned "Houston Rancher and Business Leader." Kingsville: Mr. Oscar's granddaddy's hometown. I am all over Texas dimpling like a fool.

It's a hell of a time for Mary Cowan to choose to visit but that's exactly what she's doing. I hear her at the door now, returning from her luncheon with Brute.

On a spontaneous glance toward the door my eye lights on the pictures of my grandchildren, placed ostentatiously just like Sis's pictures of my daughters were when she lived here. Every house is a depository for the only wealth women accumulate: little eggs cracking open and sending up shoots of gold and silver that look like us. Little eggs that then produce little eggs that then . . . rolling eggs that gather no money. *I* am ensconced in my role of keeper of the antiques—I, who was never even interested in antiques.

The camera caught me dimpling as angelically as the framed grandchildren. All right then, kids—I feel a squirt of power at that slang word Mother forbade—let's show them what is underneath the dimples.

My own face once looked as much like a fresh pudding as those and so did my daughters'. My cinnamon dumpling says "hi" on her way to the guest room; my corn fritter will be here any minute. I am ready to serve them.

First I intend to explain to Hallie exactly what she is doing. Like a rambunctious tomboy, she will cast aside everything that has been used once and leave the yard bare by noon. Without me, I will say firmly, Oscar and his like would have created a Houston that was nothing but a prairie-clearance project. I alone am the Texan in this family. I fix my thumb to my chest; Oscar would be pointing his finger at your face. My thumb makes its circle back to my heart. I alone understand the blend of South and West that creates Houston. I am the one who is blending it.

I intend to tell Hallie: You will lose everything if you become single-minded because you will get exactly the thing you set your sights on and you will hate it. Oscar was determined to make money and made far more money than any one man can use; still he doesn't stop because it's the only thing he knows to do. All his other parts have rusted. Now that's all right for a man but women are more complicated; they are so complicated that if they don't exercise every single facet of themselves they grow into myths like Nannie Walker. Women, I will tell both my daughters, are an intricate blend of ingredients and have to be constantly stirred or a daughter will end up as full of lumps as Northern grits. And I am here to make sure that doesn't happen to a daughter of mine if I have to grab the spoon by force.

I square my shoulders inside my new black suit. Without me Hyke would have been stuck in triviality, Hallie would have backed herself into a corner of arrogance, and Oscar would have thinned out so airily that he would have no more weight than a dollar bill floating like a kite on a southeastern breeze. All of you would fall off one end or the other of any curve you made if I let you and I have no intention of letting you.

Mary Cowan—my first born, my settled daughter (do I think of her as my good daughter?)—has offered to cook us dinner. Now she heads for the kitchen dressed in a black turtleneck shirt and black peasant skirt, black stockings and ballet slippers, and a rope and stone necklace. Her glorious red hair is unmercifully caught in a ponytail. She is going to fix something she calls Bulgarian couscous. I have too much on my mind to want to get in a hot kitchen and chop; I wish she'd let Jewell just broil us a steak instead. I take off my jacket and tie a cup towel over my middle.

Hallie is late. By the time she arrives I have chopped myself into a sweat.

"Hello, darling," I say happily as she comes into the kitchen with both girls. "I was just hoping an angel would walk in who could fix some ice-cold martinis." I am hugging my grandchildren, willing to forget everything I intended to say to Hallie.

"If you all start drinking martinis now you know what's going to happen," Mary Cowan says.

Hallie is disappearing into the card room where the bar is. "I'll fix one for Cad too—she's rattling over the bridge now."

"A referee," Mary Cowan says.

"A what?" I say.

"For the argument."

"Argument about what?"

"You'll think of something." Mary Cowan has one of those smiles on her face that say she was right to leave us down here to our southland years ago . . . but Cad is coming in and I have no time to wonder how she knows what I was planning earlier and have now decided to postpone perhaps indefinitely.

Cad has a copy of the *Chronicle* folded mischievously. She reads us part of a news item: "'Local oilman buys Louisiana plantation for one million.' Doesn't the *Chronicle* know Oscar is not an oil man?"

"Oscar?" I peer over her arm and see that Oscar apparently bought eight thousand acres near Nachitoches, a plantation referred to as "Little Eva" because Harriet Beecher Stowe stayed there while writing *Uncle Tom's Cabin*.

"He keeps his name quiet as a hush puppy," Cad says. "Thank you, Hallie." She raises her glass to us all. "I never knew Oscar was interested in literature."

I have forgotten my speech altogether by the time the first of the martini sets my cells of happiness in motion; therefore I am unprepared when Hallie brings out a batch of rolled-up papers and I ask, "What is that?"

She spreads them out on the floor; no coffee table of mine is spacious or unoccupied enough to hold such giant sheets. "You know I can't see that far away, Hallie," I say. "Am I going to have to put on my glasses?" "Yes." Her smile glistens like the beaded outside of our martini pitcher. "You not only have to look at this, you have to make any changes you want."

Returning with my glasses on, I am caught for a second by Hallie's sudden beauty. She is wearing an almost stark white linen sleeveless dress over a golden suntan and her eyes look turquoise in the last of the daylight. She looks like she has spent the two weeks since school was out playing hard and sleeping sound like Dora and Emily, growing back into childhood.

Cad is saying, "I know that land. Ella lives over there." Cad peers closely, tracing a squiggly line on the outspread paper, which I now see looks like a river. "Her house is on the bayou right about here."

"Do you have all that?" Mary Cowan asks.

"Two acres almost." Hallie sees me and scrambles up from her kneeling position. With an arm around my waist, she urges me to *my* old knees. "Look, Mother. This is the boundary . . ."

I am examining a survey of what appears to be a piece of property stretched along the bayou while Hallie excitedly describes rolling hills, huge pine trees, raintrees, magnolia, live oak, birds, seclusion, and of course those damn squirrels. Apparently she has bought it.

"I think this calls for a celebration," Cad says as if we weren't already drinking. She disappears to refill our martini pitcher.

"It's less than a mile away from here," Hallie says. "Practically next door. But it's zoned residential so there can never be apartments hanging over your boundaries and apartment children using your lawn as a dog bathroom and motorcycles racing through . . ."

I haven't seen her so pleased since she won her first blue ribbon on Truly Majestic. I have kneeled long enough; I rise to sit on my sofa where I can still peer into the astonishing rectangle of paper on my rug and prepare to ask all the right questions: How did she find it? Is she planning on building a house on it? What does she think she can get for her little house? Have the girls seen it? What school will they go to? I want to know what she paid for it too; Mary Cowan asks that.

I don't ask how she can afford it, but she tells me. She has put her house on the market and expects to get twenty thousand cash over the mortgage; she sold all her stock and bought the land and still has ten thousand left over. I calculate: thirty thousand should be enough to build a little house ample for her and the girls and maybe she will not have to carry a mortgage at all. I am a great believer in women without husbands owning their house outright, lock, stock, and barrel.

But Hallie is talking mortgage because she is still playing Hetty Green. Or Oscar, I think, smiling at Cad as she refills my glass. "To the mugwumps and her new house," I offer.

Cad holds her glass up to me with a curious smirk on her face.

"*Our* new house," Hallie says. The turquoise of her eyes suddenly looks rimmed with Indian silver. "I bought it for you. You and me and the children."

I am deafened by blood roaring in my ears like a waterfall and can only guess that Mary Cowan is saying something about me already having my own house. Hallie has taken the seat just to my right and is leaning forward earnestly. I hear her say, "Now don't say anything yet, Mother"—as if I could. I hear her say, "It is just an idea so far—a surprise . . ." She stops. She can easily see I am too surprised.

"You see what I thought was this . . ." The voice that thrills me by the gaiety with which it answers the telephone stumbles but marches on with the relentlessness of Castro shooting dissident Cubans. Since my neighborhood has already gone commercial and there are apartments looking right into my yard and since I hate having no privacy and since I have always wanted a house of my very own, she thought that now is the perfect time for me to build my dream house, to design and oversee the exact, the perfect house I've been looking for all these years. And since it seems silly for me to live in one house all by myself and for her and Dora and Emily to live in another one all by themselves, we could build a house—*I* can build a house—that has a wing for the children and also a cottage for Jewell and then I won't be scared . . .

"You know you were talking about moving into 1400 Hermann with the rest of the widows," Cad says. What is she accusing me of?

"And Cad is going to . . ." Hallie starts.

"Might," Cad says.

"Cad might be going to buy the property next door and build a house too!"

Mary Cowan says with a mixture of envy and scorn, "You'll have a reservation."

That's what the turquoise signifies.

"I am perfectly happy with the house I have."

"That's not what you told me Monday," Mary Cowan says,

accusing me again. I am sitting in the dock with six eyes watching.

Hallie jumps up as if she has won, rolls up the survey page, and starts on the page beneath. "You don't have to decide right now, you don't have to say anything right now"—but I just *did*, I protest silently—"but here are some of the ideas Betty came up with for you to look at, just to give you an idea of what you *could* do." She thrusts a sheaf of drawings of house exteriors in front of my face.

"Who's Betty?" Mary Cowan says, sitting practically on top of me so she can see too. She has been into my Joy, I notice. "Oh, this one's darling." She is pointing to the exterior of a house that could be the one we're sitting in.

"She used to be Betty Mabry but now she's Betty . . ."

"Was she short and blond with silver braces that covered her whole front teeth?" Mary Cowan asks Hallie.

"Maybe. I don't remember the braces—they're not there now . . ."

"Her mother was Calvin Hinton's sister," Cad says to me.

"She had a whippet," Mary Cowan says to Hallie.

"Did she? Yes, she did," Hallie says. "I remember when it peed in the car and I sat in it."

"Marguerite Hinton," Cad says. "She was a Pi Phi. I think she was a couple of years ahead of us."

"I remember her," Mary Cowan says. "What's she doing being an architect? She was so pretty."

"She married before she finished college," Cad says. "They lived in Connecticut for years, until Betty was in high school . . ."

"What's this got to do with *my house*?" I stood up so rapidly the sheets would have fallen if Mary Cowan hadn't been quick. I move around the coffee table, stand for a minute facing the three of them. My head is a volcano of confusion. I know I must break through this tracking down of Betty's pedigree but all my voice will do is repeat: "What has all this got to do with *my house*?" My hand is gripping the martini glass like a safety strap on a teetering bus. I drink it all and put the glass down. "I can't *think* with all this going on." I walk quickly away as if to use the bathroom.

I am staring into my mirror unseeing, standing at my bureau as if its carefully selected surface ornaments will provide ease if not answers.

How easily Hallie decided that the money she got from the sale of *my* sister's land *belonged* to her. Now she plans to give it back to me, forgetting that it is money still tainted with the scene she caused Hyke—however private, however much he brought it on himself, the money she carried out of here from that day is rank with the humiliation of my husband. I am deeply insulted that I, who have spent my life diverting the river (the cash flow, our budget committees would call it) so that some of it passed her way, should now have to *thank* her for wanting to give me a house. I will not thank a daughter. I will brook no such reversal of my natural posture . . .

Cad taps, opens the door. "The girls are getting ready to put dinner on the table, Baby, and I'm about off to Boots and the bridge game . . . what's wrong?"

She is solid and sturdy; I am only a second or two away from throwing myself against her in hysterics. I am about to break. Desperately I search for words for how I feel; wordless, my mind will swamp. "I feel like my threads are being held down by a fat thumb." My voice is low and flat; Cad and I are fixed on each other's faces eye to eye. She does not touch me; she knows how close I am to cracking? Having spoken, though, I notice I am steadying. "Are you and Hallie ganging up on me?" I don't think it came out like a joke but I smile anyway.

"Not *me*. Never. Put that thought right out of your mind."

When I first heard this expression from my mother, I wanted to obey. I imagined my mind as a house and the thought as a bad puppy that had broken housebreaking on the rug. I put the puppy right out the door. I closed my ears to its whimpering and yowling and scratchings on the screen. "Out you go," I said to the puppy-thought. "And stay there." I counted on all puppies eventually to give up.

"I know Hallie means well but I *feel* she's trying to take my *house* away from me."

"Fat chance." Cad's mouth trips over a tiny smile. "That would be harder than prying the Duchess off Oscar's neck."

"What on earth gave her the idea that I want to build a house when I have a perfectly good . . ."

Now Cad laughs and decides I am steady enough for her to sit and smoke a cigarette. She reaches for one of mine. She looks very solid today as if there were more than a hundred and thirty pounds to her (one-twenty-five according to her driver's license but women always lower their weight for that official card just as men raise their height—as if traffic police were running a beauty contest). "*You* did, I guess," Cad says. "Only this spring you were talking about how much work this house needs and how you've always dreamed of building a house that would suit *you*. In fact, if you remember you had Mrs. Galloway come out and tell you what she thought your house would bring on the market."

"But my *thinking* about building a house and Hallie going out and buying land and hiring an architect are two entirely different things."

"For some. but some others are locally famous for changing houses quarter-stream, midstream, no stream." Cad's eyes are twinkling and I decide to laugh and sit too.

"Well, but I'll do it when I'm good and ready."

"Of course you will."

"Nobody *else* is going to tell me when it's time to change houses."

"I couldn't agree with you more."

"And I'm not ready."

Cad stands up. "Then I'd better go off to my bridge game. I don't think you should ever do a thing like that until you're good and ready. And I know I'll never be ready to share a house with either of my sons and *their* children."

"Funny how I'd forgotten that part of it." We're walking toward the door; I go back to crush out Cad's cigarette—she never puts them all the way out and I can't stand leaving that smoke filling up the room when no one is even getting the good out of smoking. "Of course with a daughter, it's different. Victoria Hodges's mother couldn't *wait* to get her and her children back here and in the same house with her. Poor old Matt was hardly cold before she jumped on the train and went to fetch them."

The table is ready, except Mary Cowan is changing the salad plates, substituting others that go better with the dinner plates, and changing the napkins from the white ones Hallie must have put on to the cream ones because the dinner plates are yellowish. I go into the bar to fix the martinis.

"We're having wine," Mary Cowan says. "You don't have time to drink another one of those things."

I keep right on mixing. A woman has to take a stand somewhere.

"Do you want wine, Mother?" Hallie asks.

"Put her glass on anyway," Mary Cowan says. "It looks better."

"What did you call this, Mary Cowan? Couscous?" I am staring at a bowl of dogfood. "It looks delicious."

"It's groats."

"Groats?" I plunge the spoon in. "Pass your plates for groats."

Hallie tastes it. "Groats is right."

"It's very good for you," Mary Cowan says. "It has more vitamin B than steak and no cholesterol to speak of. The reason the peasants of Bulgaria live longer and are healthier than anyone . . ."

"Is because they don't have daughters to drive them to an early grave?"

We concentrate on doing justice to the groats—with more words than bites, I notice. I am halfway through when I see Hallie staring at me with a very shy smile. I can't get over how extraordinarily well she looks—unless it's the contrast of her clean white dress and shining suntan up against Mary Cowan's city pallor, peasant black, and imprisoned hair. Baked Alaska side by side with groats. "Maybe you'd like to build a house just for you on the same land," Hallie says. "It was only an *idea*—that we could live together. One of the houses Betty sketched out could easily be changed so the wing for the girls is an apartment for Jewell. Then if Cad buys the land next door and builds her house, you wouldn't be alone."

"Or you could do that," Mary Cowan says, "and then you"— she nods to Hallie—"could buy the land on the *other* side and all three of you could have houses."

"Like the three little pigs," I say.

"I don't think there is a lot for sale on the other side," Hallie says.

"Well, I'm certainly not going to take your lot." I decide to take a rest from my groats with a roll and salad. "After you spent your money and paid for it."

"It's yours," Hallie says. "I mean, the deed is in your name. I put it in your name because . . ."

"You what?" I am too stunned to think of anything but martini; I pick up my glass and drain mine.

"I knew you wouldn't like living in a house somebody else owned and besides if the children and I lived there too it would *have* to be in your name. I would pay for my half of the house and all that . . ."

The kitchen door swings open and Dora and Emily come in, stopping conversation and the groats eating, fortunately. I begin clearing the table and searching for ice cream for us all. After we are reseated and Hallie and I have each fixed ourselves a short bourbon and water, which will make it impossible to eat ice cream, Dora says, "Did you give Grandbaby her property yet?"

I love to hear my telephone ring and never more than at that moment. I escape with my bourbon. When I return my attention is all for my grandchildren; I will read them their bedtime stories. I will give them a special dramatic reading because I am thinking: what would it be like to see them like this every single day? What would it be like to look out the window when I am playing bridge and catch sight of one or the other racing across the lawn?

They are in Catholic school because their mother has the idea that such a school will include poor children, Mexican children, Italian children, and even Negro children soon; that Catholic education offers an honest representation of Houston's population however much it might misrepresent heaven's. Ever since she moved into her new house she is adamant that her children mustn't go to "that middle-class school" she calls it, sounding exactly like Mother: each approaching the middle class from opposite directions but maligning it with equal zest. I never misunderstood Mother; she meant by "middle class" a kind of pitiful nicey-niceness. But when Hallie explained her choice of schools to me last year, her so-called logic for the first time struck me as crazy—not nutty-like-a-fruitcake but really nuts. Now Dora has perfect handwriting and deportment (but she always had the latter) and Emily has nightmares about her sins.

I am pressed up against Emily, reading her a story about a bear who wants a house—even the animals suffer that hold over their baby selves. I shoot my mind back into ten minutes ago when I was overseeing their bath—they take a shower only at my house so it is still a special treat. What used to be the garage is now a playroom-sleeping room for them and has a stall shower, no tub. The first few times I showered with them to show them it was fun; tonight I might as well have, I am so wet. Dora with her long, thick yellow braid pinned to the hair on the top of her head, Emily with her still baby-fine hair spattered like dewdrops—my lungs lift in a gasp now as I visualize their bodies—spare young ovals, shapes called transitional—watching them my heart wanted to slip out and rush over their skin like soap, foaming and bubbling; I called it back because I know a grandmother mustn't stare.

Emily has given me five minutes of kisses and hugs until I am dizzy with her breath, which still smells like a puppy's. Dora's hugs are determined and have a definite beginning, middle, and end. Earlier I saw a telephone conversation written out in Dora's immaculate script: Hello, may I speak to Jennifer, please? Hello, Jennifer? This is Dora. Can you come over Saturday my grandmother is going to take us to the Country Club for swimming and lunch . . . Until I saw her writing I had forgotten that I used to do that. In a second I was back in 1908 with my own hair in a single thick braid (never yellow, unfortunately). I tell Dora about Grand-baby at eight going on nine. I write in the air with my finger while she watches with a smile ready in the wings.

I know I want them in my house for as long as I live.

I tell Dora about Oscar who, at seventeen, was scared to use the telephone too. He made me call for him whenever he could—just like he makes Miss Hugh do now, I say and chuckle. Oscar's young, hairless, unmuscled body at seventeen (I saw him only in a bathing suit with a top of course) returns to my mind's eye tugging for sympathy. He was so shy he couldn't ask a girl out at all unless she was a friend of Sister's and he could accidentally run into her. He couldn't telephone that I know of until he was full grown.

"It's only two acres but the people on each side also have two acres," Hallie is saying. "So it's actually about three acres if you stand in the center of your house between you and . . ."

"Who's standing in the center of my house?" I say in the voice of a bear. "Someone's been standing in the center of my house and she's still there!"

I am ready to imagine bedrooms opening onto private patios for coffee with the birds. Hallie likes the plan in which our bed-rooms—Hallie's and mine—open onto opposite sides of the same patio. They had doors opening onto the same upstairs porch in the last house we shared—and I remember fearing that if we both had our doors open I would hear something I didn't want to hear com-ing from her room.

I absorb myself in pen-and-ink houses where the question of termites does not arise. And a new house is surely a better invest-ment than an old house . . . "Oscar says he's coming over to break-fast Sunday. I think I'll just ask him what he thinks of this." I am getting up to fix my drink and don't see anyone's face. Hallie's voice hits me between the shoulder blades.

"Oscar?"

"Oscar."

"Ask Oscar?"

"He's my financial adviser," I say, turning. Her expression warns me to shut up but I am holding my brother's shy seventeen-year-oldness in my mind. "I never would have guessed that he'd turn out to be a financial genius . . ."

"Oscar is *not* a genius!" Hallie's voice is way too high and loud.

"Well, he may be," Mary Cowan says. "If by genius you mean someone . . ."

"Oscar is nothing but an upper-class pimp for a short-legged bull. *I* am a genius."

I stop partway to the bar and stare. There is pure insanity in her eyes.

"A genius is a person who becomes her concentrate and that's exactly what I intend to do if everyone will stop trying to dilute me . . ."

"With gin, you mean?" Mary Cowan's smile is very detached. "Hallie, what on earth is the matter?"

"The matter? The *fact* of the matter is that I have brilliantly managed to get you the exact house you want, the house you've always wanted, laid it in your lap. 'Thank you, Hallie.'" She stands up and bows. "Thank you, Hallie? Oh no. *You* just stand there on the edge of the road and won't even nibble the grass to see if it *does* taste greener . . ."

I have reverted back to Eudora the filly. Before I can answer she plunges ahead.

"I'm just trying to get for you what you deserve. You want a house, don't you? You've always wanted a house. As far back as I can remember you've been obsessed with houses and just when I finally get you the exact house you want, all you can think of is calling Oscar. Damn Oscar! Goddamn him!"

"Don't you ever talk about my brother in that tone of voice," I shout back. "You'd be in jail for buying that bull if it had been anyone but Oscar!"

"Jail is just a house, a house is still a jail . . ."

"Hallie, you've lost your mind."

"The fundamental things apply, as time goes by."

I could kill her. "Stop that this instant."

"I can't. I'm insane. A nut!"

But I am too hurt and furious at her for mocking my houses to let her off the hook into exaggeration. My voice feels brutally cold. "I think you're getting obsessed with money, Hallie. What kind of influence is that on Dora and Emily . . ."

"Why don't you lock me up?"

"There certainly *was* instability in your father's family," I say and turn again and head for the bar. There was; I named her for a crazy man.

"It's because you're afraid I'll get rich!" Hallie shouts.

My hand is shaking as it pours out bourbon.

Hallie's shouts now include Mary Cowan. "You're both scared to death that I might make money all by myself and not have to depend on Oscar and then where will Oscar be? Suppose I got richer than Oscar and told him to go to hell? Suppose I got so rich Oscar came to me for advice? Suppose I supported *you!*"

"Nothing could be more vulgar than the language you're using now," I say.

"Do you think houses come from the stork?"

"That's very interesting that you said that," Mary Cowan says. "According to Freud, houses are a symbol of the womb or even the vagina. So in a way . . ."

"Sell it!" Hallie is screaming. "Take the land and sell it and buy yourself a giant water tower of Joy! I'm taking my children and getting out of this crazy city where *everyone* is obsessed with money but it's called vulgar if you *think* about it."

"You know, speaking of penis envy, I think when you shot Selwyn that was a real psychic breakthrough for you," Mary Cowan says. "You never would have claimed genius like that before you shot him. Of course, you're not supposed to have to act out like that but in your case . . ."

"Take my grandchildren?" I can hardly hear through the pornography of their advanced ideas. "Take Dora and Emily out of Houston?"

"I'd rather raise them to be crass and materialistic than have them grow up crippled and crazy from this *hypocrisy* . . ." She starts toward the kitchen.

"What are you doing?" She doesn't stop so I rush after her. "What do you think you're doing? Don't you dare go in there and wake up those children!" I grab her arm; she flings it off but stops. I have never seen such fury in any eyes anywhere and I hope we are drunk.

"I will not have *my* children grow up in this den of hypocrisy . . ."

"You leave those girls right where they are."

"Not another minute!" She turns but I get her arm again. "Not another minute breathing in this two-faced, double-dealing pretense of air in this goddamned house . . ."

"If you dare, if you try for one minute to take those children and teach them that I'm a hypocrite . . ." I am choking but I have her arm fast; it is a minute before I can talk. Mary Cowan has come to thump my back. In the thin wheeze of breath left after every possible opening from esophagus to lung has snapped shut against the bourbon I gasp, "If you try to take my grandchildren out of the state of Texas, I'll see that you lose custody of those girls."

"Try it." Hallie's voice is a stab of fury. "Their own father lost trying, what makes you . . ."

"I certainly will. I'll get Lyndon on the telephone first thing in the morning and have you declared an unfit . . ."

"Mother!" Mary Cowan pushes between us as if she had never left, as if we were the original female lopsided triangle entering Houston for the first time. "You *can't*. Dora and Emily belong with Hallie . . ."

"She's a lunatic."

"I'm a lunatic!" Hallie screams in Mary Cowan's face. "Lock me up!" And Hallie runs out into the hot night and across the hills of the lawn as if we were chasing her.

Mary Cowan gets me back into the living room and onto the sofa where my heart slowly slows its thunder. Mary Cowan is trying to explain to me that Hallie's feelings are probably hurt because she thinks I don't want to share a house with her—don't like her. "I don't think you should throw Oscar up to her the whole time."

"*I* throw Oscar up to her? I merely said . . ."

"Yes, you do. As if you were *trying* to needle her." Mary Cowan gets up and as if I were on a string I follow her because I am frantic with confusion. "I'm going to make us some coffee," Mary Cowan says.

I see Hallie sitting on the footbridge which used to lead to the horses, sitting on the first stone leading up the horses' hill, facing the house. The French windows of the living room are illuminated and she can clearly see the curved beams of Sis's ceiling; the azaleas on the terrace will block the lower six feet of the room (from her depressed angle) so she can only see Mary Cowan and me when we walk into the card room.

She can see us standing in the card room: a couple of women. Of mother and daughter. Mary Cowan's slender smaller form curves earnestly toward me; I am shaking as if my strength and height were outside only, bark that will not hold. But it will, I say silently to Hallie lying back on the grassy hill among the night-feeding copperheads—snakes whose nights, as Hallie is wont to insist, are productive, active, nourishing. If Mary Cowan will pat, glue, strap me back together for ten minutes I will begin to reknit, sap rising from the waxed oak floors of *my* sister like fog from the creek.

All right, Hallie. If you lie out there you will rot from the lungs out, from the skin in.

"It's very clear that Hallie resents Oscar," Mary Cowan is saying. "Although I don't know why she has to scream at you about it."

"Because she hates me. Because she thinks she'd be a wild stallion on the range if I hadn't caught her and tamed . . ."

"Mare!" Hallie shouts through the suddenly opened door. She must have run up the hill. "Mare!" she demands and we turn to face her.

"Okay, mare," Mary Cowan says with affected weariness. "Hallie, you really don't have to shout at us, you know."

"Good, because I have a proposition to make. If I'm allowed in, of course." She intends her sarcasm to stir up anger and I clamp my teeth down on mine.

"We're listening," Mary Cowan says.

"*I'm* listening only on the condition that you don't say one word about me being harmful to Dora and Emily. You know I'd cut my heart out before I'd let anything hurt them."

I am melting with my words. As Hallie says, "I know, Mother—they love you and you love them," my reactions overwhelm me, slipping up on my blind side like that. I mumble, "I just couldn't stand it . . ." voice breaking, tears out of my control dropping on my cocktail napkin.

Both my daughters are patting me, gingerly, hands taking opposite shoulders; I am deliciously enclosed. I know but I cannot use the knowledge that Hallie wants me to love her, to see her as a special woman, a mound of perfectly whipped cream, to see her and salivate, say yumm or even ummm, wants my eyes to light up just by her presence, wants me to respond to her unique combination in the way that will define it for her, wants me to create her as a work of art by emphasizing just a touch of this here, a dab there . . . not to unravel complexity but to explain that it follows a subtle interlocking pattern which only a connoisseur . . . wants me to say "Hallie" or even "Mugwumps" and know exactly what I mean by that person.

I wanted the same thing from my mother. My voice is flat when it says, "Hallie." I repeat, "Hallie"—but now the staunch voice of my mother pronounces the word like a curse and I am naming a difficult daughter, a trial, a burden, a cross to bear, a punishment. "If I ever thought I was the kind of grandmother who cripples, like you said, I'd just kill myself."

Hallie's face congeals like forgotten soup. "Grandmother? You're skipping the very generation that needs you most!" She wheels and disappears into the kitchen.

"I'm heating coffee," Mary Cowan calls after her. "Why don't you bring us something to eat?"

Groats is not much use in absorbing whiskey.

What is wrong? Hours ago we slipped into our generational slots: my granddaughters asleep on cots in the playroom, Mary Cowan and Hallie in the twin beds in the guest room, and me in my bed with Bobdog happily in Hyke's. The children are safe because their mother sleeps between them and the front door and besides they are hidden away in the playroom where there is nothing a robber would want. Hallie is safe because her big sister lies between her and the outside world.

But is Mary Cowan safe, facing outward in the bed by the door? Am I safe with nothing but a nonbarking dog between me and the hallway?

In a few minutes I hear a very slight thumping of Bobdog's tail on the other bed, the bed my back is turned to. I sense a body quietly sitting between the two beds.

It is cold; I like my air conditioning to keep the house chilly enough to compensate for my metabolism, for the thick blood which years of living in the South has not thinned. But the story they love to tell about me is true: I do turn on the air conditioning so I can light a fire in the fireplace at Christmas.

Bobdog's tail has stopped thumping; I change my breathing to a depth that could be called snoring. A light blanket hangs off one end of my bed; whoever is on my floor moves it onto her shoulders. She repositions herself closer to the bed. My blanket is firmly tucked under the mattress at its foot. I flop onto my back, eyes still closed; I lie across my bed, chest and arms sheetless, both feet outside the sheet on the side of the bed away from my visitor. In a minute I will crack an eye open. I have left a triangle on the lower half of the bed—a triangle spacious enough for a curled-up small adult.

As cautiously as if she were laying a needle atop the surface tension of a glass of water, my visitor lowers her body into a curl on that triangle without breaking the surface. Now the blanket covers her balled body.

No adult knees can stand being balled for long. My guest inches up into the apex of the triangle until her head is by my waist and her knees half unbent. Half will not be enough; after total bending, knees demand complete straightness *now*. She puts her weight on her elbow, elbow above my arm, and lets her legs have the triangle. She bounces the bed; I utter a loud half-snore and pull my arm out from under my company—through slitted lids I see Hallie, of course.

Her face in the moonlight is six inches from my face and mine six from hers. Between us is the original smell of our skin struggling to breathe through grease. Hallie slides her arm out from under her body and sits partly up. She is staring at my hair. The strands over my forehead are pinned in circles by bobby pins, the sides are loose and long enough to cover a few inches of pillow but very thin.

I keep my eyes closed and my breathing imitative of sleep. How can anyone sleep with a daughter finding fault with your hair, watching it fail even in the dead of night?

She wants me to treat her as an equal but she throws a tantrum like a child. She wants me to be her mother and her best friend at the same time. Does she think I don't remember that the other Hallie, in a baby-doll nightgown, came into this exact room with her nefarious daughter-of-Eve schemes? Does Hallie expect me to have a sleep-over with her? Are we supposed to have a pillow fight and then sneak in the kitchen and make fudge? Are we going to tell each other our secrets? Do we have each other's pictures in our lockets? And suppose she starts liking that new girl better than me . . .

I flop my face over as if in a dream because I am afraid I will start smiling, even giggling.

With my eyes closed I remember the picture I have of Hallie which she loathes: a gold-oval-framed face in blue hat with veil and blue draped wedding dress, tinted to look as much like Pat Nixon as possible. There is another picture which Sister kept: Hallie on a swing at two, knees locked, belly out, two front teeth overhanging and the heartbreaking eyes of the born nosey—looking nothing like Shirley Temple, not at all like a fairytale princess; every staunch bone in her body seems to announce that she is on her way, world, look out. A mother must do everything she can to reshape such a daughter or her life will be ruined.

I will try no more. I certainly have no intention of living in the same house with a woman who mocks me as if wanting a house were an aberration, a queer notion of mine. She can *sleep* on the range for all I care. Stare at the stars until she goes blind with rage.

Scream at the animals and be as honest as the day is long. Let Dora and Emily fend for themselves—they're not my concern. It will be nice to have some peace around here in the time I have left . . .

Peace in our time, I hear Chamberlain echoing and see the banner headlines of a very old newspaper.

Well, I am not speaking out loud, I tell Chamberlain. No one is going to put my remarks on the radio and make me stick fast to them. But it is absurd—Mary Cowan is being ridiculous when she hints that I want to needle Hallie. And if I did—isn't it only for her own good? Isn't it important for her to get independent of me, to break away, to live her own life? She would stay little forever if she lived in the house with me, always wanting more than she can have. Always trying to catch up.

I feel a horrible raw well in my chest. The mattress is rising; Hallie has gotten up and is tiptoeing around Hyke's bed toward the door; I hear Bobdog's tail thump and then stop; I hear the door open and shut like a whisper. I stretch out akimbo now that I have my bed back to myself.

I rearrange my sheet but I cannot arrange my heart. It darts forth to stare at Hallie's head bent over a drawing, blushes when her head raises its face to mine. In my daughter's eyes is the land, the gift, the present I have never believed would be given and I am melting to my toenails. She is crisp and tan in white linen, her hug is like a python's but I am too tall to be squeezed; still she squeezes, imagining my gasp comes from that. My nose is in the grass smell of her hair. My mind buries itself in her mind.

I was with you when you went reeling through the streets of Greenwich Village after taking benzedrine from an inhaler and dissolving it in coffee—running to connect with mother. I heard your silent scream: *I'm sorry mother I don't want to hurt you—now I have killed myself you will not understand. Mother! Listen! it was an accident—I didn't mean to, it was an experiment. Now my heart my brain is throbbing and dashing against my skull—I am running—to my sister's apartment six blocks away—I hope she is home and will save me—I am too young to die alone.* I was there when, on Sixth Avenue between Eighth Street and Waverly, the brain subsided, the heart called attention to its steady slap-slap, you stopped. You felt your aliveness, you knew you were too alive to be dying now. You were glad for me, but you were mainly glad for yourself. Now you had one more chance—one of the hundred million one-more-chances you have already squandered.

Hallie. I told you then as you paused at Sixth Avenue by the subway entrance. *You are separate from me.* You stood like a horse seeking a pasture corner after a beating, wheezing, hypnotized, eyes inward.

I do not want to hug her right at this minute although she wants to be hugged. I want to scratch the soil around her heart and mix it with Sister's bonemeal and ground-up egg shells and dried coffee grounds and last summer's preserved aged horse and chicken contributions so she will shoot for the sky. I do not believe she wants to hurt me or herself; it is her mind that is terrified, fearful—because I have never confessed that I enter it—can enter it at will. She suspects. I have felt her pawing at my mind—a baby hoof tentatively inside, probing like a timid tongue, touching like a left index finger. I phase it this way because it never happens this way: she enters boldly through my eyes instead like clear yellow and circles my prehistoric humps until my skull is numb and deaf with a burr like the throat noise of a giant cat and I am sailing weightless over a table, a rug, a highway; I am wrapped in her mind, I am safe, I am immobile in her cocoon, I am central in a spin of goldenrod pollen like faint, fragile electric charges.

With a muddy primeval instinct, with an overriding sense of tragedy, I wrest myself loose and her mind hurries away.

I ACCEPTED OSCAR'S money for my bull and decided to take a trip to Europe—I hoped with Cad. She had to choose between the trip and running for the Texas Legislature; I understood when the trip won. Cad is not really aggressive enough for Texas politics; as she puts it, she is too old to be insulted in public and have to smile like a lady through it all.

We revisited all the places we had been to in our twenties and added Yugoslavia and Greece. We had six weeks altogether: the sixth week in Paris.

In Paris, disaster plunged like a hawk from a baby blue sky.

We were in our nightclothes preparing to read. Cad was arranging the bolster pillows, borrowing mine—I have to sit up straight in a chair to read or I'll go right to sleep—when something about her movements arrested my eye and my thoughts caught on her gracefulness. I was staring. She lifted my bolster over the fragile-looking French lamp between our beds and settled it over her bolster in a motion so precise, so unified I thought I was looking at yet another statue, this time in a navy-blue nylon robe.

"Tomorrow let's go back to the first shop and buy you that nightgown and robe," I said. We saw it in a boutique just off Saint Germain: a silk almost stark nightgown in lavender and cream—colors indigenous to Paris, a matching robe that folded in on itself like unbaked meringue when Cad put it on. "You look absolutely delicious in it."

Cad said with her back still turned, "Hungry again? I can easily imagine that. It's so hard to find anything to eat in Paris."

Although I had gained five pounds, I indulged my literalness. "Do we have room service? Would you like some Roquefort and brandy?" I wanted some Roquefort and brandy. I was reading *Lolita.* But I was so entranced with watching Cad arrange her bed as if she were Gertrude Lawrence on an opening night stage that my mind placed lavender and cream on top of green and gray.

"Gown and pegnoir. I have never seen anything so beautiful."

"Well, why don't you get it, Baby?"

"No French woman is five feet eight and a hundred and thirty-five. Or forty." I felt the roll around my middle. "Maybe forty-five after today. That's the reason trips to Paris are economical for me."

"But apparently not for me if I have to spend a hundred dollars on a gown and pegnoir."

"I'll split it with you."

Cad turned and looked directly at me with something between an appeal and a stare. "I don't want it."

"Well, you're wrong."

"I'm what?"

"You should want it. It was made for you."

"For my life in the boudoir? For the times when I'm locked up overnight with the Grand Jury?"

"The Grand Jury is over." Being in Paris validated Cad's proportions in an amazing way: suddenly instead of appearing undersized as she does at home she looked delicate—definitely lavender and cream, certainly silk meringue. "Who knows what's in your future?"

"Possibly a king. If so, I can have my pegnoirs made when the time comes."

"You have to think pegnoir first to attract the king. You have to turn yourself around to lavender and cream . . ."

"Unless I don't want a king."

"A duke then."

"Or a duke."

"Well, you certainly don't want a dirty old man like Humbert Humbert."

"No."

There was an edge of patience in her voice which she uses when she wants to tell someone she is suffering a fool dutifully. I was suddenly angry. "What's the matter with you tonight? I just want you to be happy, to have the best . . ."

She sat down in the blue and gold chair matching the one I was in, across the table that was to have held brandy and Roquefort. It held only *Lolita* unopened. "What do you think of me, Baby?"

"I think of you as a beautiful woman . . ."

"But not apparently as a productive one." Her hand was lying wide open on our table, a deep head line cutting straight across her palm. "You were glad when I decided not to run for the legislature."

"Yes, I was glad."

"You thought I would lose."

"Maybe I thought you would win." I know that was a silly thing to say but I don't think she was listening. I'm not sure she was talking either—she delivered a speech as if she were in the legislature now and I, the hated conservative opposition.

"I hate you when you don't back me up. I hate my best friend pulling me down into the pillows when I am trying my best to do something for the world. You want me to become you because then you feel justified with your life. I don't want you to be me to justify mine. Why can't you be on the side of my strengths? Why couldn't you have urged me to spend a hundred dollars on a campaign manager, a thousand on a fund-raising party instead of this trip? And you don't even want me on this trip with you except as a substitute for a man. You're acting like we're post-debs off to Europe to buy our trousseaus before we enter that grand life of marriage and babies—you're behaving exactly as if we were dumb twenty-two-year-olds. I would have expected you to understand that I was scared to run for the legislature, that I felt trapped in my own ambivalence, and that if you really loved me you would have egged me on, knowing I have no respect for quitters or for timid women. You urged me out. I am here instead. And all you think about is not what I've lost but a pegnoir! A pegnoir for what? To die in?"

I felt sick. My brief moment of anger visited like a sour eclair leaving nausea in my bloodstream. I wanted to jump out of the window. There was nothing, nothing I could say because everything she said sounded exactly true. I did imagine us as twenty-two-year-olds. I wanted to recapture our first trip with all my heart. I still did at that moment. I reached over to take her hand but her eyes were fixed on mine as if she were looking at a stranger and I was prevented. "I'm sorry . . ."

A smirk told me how inadequate that sounded. My lungs and heart were collapsing inside. "Oh my god, I am going crazy!" The blue and gold, the delicate painted pastels of our Parisian hotel bedroom were about to burst into a violin serenade from some comic opera. The audience would laugh. Or we were best friends reciting a scene from the theater of social realism. Or we had been sprayed onto a page of *True Romances*. My reflexes were poised to bring on a flood of tears. I wanted to beg forgiveness and be held and told that it didn't matter.

I said, "I would give my heart to undo what I have done." It was my heart that did it, I saw—my greedy literal bossy heart. "I've ruined your life." I saw scorn in her eyes. I was not important enough to ruin her life?

"Hardly that," she said unnecessarily.

And I was furious. Trapped in Marie Antoinette decor with love creating havoc in the city outside and only hate here. I picked up *Lolita* and clenched my teeth.

She arranged her miniature self on our bolsters and dove into her book. She probably read it. I couldn't read a word. If I'd been home I could have gone into another room, gotten in a car and driven home. Here I was caught. I couldn't get dressed and go out into that impossibly romance-geared city. In a minute I went into our bathroom and took a needless bath. When I came out her light was off—at ten o'clock, Cad? With four reading hours left of the night?

"Cad." My voice was weak but neutral at least.

"Dammit, Baby, go to sleep." The way she yanked the covers over her body like a shield was as violent as a slap, a scratch, a mean pulling of hair. The sight of her upraised back left me suffocating with fury.

I was barely asleep when they came—nurses and gym teachers from childhood with mean laughs. They surrounded me, held me down; it was an initiation, a ritual of pain, a show of terrible power. At the center of their circle I was pinioned like a foolish cricket. I knew they would not kill me, they would do something much worse. I exploded in what I have to call a "wet dream" because I know no other term, although I am sure women don't have them.

The morning was nervous, polite. Fortunately we were meeting Gracie for lunch, then flying home.

Houston Intercontinental is announced by our captain; Cad says that as soon as Dallas gets one and names it Dallas Interplanetary we will retaliate with Houston Intergalactic and I think I smile.

The new airport is huge; I have to walk miles at Cad's side—I try to keep at her side, she is walking deliberately fast. Her back is deliberately sturdy, her shoulders deliberately square. My chest is like wire.

I do not want to go home; my mind is tied to a post by baggage claim like a dog. I can pull it or entice it but it won't come out of its rope's radius, I don't know why. I decide to leave it there, abandoned, yowling if it yowls.

Hallie left me in the only way she could; she decided to write a novel.

UNCLE DOCTOR'S FUNERAL was this morning. It is now three o'clock on Saturday afternoon and Hallie has disappeared into the guest room. You can hear the clicking of her typewriter from the front hall or from the bathroom.

Emerging from the bathroom, Oscar says, "Baby, what is Hallie doing in there? Is she taking a secretarial course?"

"She says she's writing a novel."

"Honey, I believe I will have a little drink." I ring for Jewell. "What's her novel about?"

I hate this subject. Every time I think about Hallie writing a novel my eye twitches. I know that anything I say can reappear in print and stick to me forever like the farmer's wife's nose. Most of the time I successfully pretend Hallie is not writing a real novel— that the clicking is knitting needles or mah-jongg or something mysterious in the duct work.

"I don't think it'll get published necessarily," I say.

Oscar thanks Jewell for the drink and waits.

"She says it's about Houston," I say.

"Houston?"

"The people in Houston."

"Which people in Houston?"

"She says they're all made-up people."

"Uncle Oscar, if you're through with that cigarette, I'll take it," Dora says. Oscar thinks she is indulging the fastidious nature of little girls and holds the ashtray out to her. Dora picks up his butt and slips it in her shirt pocket.

"Honey!" Oscar says. "You don't want to do that. Cigarettes are dirty."

"Then why do you smoke them?"

"I don't very often." Oscar tried to quit after his coronary occlusion and now smokes only one or two cigarettes a day. In the silence the clicking from the guest room comes through like an accountant with an abacus at tax time. Oscar pulls out another cigarette and fits it hastily into his holder. "I'll just hold this one," he says to Dora, who is eyeing it.

I am almost through with my Chesterfield. "For heaven's sake, Dora, I can't enjoy my cigarette with you standing there waiting to snatch it up like a vulture the minute I put it out. Go on out in the kitchen and hover over Jewell's cigarette if you have to hover." Dora doesn't move. "Now I mean it. You can have the ashtray when we're through."

"You promise?"

"Of course I promise. What do you think, that people are lining up outside in order to get first dibs on these cigarette stubs??

"If I come back later and the ashtray's empty I'll know you lied," Dora says. "Dora! Don't you talk that way . . ."

Dora disappears behind the swinging door to the kitchen. I put out my cigarette and immediately light another. "It's enough to make a woman switch to filters."

"Do you think she's writing about us?" Oscar says.

"I don't know." I know full well that she *must* be. Where else would she get her material? Or her power. Who else could she hurt as much as she could her own mother—and art, I know, has to be motivated. The clicking seems to be faster, steadier today. "Maybe she's writing about Uncle Doctor. She was very fond of him, you know. She does seem to be going at it more forcefully than usual."

Oscar rattles his ice. "She wouldn't say anything that would embarrass us, would she?"

I read a few pages of Hallie's novel at first. She complained that her own mother wasn't interested in what she was doing and made me prove I cared by reading at least a small section. Unsure of exactly what I was reading, mostly I felt that the pages contained sex and pain. It hurt too much, being confronted with pain I had not been able to shield my daughter from, and I think it is unseemly for a daughter to tell her mother sexual details. I handed the pages back to Hallie, telling her it was well written, and had read nothing since. "I think it's mostly about her," I say. "Aren't first novels always autobiographical?"

"She can't write about her life without at least giving herself a mother." Oscar leans back, resting his hands on his charcoal paunch. But Hallie doesn't necessarily have to give herself two uncles. A confirmed nonreader of fiction, Oscar believes (unlike me) that her obvious preference for Uncle Doctor means she will concentrate on the D.R. in her books.

"All first novels have a mother," I agree glumly. The very mother who is making the novel possible by keeping the children while daughter creates. Sometimes I realize that biologically I could have two girls at the ages of Dora and Emily and swear that if God were really smart the menopausal reprieve would occur at thirty-five or younger. I felt exactly like killing Emily last week when she walked behind me at the bridge table and said, "Look, Grandbaby, all your cards are *red*."

"Has she said anything about me?" Oscar asks.

"No. She just asks a lot of questions about Mother and Daddy. Particularly Daddy."

"What questions?" Oscar's ice is poised.

"Mainly about Daddy's will." I see him start. Now I know Hallie doesn't know enough about law to include it in a novel but Oscar doesn't. "She seems to be interested in the community property laws of the twenties," the devil makes me say.

His ice is rattling violently and I ring for Jewell.

NOW EVERYONE HAS read that book. One newspaper didn't review it—just interviewed Hallie—and the other, although they did both a review and an interview, hurt Hallie's feelings by calling her heroine self-indulgent and shallow. Since a heroine has to be the author, *that* got my dander up. A family, before going public, should anticipate the voices of those who will now feel they have a say, should make certain the family retains control. Hallie foolishly sprung this on us before we had time to line up our proxies.

Every day I hear of some additional woman throwing her copy into the garbage like junk mail. Drukie asked Cad confidentially what certain obscenities meant. The Tennessee Walking Horse, now in an unmarried interlude, asked Hallie for a date. Selwyn's family blocked her appearance on a local television show. Her fan mail consists of anonymous letters demanding that she repent. Some wives even think Hallie is describing, under the guise of fiction, her own affairs with their husbands—and if true, do wives think husbands walk in their sleep?

Hallie is wearing a pale yellow tweed suit that is much too heavy for Houston but is lined with yellow- and gray-striped taffeta and she knows her power in it. When did she start wearing yellow so often? Her eyes are the fresh shiny green of a new Crayola.

Oscar's are a smoldering black, as dark as Mother's; unlike Mother's, the puffs and dips of flesh around them do not soften their bullet-hole shape. Oscar's paunch belongs not to a man who loves food but only to one who lacks exercise; had his flesh popped up from undisciplined eating it might tug for affection . . . but I am just pushing him away from my heart with these thoughts because I know he is mad at me.

His eyes are concentrated into Welsh coals now. "Of course, it's your concern," he finally says. I know he would ordinarily say "your business" but the business to which his sentence refers is too starkly *his* and exactly the one he thinks I betrayed. I almost smile when I understand that a substitution of "affair" for "business" is impossible after Hallie's novel.

"That's a nice old-timey word: *concern*," I say sweetly.

"Your concern," he repeats. "I wish you had let me know what you were thinking about though; I would have been happy to advise you, Eudora."

I hear Hallie's angry insuck of breath. "You don't have to call her Eudora."

"I like it," I say, trying to dimple. But no one likes a sudden name change in her sixties. Oscar pronounces it *Eu*-dora, emphasizing "you" like Texans do with *Eu*-gene. Of all the ways in English that one person has ever called another person, I hate "you" above all. While I keep my surfaces smooth in case a colleague or competitor of Oscar's is within range, Oscar tells me, in his careful way, that he hates me for doing what I did.

I sold two thousand shares of his company's stock (which he'd given me once) for thirty thousand dollars.

When he pauses, I hear my voice saying, "Wasn't it mine to sell, Brother?"

"Of course it was, honey." Honey gums up his words, checks his train of thought. He is nodding to the head waiter. I see a sigh in the hunch of his back, meaning I have lost my mind (my money) but he will somehow get it back for me.

Walking through what looks like the waiting room of a hospital atop a spaceship but is called the Petroleum Club quiets Oscar and me. We may be skirting interested ears. I am surprised to see, after we are seated, that Hallie is practically twitching.

"Uncle Oscar," she says, ignoring the black satin menu that the headwaiter is trying to hand her, ignoring his ears too, "Mother didn't sell her stock to buy a new hat. We signed a contract on thirty acres of land on Post Oak right next to Auntie and Uncle Doctor's old land . . ."

Oscar has his back turned to her by the time the head-waiter leaves. "I think you did a very foolish thing," he says to me. "That stock should go up steadily . . ."

Do you think land is going to go down?" Hallie says.

"Real estate is a tricky investment . . ."

"It isn't 'real estate,' it's *land*."

But our waiter is near; Oscar will not speak until he leaves our drink orders. "I know a lot of people have sentimental feelings for land because it's real and they like the fact that they can see it. And

I know you always had a special warm spot for that land of your Uncle Doctor's, but honey . . ." He is looking straight into her eyes, a thing I could never do when they are the light pistachio green they are now, as if all the color in them has fled for safety. ". . . is only valuable if you have the know-how to develop it, put up buildings, a shopping center, get other men to invest with you and have enough clout to persuade big tenants to relocate in your development. Too many people now are sitting on land they paid too much for wondering how Houston passed them by. You know that strip of Westheimer by the Tower Theatre? You could have bought anything on those blocks twenty years ago for practically the same thing you have to give for it now."

He is persuading me. I never have understood why those few blocks are such a Jonah. I wish I'd ordered a martini. Bourbon's all right if you're in high cotton but the terrible first taste of a martini is the only thing that puts enough fight into your mouth to save thirty thousand dollars.

"It's a natural mistake to make. I'll see if I can find someone to take that parcel off your hands—of course, I can't promise but I do know a few of the developers. You wouldn't even need to get full price—the market's down right now and you could get that stock back for a little less than you sold it for."

The bourbon is right after all. I am so relieved that we are not going to have to suffer for our mistake that I want to drink a toast to Hallie's next book . . .

"How much less?" Hallie asks.

"A couple of points, I believe." Oscar can't shake the ice, it's imbedded in scotch. He gives the glass a little twist, sloshing scotch, which he pats up vigorously.

"Two points?"

"Actually, three today. But tomorrow, of course, it may . . ."

Hallie holds up her glass to me—a toast to *my* next book? "Mother, you sold stock at twenty which is now worth seventeen. You just made fifteen percent on your money in two weeks. Unless, of course, it's actually down a little more than three?" I've never heard her voice so cold; I think it's because she doesn't drink anymore.

"You mean we could buy our stock back for three dollars a share less than we got for it?"

"If we want to," Hallie says.

"Of course, you'll have to pay taxes on that money . . ."

"Uncle Oscar, I'll be happy . . ."

"There's Cad!" I start waving. "We're waiting for you like one pig waits for another," I say, hugging her, beckoning our waiter at the same time. "What about a drink?"

"He was very nervous," I say. "I think he read it three times—probably the first novel he's read since *The Five Little Peppers*." I am listening to the sea gulls raucously warning each other that a storm is brewing although nature has already made that obvious: the Gulf is as heavy with waves as a real ocean. To our right the sky is iron gray; I cannot tell if it is slowly darkening or moving closer. A lone cylinder of sunlight remains to the left.

I am sitting on the glider, well back from the edge of the porch. Hallie has wrapped the string hammock around her like a blanket, leaving one foot free to keep her in motion. She speeds up her swinging.

"It doesn't have anything to do with him," she says.

"Of course it does. He's the major villain." I chuckle at the picture of Oscar snarling "You *must* pay the rent!" with a ferocious rattle of his ice. "Unless I am the villain?" Hallie had mothers in there as battle-axes, flirts, totem poles, puppies—as many mothers as a worn-out roof has leaks; she tried to get me to see what an interesting character her composite was. My friends waited to see what I would do. Do? I could hardly breathe.

"I forgave you when I saw your picture in *Time* looking as sweet as I always knew you looked." Instantly I know I have said the wrong thing but a pure prolonged zag of lightning splits the sky down the middle and I think, with the thunder: I say what I mean.

Hallie sits up in the hammock's now-sagging middle. The cone of sunlight is at her back; I cannot see through the shadows on her face. "You think art is motivated by revenge," she says. It is a sentence with *glum* for a period. "I don't *think* that's true but it probably is."

"I do not think that." I do.

She knows I do. There is too much electricity in the air to expect thoughts to stay separate—they are crackling from brain to brain like innocence.

"I wonder if that has to be true. I wonder if a novel could be written only from love—no hate at all. Of course, hate *is* easier." It oils the parts, lets the words slip out ready-greased.

The sunlight has disappeared and I can see her face but I can hardly hear; thunder is too frequent. I fidget as the rain walls our porch off from the beach; I am ready for a drink myself.

I wake up abruptly. There is a curious lightness in my head as if all my muscles were sixteen; they are laughing; I am drenched. The storm is coming into my bedroom in a gale of water: I might as well be under a shower. The window is flapping wildly. Hallie is standing in the doorway, alarmed; then she is laughing. I think I have never been so wet: my nightgown sticks to my body in patches and creases, my hair drips, the sheet is transparent; I am making puddles on the floor toward Hallie when the window shatters.

"Put on some coffee," I say.

"I've got to get this stuff out of the rain." She shoves furniture across the room.

I am at the bathroom door. "Watch your feet."

The windows in her room are unendangered—in fact, they are almost dry. The gale is near horizontal but we are safe in our ark.

"Are we what God had in mind?" she asks.

"Well, certainly. If He hadn't wanted us on board he wouldn't have left us with one dry bed, now would He?"

I am wide awake now, cajoling my spine into accepting one pillow, vertical, as support enough. It is strangely airless, almost hot, on the leeward side of this storm. Hallie is dressed in her underpants, allowing me to admire (but it is closer to love) all of her: her shoulders squared at the ends so nothing can slip off them unaware, her breasts much smaller now than when I saw her as Persephone in a trousseau gown, the little snake of flesh circling her waist when she sits like this cross-legged on the foot of the bed. Her hair is short and straight as a pin, wet threads now. She is waiting for me to say something.

I feel her waiting. There is a layer over her eyes, a transparent second eyelid; she has not opened it for me since the night she tried to give me a house. She thinks she prevents me from seeing into her mind.

I am telling Hallie that I will not try to dominate my granddaughters if she won't take them away; I have no power to force.

She is explaining to me that she really has to leave Houston.

The room is brilliant with a series of lightning jags, on top of us, close behind us; thunder rolls and claps simultaneously; I smell rust mixed with ions. The power goes out; between flashes the house is lightless. I walk through the living room thinking of chiaroscuro. Hallie rummages for candles; I search out the bourbon.

She is so remote: here in the weirdness of erratic lighting this cottage becomes a horror-story setting; her face, now lit from below by the one candle she found, is a stranger's. A clap of thunder unaccountably frightens me: I remember she once told me she had imagined a plan to murder the Duchess so Oscar would be free and I would not have to worry; she said she abandoned the idea because she was afraid Oscar would be blamed (she knew no one would ever suspect her). No one would suspect her now, although she is thirty-five, if she decided to kill *me*: daughter who loved her mother to death.

Now the thunder is in the room, lightning seems aimed at the house, at the kitchen where we stand. I am hugging her, holding her against my body as if we could insulate each other; I am frightened even as I understand that fear is a mask for loneliness.

Holding the candle over the sink she returns my hug with her other arm; her front deflates against my chest; her back is as rigid as ever. I am stroking it. I am kissing her hair, her neck. I feel her youth transfer itself into my age. Thunder vibrates against my ears. Then there is another noise—the sound of a hundred hooves stamping on our roof. We are being pelted from above: hail.

Although one room, one position is as dangerous as another, like babies we choose to huddle together in the bed, drawing the sheet around our shoulders, fixing the candle to a saucer and placing it on the dresser where we can see it. Fear unmasks itself. I am a fire of loneliness: no longer the gluey gray mud of yesterday, loneliness rages through my veins like hot rain, like flesh.

I am kissing my daughter like a lover.

PART V

October (1963–1964)

NINETEEN SIXTY-THREE will go down in history as the year our president was shot. The state of Texas—host to the assassin, scene of the murder—gained by death a native son in the White House. Some Houstonians tried to dissociate themselves from Dallas, claiming that Dallas had not handled its Birchers, its Minute Women, its White Citizens, its police force, its blinkered fundamentalists, its undiversified oil money, in time to prevent such a horror. But President Kennedy had come to Texas in the first place at the request of Lyndon Johnson, who hoped to heal the split in our Democratic party by the visit, and Lyndon is close friends with Houston's leading citizens. Together they got the Space Center for Houston, Rice put in the first Department of Space Science in the country, and Oscar and the Duchess were Lyndon's guests at Cape Canaveral when the first U.S. astronauts were rocketed around the earth. We all feel personally guilty here and my heart aches for poor Lyndon, who always wanted to be president but not this way.

My heart is curiously unmoved, however, by the danger to its own body. Although everyone is too preoccupied to notice—Hallie is in Paris with the girls, Mary Cowan harried by the twins and little Bobby, the widows preparing Christmas for their grandchildren—I can no longer swallow without pushing each bite down my throat with my fingers. My heart has dissociated itself from the failing apparatus adjacent to it; heart thumps happily and makes me laugh when someone remarks that I have lost weight and I announce that I have finally found a diet that works. I'm sure Jewell knows. I'm sure it is only a matter of time before others notice. Meanwhile we wait, heart and I, strangely excited about our approaching finale, our devastating conclusion, our powerful final chapter.

Today Cad pops in just before lunch and announces that she hasn't eaten. Of course she will eat with me. Lunch is cold soup, scrambled eggs, soft rolls. We are almost finished when Cad pretends to retrieve her napkin and suddenly changes her eyes' direction and watches as I reach for my neck as if I am adjusting my collar and surreptitiously squeeze the front of my throat from halfway down to my collarbone.

"Baby, Catherine told me you were doing that."

"Doing what?"

"Pushing your food down with your fingers."

"Catherine? I haven't seen Catherine for months . . ."

"Jewell told her."

Suddenly I know I am not ready yet. I stand up tall over my sister's table, push down on its surface with hands that are still stronger than any woman's I know. "Well, if you think you can sneak up like this and *catch* me, if you think you can trick your way in here and start criticizing the way I *eat* . . ." I leave the table. I am standing stock-still in the middle of my living room; I feel Cad following me and prevent her from coming too close by a violent shake of my shoulders. Of course I succeed; she stops two feet away.

I am controlling this silence. I alone can break it. I wheel and face Cad. "I will not be operated on. I won't have that whistle thing in my throat like the Mogul. I won't wear a bag under my clothes like Titta. I am not going into one of their hospitals and let them cut away at me and leave me to cart myself around in pieces. I'd rather . . ." There is too much blood being pounded into my ears and I am deafened.

But I went. The entire human community banded together to push me into the arms of the surgeon who expertly slid me into the hospital and began cutting early in January. The operation lasted four hours. They cut a foot-long gash in my back skin. They removed two ribs and entered my chest cavity through the back; they sliced off the diseased section of my esophagus and pulled my stomach up so the shortened tube could be joined again. They lay my skin back over my back and then sewed up the two-foot gash.

I did not die on the operating table. I recovered consciousness in intensive care and tried to comfort the terrified faces of my daughters. I was wheeled into a small room of my own and almost immediately pain raced through my body unable to localize itself. There was bone pain where my ribs had been severed, chest pain where my esophagus was cut, abdominal pain from rearranging my stomach, muscle pain in my entire upper torso, and finally skin pain where the stitches pulled against flesh. I smiled and held the hands offered to me. But as soon as I entered a brief sleep from a dose of painkiller, I must have screamed. The scream woke me up. I looked into the raw eyes of my daughters and tried to explain that I must have been having a nightmare.

Mary Cowan came back in April. I didn't want her to come before then because soon after I got home from the hospital, just as I was feeling that I had beaten it (although I could barely eat), I came down with serum hepatitis. It was a struggle to expel that cloud of yellow from a body which, apparently outraged, cooperated dimly. By April I was as thin as I'd ever wanted to be.

And I was well enough to begin the chemotherapy treatments. I go Mondays and Thursdays at noon; I am almost recovered from them by Wednesdays and Saturdays, but on Sundays I feel marvelous. On Sunday my heart settles back to its hard sure beat and the joy of every second makes my blood skip through its hoops. It will be a lengthy final chapter, heart and I decide. We eliminate the rest of the week. I merely smile when Mary Cowan says I should sue the hospital for using blood plasma when both she and Hallie were right there with the same blood type eager to give me a safe transfusion. She will be here for only two Sundays, for only one Wednesday and Saturday, and even on my best days I must sleep or rest twelve hours. I tell her the doctors say I am doing fine; I am doing exactly what they tell me to do. I would be dead by now, I think, if I had not gone for my operation. Instead I have one hundred and seventy-two thousand, eight hundred seconds of Mary Cowan right now. "I want you to bring all my grandsons down at Christmas," I tell her. "Will you?" That's what this house is for: children and grandchildren and all our friends. She has pictures of them, and drawings and poems from them. Already I sense their presence here in the hot sunshine of next Christmas. "And how is angelbaby Ed?" I ask, knowing they are happy by her face.

I called her. Even though they were on some Greek island and I didn't know exactly where it was, I know I woke up one night in the dead middle of darkness and heard my words ringing off my brain: *Come home soon.* I was too self-conscious to repeat them now that I was awake, but I knew I had just called Hallie wherever she was. And I believed she heard me. I hope I never have to speak of this in front of scientific minds. I was very agitated. I wanted to assure her that there was no emergenncy, that I was fine, but whatever tunnel I had spoken through was gone. Nothing more was necessary in any case: I had clearly said *soon,* the correct nonemergency word, and I was certain now that she heard.

She is arriving today. I am glad she left Dora and Emily with Mary Cowan on her farm; I want to see them later. I know all our letters to Hallie have told her how well I am doing; I am afraid my diminished self will be a shock. Even I am surprised when I look in a mirror—was I never a raw-boned Texan? With the supporting flesh gone now, the bones themselves have shrunk into a useless aristocratic delicacy. Brown eyes which used to fit symmetrically into the whole large structure are the only large things left and dominate an unfamiliar tiny face. I try to keep them soft to make up for their conspicuousness.

"You're so thin!" Hallie says it lightly, as a compliment to someone who has succeeded on a diet, someone so firmly placed in life that she can indulge vanity. but I feel, as we hug each other, how carefully her arms rest across her mother's shoulders.

Like a lot of women who take their time defining themselves, Hallie has grown good-looking now that she is over thirty-five. Her mouth is still soft but doesn't wander the way it used to, her puppy flesh has dropped away leaving definite cheekbones, her eyes seem to assert themselves in spaces carved only for them and their balance has changed: intelligence now dominates sympathy. Since it is a daughter's face I can be used to its difference in a second; still I smile and wait. I am sitting on the gold brocade Louis XV sofa and waiting for Jewell to bring me my tea. For the first time in my life I belong here visually. I am wearing a gold chain belt around my waist over white silk; it has been forty-five years since I had a waist ready for a gold chain. My eyes glisten when I think Hallie must see how perfectly I now fit into my sister's living room. I am waiting until Hallie gets used to my difference: then we can begin.

Light flickers across the room's tapestries and rubbed woods, objects from a hundred lives like an audience watching us: antiques from ruined or ignorant descendants of English and French wealth, portrait of my father (done from a photograph after our family produced its successful businessman) over the mantel, and my own multitude of things from Mexico, inappropriate now. The air is machine cool, empty and soundless.

Suddenly the unit goes off at a thermostatic command. Suddenly the room is alive with the sounds each object makes as it settles to rest—tiny sounds natural to the material itself, patterns characteristic of each molecular construction, rhythms of brass or oak or oiled canvas or linen weave, sounds of hair and dust, of glass, silver, ivory and wire and aging china. I wait for Hallie to hear the sound she does not want to hear: the brush and crack of my bones shrinking, the collapsing lisp of my cells as death reaches out to digest them. My hands are only bone and vein, backdrop for museum jewels; while we wait they suck at unaccustomed emptiness, cupped idly in my lap.

We chat through our first night's miniature supper and then settle into place in the living room where even the ashtrays are clean. I think it is time now for Hallie's brain to have reconnected itself to a present Houston socket. I think she must know by now that my minimum flesh contains a giant anger, unpardoning and betrayed. I think she herself feels exactly the same way. With no alcohol possible to bring an argument to furious and forgivable surface, no cigarettes now to shrink the blood exploding in our bodies, how will we engage each other?

I begin. "I guess everything turns out for the best." I have often said this sentence with the Southern rhythm because, like Southern cotton, it suspends its seeds in white clouds. I mean (now) that Hyke died before my illness: men are not good at nursing; they are too afraid the patient will die. I speak of Hyke for a few minutes. I like to remember that on his last Christmas on earth Hallie gave him a pair of pink silk pajamas and matching robe, proof that she loved him, that she wanted him to be the pink one sometimes, and especially that she entered him by such a gift into the boudoir.

"Of course, I didn't invent this cancer to get you home," I say lightly, "but I'm very glad you're here."

Is she telling me that she thinks I am going to die? "I have every intention of getting well. Nonrustible and indestructible, as Gaius used to say."

"Doesn't he still say it?"

"Yes, but you can hardly understand him now—he's never sober. Nondustible and inderustible."

I win a laugh and try again.

"Nonmumble and indenurnur." It still feels strange for my hands in my lap to be resting on hipbones.

Hallie moves to the couch beside me. She sees I see how lightly she lowers herself; she says, "You look like you would break if I'm not careful." She smiles.

"Very boring too. I can hardly wait to get back to my bad habits."

"I've lost mine too," Hallie says. "I must be boring too."

"You are not. I like you better with roses in your cheeks but you certainly never bored *me*. Darling, would you get me a glass of water?"

"Of course, Mother."

The perfectly equipped bar is spotless now with bottles lined up; no one dares really drink in the presence of cancer. Hallie says, handing me this water, "You're wrong about the roses, Mother. Sun isn't the only thing that has beauty." But sunny Dora and sunny Emily sparkle and delight; it couldn't be only me who notices how odd that sunshine seems beside their dark mother as if they sucked her lightless. Hallie's mind pushes to the front her hollows and lines and clouds. She thinks she earned them. She wants them respected. She wants to come as thunder and a close, low sky and have me huddle under with her for my final taste of the earth. Only my death will fit such seriousness.

My mind begins: What do you think we have you for? You could have been my lifelong friend like Mary Cowan, a normal daughter. We could have exchanged love at holidays, adventures at odd meetings, loyalties at crisis. We could have claimed each other in communities, upheld each other in the social eye. You are not so wild that you could not pass—and for everyone who resents your blurting out the truth there is another wrapped in silence, huddled in protective wedlock, who is secretly clapping to beat the band. Texas has absorbed worse mavericks and Houston positively sends out invitations to such as you. Did you seek out the timid to disprove this? Did you ever try to mate with a heart as thundering as your own?

"Houston seems so big to us now but it must seem very bland to you." I am scared. Doesn't Hallie see that?

"Not bland. Too boisterous for me, if anything."

But I spent my youth hammering away at your senses, at your mind—I practically took a corkscrew to unplug your heart. I never wanted *friendship*—Mary Cowan saw, Cad, Auntie, Hyke—you all saw. *You* spent my youth with your elbow in my chest holding me off for my sake. And still I came with a hammer, a feather, a promise, a tantrum, even an offer of a house. A gift of a house. Nobody had ever given you a house of your very own to create on your own in good taste or bad to suit yourself. What did you think the house was *for*?

I heard you say house once. I never heard you bring up the house again. I never heard word *house*. I saw a daughter using my old house to write a novel housing—distorting—a mother who loved her. Taking the money from that novel and running to Paris—didn't you know I would like to be offered the house again? To share a house with my daughter the novelist silences all criticism—but you never considered critics. What wouldn't they have said! But once you became a published writer—and since I had become for the second time a widow and was at an age which might be considered old (although I was barely sixty-one)—I would have been forgiven for sharing a house with you (as long as it was my house) by most of my friends—except the old beaux, of course. But then *you* chose not to see. A lifetime of knocking, ringing, rattling and when the door blew open by itself you slam it shut and run. *My* daughter.

I see she sits away from me in her chair. "Well, I guess living in Houston does require optimism. Fortunately, I have enough of that for both of us." More than enough, and still you left me, although I had stamina for us both too. I understood that you didn't inherit that from my side of the family; I gave you my wide back to follow, to cut off wind, to provide that shade you love.

There is no house, Mother. You wanted a nest, a cave, a secluded hollow where you could be safe—protection we need only when there are young in the nest. You never understood that you haven't needed that for years. You wanted a shelter against Oscar, against the money-makers . . .

I wanted what? When you showed me that drawing and said, "This one is nestled in the pines," I was furious. *Nestled?* You and Chanchy were the ones mooning over your lost homes. I never looked back on a house in my life. I wanted a house like a dress to decorate me so a husband would come, roof like a hat with daring plumes, walls like a veil dotted with mystery—I wanted a castle

so I could entice me a prince: spider's parlor, witch's gin-
gerbread, siren's rock. I certainly never wanted a hiding
place.

"I may never be as strong as I was before but when I get well I
certainly intend to gain some weight back."

And I wanted you to come with me, play in the Gulf like
the porpoises, roam the seas with the whales—there are
no real castles for women without princes, Mother. Houston as territory belongs to the men.

She has already told me she wants to live in New York now—
for the children, she claims. If I convince her I will get well, she will
do it. If I pretend I am dying soon she will stay. "I hope you don't
think for one minute that I'm not going to get well?"

I would have come. You never asked me. You never once
suggested I go to Paris with you all.

From here I shiver from the ice that suddenly crusts Hallie's
face—a second only: she gets up and wheels toward our former
card room–bar, knocking against the end table, unbalancing the
lamp, I see her frigid back disappear through the doorway. I feel
my body rejuvenate with the return of old fury.

Cells rise up. My lungs feel strong as a bellows. The
sweetmeats you save for yourself, I tell her in my mind; I
am supposed to be happy with a house nestled in the
pines, a baby house?

At the exact moment when I needed you, you took your
ill-gotten gains and absconded to Europe—abducting
my grandgirls, opting for your own adventures, as if you
had a right to live your own life. You might as well have
flagged down the next bus—any bus with its obnoxious
fumes trailing then behind you, in my face as I ran after
you and you chortled, you could tell your mother-tale
translated now into French for your new Parisian audience. You might just as easily have sided with the waiters
at "21" who held their Manhattan noses high as if Spanish were declassé, not their language (although their

mother tongue). But live, Hallie, my daughter; my tongue
is bitten back. Texas raised you, Houston tattooed your
heart; no impress now will turn you French, or free. No
mother ever says different: go, grow, take your own path
(the clichés come with our milk): but you protested—
how you yelled and carried on: I want to share a house
with *you*, you said (Didn't you mean life? Did you think
that would rock along forever, awaiting your mood, your
moodiness? And didn't I call your bluff?)

She comes back to the sofa to hug me. "Of course you're going
to get well. I have a lot more optimism than you've noticed yet."
"You do?"
"I keep it hidden sometimes so you won't pounce and say I'm
just like you." She smells the same—a fresh grass smell pouring
through whatever Paris scent she's smeared on top.
"Mugwumps. I'm so glad you're here."
"I want to stay until you get well."
"You do?"
"Tomorrow I'll try to rent an apartment across the creek.
Emily and Dora can go to school here this year . . ."
"Feathers! It's certainly not going to take me a year to get well.
I'll be looking for a girdle to hold in fat long before Christmas."
"Then we'll just have to leave." Hallie's eyes are glistening so
they don't look nearly as intelligent; they look like old pleading
baby eyes again. "As long as we keep leaving and coming back,
we'll love each other forever, I guess."
"I guess that's what a daughter's for."
"A yo-yo? I knew it had to be for something."
I'm exhausted. Victory used to shoot through my veins like
alcoholic sugar; now it arrives with a hangover in tow, its after-
effects in its lap. I lean back and close my eyes even though she will
see. She must already have seen that my life is too diluted to dominate her life; she can safely stay with me. And she will have to
forgive me for trying to drive her like an oxcart through the under-
brush and mud.; I am too thin not to be forgiven.
"I'm supposed to go to bed now." Hallie gets up and follows
my lesser steps to the bedroom. "You don't need to help me. Millie
will be here any minute now." At that moment we hear a car drive
up and stop.
After supper every night Millie bursts into our elegance like a
strawberry roan in a lush summer. Her grin shakes the crystal

drops of the sconces and sends my face back into a childhood giggle. Millie's job is to bathe, massage, change and medicate my body; she also tells me tales of her own earthy life until I fall happily asleep. Millie carries her health as loudly as if she had earned and deserved it and flings it around my sere, creaking house like tough overgrown zinnias. Her freckles wink, her hair is cut like a scouring pad, her voice records to the walls every change or sameness in the condition of my scar tissue, pale bowels, frozen feet. It was Millie who traded the percale sheets for no-iron contour ones so my medicines could be washed away easily.

Tonight Millie opens the box of wash-and-wear shorty nightgowns from Sears which she ordered. I was going to put on one of my satin ones since Hallie was here, but Millie frowns.

"You know this lotion I rub you down with stains."

"Oh." I see Hallie looking at the sheets; their pastel doesn't fit the room.

"The lotion stains the sheets too," I say to Hallie.

"That's right," Millie says. "You don't want to do that."

"Why not?" Hallie says. "Let her stain them—they're *her* sheets."

Millie's face looks alert.

"Oh no, Hallie, I don't want to stain them." My voice comes out in a singsong. I know I look ridiculous in my pink seer-sucker shortie with my huge head wobbling on a stick frame, my face greased with Millie's lotions and my hair tied back with a piece of pink yarn. I walk over to the bed gingerly because my foot bones press directly on the tender skin of my soles. I have the nightgown on with the opening up the back. I giggle again. "I won't even stain this."

Millie's card stands by the bed, her bottles and drops and lotions which stain covering the entire surface.

"It looks like we have so many potions and lotions that if we don't cure me we can embalm me," I say to Hallie. I feel her anxiety. Does she think Millie wants to kill me?

Millie calls Hallie "your daughter" and explains to me that the lotion she's going to use first is the one I like best. "Your daughter can stay with us while we get down to our bedtime work," Millie's voice sings out to my soft white back skin, slashed diagonally from backbone around under my ribs with a scar still vivid red, puckered, trivially painful. "We talk a lot about things which might bore someone as sophisticated as your daughter, so traveled and all; old ladies' talk, plain old talk . . . and I don't want *you* talking any more now, it's time for you to quiet down now and get ready to go off to sleep."

Since Millie spends the weekends with her own family and won't return, after tonight, until Monday, I have two days to explain to Hallie that Millie is good for me. I am falling asleep under her hand. I am too sleepy to explain to Millie that Hallie . . .

Hallie is standing by the piano looking through the leaded French windows at the black trunks of giant pines which stand like stilts over Sister's hills. She is sitting on the sofa pretending to read when Millie comes through the living room. The absence of sound when she stops in front of the sofa is unmistakable.

"Do you want me to get you the tv? You mother won't be watching it any more tonight." Millie pauses until Hallie looks into her shining eyes. "Oh. Of course you don't watch tv, I see. I didn't notice your *book*."

"Mother doesn't watch tv either," Hallie says foolishly.

"Are you feeling all right? You look ill." Millie's face is as near a smile as it could get without actually looking happy.

"I have indigestion, that's all," Hallie says.

Millie disappears and returns with a bottle, shaking out two pills in her hand, explaining that this is the newest, the only effective hospital-tested way to relieve gas. She stands until Hallie takes the pills from her and puts one in her mouth; as Hallie begins chewing Millie grins and leaves.

Very soon the slight indigestion becomes a total sickness like only a child feels—shivering nausea and weakness from the bones out. Millie is gone; she will sit in my room, door closed, watching tv with earplugs in until all stations go off the air.

Hallie stands in the kitchen, gripping the wooden table she has known since childhood as her aunt's, and accepts the fact that she has been poisoned.

At midnight she prepares for bed but not for sleep. The pill had only a hint of the poison, was meant to tease—to show Hallie that Millie is in control and can (but does not even need to) kill Hallie if she interferes. She does not need to kill Hallie because she has already persuaded me to change my will, giving Millie all those sheets and nightgowns she has been so careful to keep unstained. Nightgowns? The house itself and everything in it. She doesn't need to kill Hallie; she only has to kill a frail and trusting me and reap her reward for devotion. All my friends will say: Wasn't it a blessing that Baby died peacefully in her sleep and was spared the awful lingering death of the cancer?

Hallie! Millie may already have done it! Hallie hesitates before the closed door and then opens it quickly. Instantly Millie's diabolical grin greets Hallie as if she were expecting her. Hallie whispers, "I'm going to kiss her goodnight"—politeness automatic and dangerous. Run headlong to the bed and drag me to safety, Hallie! Millie frowns briefly.

I am curled in an arc so tiny with my head turned away from the door that at first it seems no body is in the bed at all. Hallie puts her lips to my forehead and smells the new, unfamiliar Millie-cream; holds her cheek to my nose and gasps when she understands that the tiny flutter on her cheek is breath. After a moment she leaves the room. Millie is reattached to her tv screen through her earplug and does not look up.

The "medicine" she is giving me hasn't finished its job yet, that's all, Hallie understands. She's timed it so death will occur in the early morning hours in case I wake up during the night.

Hallie calls Mary Cowan and tells her that Millie is dosing their mother to death, that Mary Cowan has to come now.

Millie has gone. I am sitting at the table drinking my tea when Hallie wakes up, cramped and stiff from spending the night on the sofa.

"I had a dream once when you all were just about teenagers," I tell her. "We were all at the beach, in the ocean, and there was a terrible undertow. You and Mary Cowan were wrapped in bicycles. I was trying to pull you out before the water dragged you under; I pulled and pulled but the water was winning. Then all of a sudden you all stood up very tall and pulled me out! I loved that dream. It's a turning point in a mother's life—when the children grow stronger than she is and save *her*."

I love dreams when Cad isn't around to sexualize them. Now Cad comes down for her Saturday morning visit. There is a special fuzz in the air and we decide to go to Rudi's for an early lunch, the three of us.

After years of overpowering Cad's minimum flesh with mine, I cannot get used to our bodies' new relationship: mine tiny and skinny, hers sturdy, robust, reflecting vigor and optimism by contrast. I accuse all my friends of exaggerating their heartiness.

Since Rudi's is only at the end of the lane, I ask Hallie to drive us to Jamail's first and pick up some crabmeat. "I know they don't have our lump crabmeat in Paris," I say for an excuse. I just want to see my town.

"Shouldn't we also show Hallie where Oscar's new building will be?" Cad says.

We saw the pictures and final plans just last week. "Oscar is happy as a grig," I say. "He thinks his will be the most beautiful building in town but you know he never was any great shakes as an esthetician."

"I'm sure it will fit right in with what's already here," Hallie says sweetly. She will not argue with me now.

"And what's here is the personal signature of every banker, insurance man, and construction mogul," Cad says. "Our skyline represents the Ten Penny gang when they're not at the bridge table."

"*Gang.* Honestly, Cad."

"Round-up? Squad?" Cad's whole face is twinkling.

"Posse?" Hallie says.

"Their last erections?" Cad whispers to Hallie.

"I heard that. But I won't listen to any more," I say. "You all are just jealous."

"*I* am certainly jealous," Cad says. "I don't even have a corner named for me much less a company."

Everything is coming to rest in my body. I see a large black dog on the edge of the street, a shorthaired male—maybe a labrador; his front paws are akimbo over his eyes and as we pass I see a rectangle of hairless hide where he was hit on his shoulder. A burn whips through my shoulders, upper chest, neck, and lower head simultaneously with the unspoken words *oh poor thing.* I am talking to animals today: an excited golden retriever pauses on the curb as we pass Bellemeade; I tell it out loud to go back. Only a baby squirrel, unrecognizable until the car is almost over it, it is so tiny, produces thoughts that are all thought: we have too many squirrels already. I do not especially like squirrels.

Now turning back onto Post Oak, I shift my weight in such a way that my panty girdle catches a tuft of pubic hair and causes a twinge which spreads through the part of my body uninvolved with the "poor dog." I know what this day will bring. We will go into Rudi's and I will feel that soft glue on my tongue as soon as Mr. Lucia smiles at me. I have always cherished these arbitrary hours of life when I feel threaded into every other life I meet although I make sure I am safe when I feel it coming on me. I think of "it" as a microscopic epileptic seizure which unites me with my Idiot; at its best it remains as a burring tingle just underneath my skin, a sensuality which speaks to a uterine memory, a minus-thought. I hear and don't hear Cad and Hallie speaking. A mere glance at either of their faces makes my heart want to burst.

I sleep for two solid hours with the afternoon sun on my face.

It is the Tennessee Walking Horse's turn at the cocktail hour. I know Cad wants to stay but she adheres rigidly to her own rules: two at a time, appointments made by her. I can no longer hug our walking horse; I have shrunk too much to reach his cheek.

I tell him he signed up for two and where is his wife? "We all know you're dating, don't we Hallie?"

He gives his old sexy laugh and admits she's in the car.

"In the car? A dog would die in the car on a day like this. Go get her." I know he really wants to appear single in front of my daughter, whose sojourn in Paris excites him.

Everyone wants to hear about Paris. Hallie says, "They are so visual they name a loaf of bread a 'wand' because it looks like a wand."

Her stories are clipped now, unnaturally short with quick points. I like stories that go on and on.

"I guess they know their bread tastes so delicious they don't even have to mention that," I say.

"Well, it certainly rubbed off on you," Horse begins gallantly. Hallie laughs. "The bread, you mean? Around my middle?"

Horse grins in confusion—he knows his grin is his major attribute. "The visual, I meant. You know I meant that." He is looking too long at her compact body in its simple little Paris frock.

I say, "If I don't gain all that weight back after I get well maybe I could fit into Paris clothes too. We'll go on a shopping spree," I say to the mare sitting on my right. "For your third trousseau."

"Oh, I don't think . . ." Her laugh *is* something like a nicker. "Fourth, isn't it?"

Cad only allows my visitors to stay an hour; today she telephones to remind them that their time is up.

"You all come back, you hear?" Hallie drawls at the door.

"We won't get another turn for two weeks." Our horse is desolate. "How long will you be here?" The desolation is not for me this time, but the mare and I prevent him from asking her out to lunch.

"A long time, I hope. Jewell is getting bored to death with this dull life. Aren't you, Jewell?"

"Yes ma'am that's right I thank you yes ma'am." His grin displays new teeth but otherwise I think he is exactly the same as the day I met him.

For dinner Hallie fixes me the tidbits I call meals. "You will starve if you try to eat what I eat," I say, heaping her plate with our lump crabmeat and homemade mayonnaise. We are smiling at each other as though we had spent our entire life together and today is not even my best day. I am heady with anticipation of tomorrow— while Hallie rubs Germaine Monteil body lotion into my ugly scar and massages my icy feet with estrogenic cream. We are smearing my best satin and ecru nightgown. I tilt my ear up and she runs to get my Joy. She dabs behind one lobe. "Now turn the other cheek," she says. We are laughing like children playing in mother's makeup.

I want to stay awake. I am fighting sleep. She has told me the girls are thrilled with their Paris adventure but are glad it is over. I always feel that way too. She has told me enough details of their year that I should be able to picture Dora and Emily a thousand ways but instead I am seeing pictures of Hallie as a child. We are in Memphis and Mary Cowan's class is putting on *The Taming of the Shrew*. Left out and ignored, Hallie has been screaming her hatred of Shakespeare up to and through performance day. Just after, she began a campaign against using any word bigger than a substitute she could think up. What does that mean? she asked as often as possible. When I told her she argued: Then why use the big word when the small one means the same thing? For variety, I said at first. To make people who don't know the big word feel dumb, she screamed. How do you think Chanchy feels when you use words she never had a chance to learn? Isn't the point of language to *talk*?

She was nineteen when I slept with the major. He took Hallie, Mary Cowan, and me to a matinee of *Kiss Me, Kate*. I was so proud that my charm could provide a Broadway play for my daughters that my very breath was electric with self-congratulation. Breathing quietly over their glossy mesmerized heads in a dark audience I blessed them with the fact that what they required I would get for them. And I got it too. "Didn't I get it for you?" I say aloud to Hallie who is down by my feet rubbing. "You always did," she answers as if she knows I am talking about Shakespeare. I don't believe for one minute, as Cad slyly suggested, that I really wanted a romance with the major and used the edification of my daughters as an excuse.

Nor did I ever believe Hallie wanted her stallions. After she saw *Kiss Me, Kate*, she sang the male songs with gusto: *"raising an heir can never compare with raising a bit of hell"* and lines like that. At nineteen she knew that a shrew is a small animal but her flipflop labyrinthian mind metamorphosed the weasel-like creature into a wild mustang. It was herself they caught, she felt, and almost tamed. As soon as she acquired two heirs of her own she returned to the untamed herd; although her coat is still glossy and her mane has not reverted to a matted hair of the prairie, she chooses her stallions when she pleases as she pleases and everyone has been seeing that for years. "It does not matter what the world thinks of you," I say—to myself more than to her. "I know. Or I finally know," she says. "Obviously, I *almost* know." Her laugh blows on my cold feet like honey.

Besides, she had a perfectly good stallion at home who was—in spite of Mary Cowan's latterday opinion—flawless in that respect. What she wanted was the power of the honey pot—watching stallions become ants swarming around her by her merely walking into a bar. "I am very proud of you for buying that land," I say. It has tripled at least. "Should we sell?"

"We'll sell when its price is enough to pay all your doctors and all of us take a trip." She squeezes my feet and begins rubbing my calves. "I think that's now."

Money no longer interests me (did it ever really interest me?) but I try to talk about it for her sake. For me, money has been getting thinner and thinner like my body; the more I have of it the more I spend. Squander. Hallie gets her own money for her daughters; no stallion is allowed to provide so much as a mouthful of grass. She told me once that, during her religious period, she was raped and used her will to turn that crime into a sacrament by loving the man. I am still horrified when I think of that; although she assumed my shock came from the sexual subject, I saw only the insane extreme of self-power manifested in my own daughter.

"I'm leaving everything I have to you and Mary Cowan, divided down the middle." I am so sleepy I wonder if I am speaking through a dream.

"Tomorrow I'm going to wash your hair and set it for you."

"There's not enough left to waste bobby pins on," I say. "Not that there ever was all that much . . ."

"We'll sit outside and sweat. We'll sweat so much you'll have the most bodyful head of hair in town. No one will know it isn't thick as a skunk's."

My own chuckle wakes me up. "From the smell?"

She turns out the light after a kiss on my bald head-top. I am seeing Hallie as a very old woman at her death insisting in a very firm voice: Now *I* am choosing to die.

———————

It was my very best day, possibly the best day of my life. Oscar and the Duchess came for an hour at lunchtime. I listen to her tell me about her luncheon for Princess Grace while Oscar brags about his new building to Hallie, insisting she examine every architectural detail. Since it is not an original building, they can finish in an hour.

After my nap Hallie and I have the evening to ourselves. I feel myself exploding with health. Hallie is telling me that she believed Millie was poisoning me—"your marvelous recovery since she's been away almost proves it," she says—and I have the curious sensation that I knew she thought that already. I don't know how I knew. As if my mind scorns so meager a body after its lifelong habitation of a full-size one, mind is floating off on its own errands. I am growing accustomed to being without mind altogether; I like it. "You always liked to think," I tell Hallie. "I hate to think." It excites me that my mind is invading other minds so shamelessly. "I wonder if I've been wrong about that. Dammit, I have been wrong about that. I'm only sixty-four. That's not too late to start."

I am now very excited—overexcited: I feel red spots popping out on my cheeks. "I'm sure I'll think just like I dance—plunging across the floor, knocking everyone down. No partner will have me."

Hallie has figured up what we could make selling our land right now. So that's what she was doing while I napped. She says, "You have, all by your personal self, ninety-eight thousand dollars. After commissions et cetera. Think about *that*."

I wave my arms. "I am swinging thoughts around so fast they've left the floor."

"And that stock you sold has just now gotten back up to the price we sold it at."

"I'm going to buy some ice cream."

"You're going to buy some jewels."

"And dresses. Everything I have has been cut down from a bigger size and looks like a hand-me-down."

"We are going shopping first thing in the morning. I'll call Esther Wolf's and tell them to be ready for us."

I get up and pull her up. I want to use my last breath in a twirl certainly modest compared to my old days but a real twirl nonetheless. "My thinking period didn't last long, did it?"

"Long enough to solve the big problems," she laughs. "Why

should you have to think in rags?"

"*Rags.*" I pluck at my old Trainer Norell suit, which darts suddenly in below its shoulders. "I think—after I get my new clothes, of course—that I will write a book. I'll never be able to carry on like I used to anyway, and who's left to carry on with? I think I'll buy a dress for writing a book in."

"Mother, I've never heard of anyone writing a book in a dress!"

"Does it get in the way of the typewriter?"

"It gets in the way of the stomach. You have to push your stomach way out when you're writing a book—way out to here. You have to leave lots of room for churning."

I know, because I am not hungry even after this talk of ice cream and stomachs, that I still am not fully well. "Now you be quiet a minute. I have to think about what I want to write about."

Hallie is calling Mary Cowan—telling her not to come? She *did* think Millie was poisoning me. I let my book wait to listen to my daughters praise my recovery, restate my constitution of a horse, marvel at my powers of regeneration. I feel my heart pumping harder with every lilt.

We are at Esther Wolf's at nine-thirty the next morning. They have persuaded me to buy all three of the very expensive dresses I was going to choose between. I said I couldn't afford them; Hallie told dear Miss Matthews to charge them to her then. It no longer matters that I have to go to my chemotherapy without my morning rest; I am in love—with my body and my mind, with my daughter and my saleslady, even with my own hideous feet. I have slipped back into happiness as if I were ready greased; there has been no past year, no betrayal, hardly more separation in fact than the time it takes a quick woman to go to market.

I do not know whether I am awake or asleep. After vomiting from the chemotherapy I must have slept. The shadows look long enough for late afternoon. I am dropping through my bed in a stomach-wrenching fall; my chest is locking. I remember what the doctor said about trying to breathe normally, do not pant, do not gasp for air. My hand reaches up miles and miles and finds the bell on my bedside table—do not gasp, do not fight—and pushes for a long time. Run, Jewell! Run! I cannot reach my oxygen.

I must have slept again. Two men are here with a stretcher; they are going to take me back to the hospital. I made Hallie promise she would never let them take me back, never—now I see her bruised face and want to tell her that I know it is a promise she cannot keep. But I have strength for only one thing: "Hallie," I whisper around my oxygen mask. "Bring me a piece of paper and a pencil. I have to write something before we go."

Let them wait. I cannot write fast now and I must get this down exactly right. I want to cancel that bequest I have in my will for Christ Church Cathedral and leave the money to Jewell instead. I want this in my handwriting and I want it witnessed—one of those orderlies will have to do it or I won't go.

Cad is in the hall. I hear Jewell telling her, "She rang the bell hard."

"Sign it right here." My eyes are closed but I know my pencil is pointing at the right place. "Did he do it, Hallie?" Tell Jewell I'll outlive him just the same. I don't think I speak this.

PART VI

October 1964

SOMETIMES HALLIE TRIES too hard to make conversation.

"Now you be quiet for an hour. Why don't you go down and get lunch?" I have a lot of thinking to do—about my book. I have time now to write the story of my life but first I have to decide what my life is.

Hallie sits by the window. I close my eyes and block her out.

She won't go. Her enormous healthy body looms off her chair. She is blocking my air. She is one-half my total offspring sucking against my strength; she is the design of a malicious mother nature meant to live after me, live off me, live right on top of me whether I smother or not. She has not only used up all the air in the room, she has substituted a vile smell of green putrefaction. I can't breathe here. My chest muscles are waterlogged and limp like dishrags. Hallie, *move.*

"I'm expiring." My voice is barely a whisper. Hallie's face is on top of mine, her eyes fixed on my eyes as if they had voice. I can't say the words again. Run, Hallie. Race to the corridor station, order, pull, insist that all doctors and nurses come immediately, that my doctor be found now; with all your schoolteacher's authority to children dare their young health to betray unconcern at just another woman's possible death.

They come but not urgently. They set up their machine and suck fluid out of my lungs. I was drowning.

I'm expiring: two words I have never heard spoken by or attributed to any human being or literary character in my entire life. I'm expiring. I meant I could not breathe another breath. With air for four whispered syllables only I chose the precise word.

From that day on I began to think of myself as a novelist. I announce this fact the next day—in a huge round scrawl across the sheets of blank pages Hallie brought me by the packet. They had, of course, done a tracheotomy: opened a hole in my neck and put a tube down it to make it easier to pump out my lungs. Although I made Hallie promise me to consent to no more operations, they persuaded her that this was not really an operation, that the hole can be closed back up after I get well. It is another promise a daughter cannot keep. They took away by dying voice but I have my pencil.

Turn me over, I write. Pain so bad. Slept some last night. Like Mrs. Greer but don't like that new afternoon nurse Barbara. Mean. How're the girls? Tell Bobby that they feed me through my foot. He'll laugh. Say: Bobby, imagine Grandbaby eating through her foot!

When Hallie reaches this sentence she glances up. I smile and stick my foot up, wiggling it and the tube stuck to my ankle vein.

Barbara shouldn't be a nurse. She doesn't have to. Doesn't know she doesn't have to. I'm telling her that in my novel.

My novel progresses by about fifty words a day, faster than many. The characters are my nurses: besides Barbara there is Mrs. Thomas and Miss Baugh as minor characters and Evelyn Greer, the Negro evening nurse, who is my favorite, as the main character.

I know my Houston world wants me to die. My death will release them into a ritual of a magnificent funeral (it had better be), into the memories from which they can create a Baby myth. As long as I drag out my life they are helpless to do more than arrange their visits—each friend taking a different day of the week (only one to a day now and some eliminated) so they won't create a jam-up by my bed one time and an unsociable absence another. I don't need them to come but I understand why they need to. As long as I remain alive that afternoon nurse named Barbara will continue to simper each time Oscar appears—she thinks he's Houston's most important capitalist. As long as I continue to weaken before their eyes they will be forced to look on my disease, my wasting body about which they can do nothing, the image of which will soon begin to erode the real Baby they want to love—the vigor, health, good humor that provide the optimism necessary to live in Houston.

———————

Vignette
1. Dr. S. not only great Dr. but a good man. Has people who will work for him any no. of hours.
2. Nurses—worst of them (even when RN and tops) WASP—trying to vindicate position. Best Mrs. Greer—smart, kind, intuitive. I'm going to sleep now come back later.

It is hard to explain my novel to Hallie although I must. In case I can't finish it. It is hard to write, easy to imagine. All night Mrs. Greer and I sit together with our minds spinning around through our pasts, recognizing each other. I am Chanchy's size now and Mrs. Greer is my real size. When I feel I cannot bear the pain of my own skin anymore I let my mind slip into the vigor of her body. Then she comes and turns me over. Her hands cradle as if I were a puppy. All my senses dart to the spot she is touching and there are none left to listen to those messages of pain.

I think they are giving me drugs. My novel unfolds in images and smells, colors, motion; a whole night passes without a single chapter dressing itself up in words.

Name of Book, Meet Mrs. Greer—observe her. Negro. Observe. She's most interesting and wonderful heroine (someone may have to help). She's smart, poignant, & practical. Talks very little you'll just have to get feel. 5 boys 2 girls. Boys probably (?) like her, (I hope) girls like Valkyries. She quietly rules with iron rod.

I hand Hallie the page. *Observe,* I say with my lips. I nod my head firmly. Hallie will have to send her mind in here during our nights and put Mrs. Greer into sentences for me. We must not lose her story.

Hallie nods and says she has always known I would end up a novelist. She says it is because I am not wearing a dress. I stick my stomach out inside my hospital sheet. It barely humps.

I write: *I slept a good deal today and feel fine now. Later I want to hear about your day. I may take small amount cool sweet tea—perhaps an ice chip. Not now.*

I spend another night with Mrs. Greer. I do not let her see the tears but I can't stop weeping at her strength. My life has been too easy. I haven't had a chance yet to show what I'm made of. I spend the night in her life, my shoulder next to hers, pushing.

Both my daughters are beside my bed. I take a page. Across the top it says, *I wasn't scared just wanted Dr. S. not that goon and that nurse. If anything happens again just call Dr. S.*

Below that it says, *Tell her not to lean on me, it's heavy and hurts hand.*

Mary Cowan gives me a clean piece of paper but I smile and use this one.

I feel better than in months. Can breathe easily, no pain, or discomfort. Even took 3 sips plain dead water which tasted delicious! But I told Dr. S. I would soon want something STRONGER.

Why don't you all go to the Bayou Club.

Mary Cowan's face is as frozen as a hand before my eyes.

This trachea thing is temporary. But I am breathing so much better. He is going to put a stomach tube this aft but not like the first one that made me so sick. Where did you have lunch?

"We found something in the freezer marked 'Drukie's chicken hash' but we didn't know whether we should eat it or not so we had eggs," Mary Cowan says. Her hands gripping her purse have white knuckles. Her clothes look ironed onto her skin. I reach for her hand and make my eyes knead her eyes loose. Now they are watering.

I write, *You can have it. Where are the children?*

"They want to come whenever you want them," both daughters begin together; Hallie's voice drops out in the middle.

I want to see them tomorrow. I want to see the children dressed up once. Not tomorrow. I want see them tomorrow just plain. Sunday.

Now Mary Cowan's hand feels ironed on to mine.

They suction thru the tube about every four hours. I would have died if everything hadn't happened as it did. I had given up. But am going to try to stay on and fight for you and children, Hallie & children. And Oscar.

The Judge is living here too. He goes to town everyday, to his bank. He and Nannie Walker same age. She was 88 when she died. I'm sure Oscar has heard from Mary D and Dan tell him to give them my love. The Fascinator's birthday is sometime this weekend try to find out from Elise Minor she's MO 84660 & send her a message from me.

Now Hallie is telling me that everything is fine at home and Mary Cowan that Ed sends his love and wants to come if he can help and Hallie that the children are making a book for me and Mary Cowan is asking what she can bring me and they are very beautiful but I am out of strength temporarily.

You all are making me well. Just come in & out but don't stay here all the time.

I am sleeping while everyone eats. It is quiet here; there is only the sound of my breathing inside my oxygen tent, the crackle of its plastic, the whoosh of my tube.

Mrs. Greer's face sprouts just the other side of my plastic. She reaches in to turn me without asking. She moves the pillow under my neck.

Thank goodness there are just you and I here tonight. Off with the biddies and others! Do nurses ever have to take a refresher? to renew license?

Mrs. Greer shakes her head while she laughs. She laughs and shakes her head. "Not even if they can't see the patient with their glasses on. Not even an eye test for that."

Those 2 biddies are dangerous. Miss Baugh is nice but doesn't know much. Mrs. Thomas is an RN; she worked for the Yanceys once and I couldn't stand her then but was so sick didn't say anything. Mary changed IV at 5:30. Not changed, refilled. Will that other be on tonight?

Mrs. Greer does not know. But she promises that she will stand right beside me. "I can tell by looking at her hands that she shouldn't be handling anything lighter than a bulldozer."

But we won't need her I hope. That resident shouldn't either—but the minute Dr. S. touched it everything was ok. So if we do have any more trouble just say I insist upon Dr. S. at all times. I told Barbara that and she just stood there nodding her head.

I laugh with a bumpy rasp and Mrs. Greer answers in a soft chuckle. She doesn't talk much because I can't answer her easily. She understands power. I want to tell her that I understand power too but I'm not sure that's true.

We are together in near-darkness talking without words. My pictures have taken me back to Mary Cowan's birth; Mrs. Greer is also birthing her firstborn, Ellen. I am telling Mrs. Greer that I expected myself to grow fat as naturally as a pumpkin, to drop this baby like a feather which would float down into a loving doctor's cupped palms. I expected my breasts to fill with warm vanilla ice cream which my baby would kiss out from them while my face smiled like a sunset. I expected that in a few days I would be keeping my house again . . . Her laugh interrupts. *Keeping it?* She makes me laugh. *Keeping it*—while I sang to my lace-trimmed baby (I created babies ready-trimmed) until it grew into its Sunday school piqué, at which time I would gently expel a second lace-trimmed feather of the opposite sex. Whatever that is, she says, and for a while the babies romp across the screen pelting each other with miniature wee-wees. Then the feathers would stop but not the tickling, of course, I say. Oh, not the tickling, she agrees. Not the tickling—which we are laughing under right now, not the goose bumps from the goose feathers, and she says, I would like it if you would call me Evelyn and I say, Then you will have to call me Baby and she shakes her head sternly and says, No, I can't do that, you know I can't do that.

They are lined up beside my bed: Dora and Emily and the twins, George and Teddy. Bobby is absent. They are very tall and beautiful. I look from face to face. I see you, I want to say, but they are all talking and I am just smiling.

You all look beautiful. I am so very happy to have you all here. My heart is full of joy & gratitude. To think of all of you in the house we all love. Don't let Bobby feel left out. One of you draw Bobby a picture of me being fed through my foot. Funny? How do you like school?

I am asking Dora and Emily who have just started their new Houston school but each one thinks I'm asking *them*. It is a bonus, this writing everything down, because no one knows who's being addressed; I get answers from all four.

Just think of my breathing difficulty like pulling a horse out of the mud, I write for Emily.

There's lots of delicious cheese. The twins grin and shake their heads. "Not any more, Grandbaby."

All gone? Good. Cheese shop at Foley's. Tell your mothers. Gourmet shop. Charge to me.

They have brought me a book they made. It is tied with leftover Christmas ribbon and has a picture of the house on the front. I pat it and nod that I will read it later. Dora says it is to keep me from being bored.

Too sick to be bored. Take the roses if you want. I don't need them. Don't touch me but throw me a kiss. So glad to see you. Have fun and do what you want to. Glad you're home.

Barbara is not perceptive enough to see that I am exhausted after their visit. She wants to tell me about each of the four of them.

No hurry but when you have time call my house NA 10996 and give Bobby my love. He didn't come & in excitement forgot to ask.

But when she returns I am not asleep. Barbara's voice is like a sticky child yanking at your shirt. I try to smile; my eyes ache from looking sideways at her.

Give me something to quiet me down so I can sleep if you can. If not ok. Head up a little.

I can't control it. Tears burn my eyes while I wait for my shot. I know I am lucky to get the shot. My body disappears and pictures return to my brain; I think I sleep.

Cad is here. She walks in like cardboard. She puts two new baby pillows in plain cases under my neck, barely touching me.

"Jewell says to tell you that he took all the curtains and bedspreads to be cleaned before the children got here."

I feel a surge of warm bubbles running through my veins as if I were suddenly carbonated. I think I bounce. It is Cad's voice, just the sound of it, the rich tone, the oldest unchanged voice I know. I cannot bear the pressure I feel to explode from the sound of that voice. I am afraid she will and terrified she won't speak again. I scribble, *Gaius always said I was nonrustible and nondestructible & it's beginning to look like it. Now I don't want to destruct since I can breathe.*

She smiles and nods. As if she knows I will splinter if she speaks again, she takes my get-well cards and letters and sits by the window, noting down names.

I sleep, bombarded by flowers in brilliant colors which sail over my head. None of them are words. I don't know how many words are left. I think I may have used them all up. I think I can make a few dozen more very large on the page, a few important words to every page.

The portable tv is Millie's. I have only one. I don't care for tv. Let Barbara do the tea. You have too much to do and I'm in no hurry. The nurses are out. Tell Teddy better stay off horses. Don't try to come back tonite. Late for me. After dinner. Dr. S. came. I told Hallie about the curtains & furniture. She will explain it to you. He came at 2 am. There was no danger. Temporarily. Sometimes happens. I didn't know it. Barbara saw it & held it. He's so gentle & good. It could be serious if you were alone. Mary, I am leaking. Put a little towel . . .

I'm just generally uncomfortable, the way when you wake up drooling, bedpan, etc. I'm all right now. Tell Barbara they give the therapy now. And be sure she understands about cleaning the trachea thing. When we settle down I might try a sip or two of water if you think so. I will look at the flowers & then the girls can take them home.

I am uncomfortable again. Dr. S. wants one of you to watch me all the time so I won't be nervous. I don't know. I am sorry to be so contrary tonight. I am asleep and these things wake me up and then my throat—

I'm sorry I've given such a bad nite. Let's wait a minute before we close up. I have slept just woke up.

Dr. S. is going to put in a feeding tube to my stomach. Reli-

able but need more food. That's mostly liquid & dextrose, some medicine.

I had a bad nite but it was no one's fault but my own. I was so restless, would sleep an hour and then turn. Don't know what the trouble was. It could have been the food. It didn't disagree but a change—

Don't you remember Mary Cowan when the twins first visited & then went home they were afraid the house, mine, was going to disappear. That was roots and home and they wanted it there. Dora and Emily told me later. It's a great house. Fun and love house. I won't be there for some time you know. I have to take all of these treatments, but I am going to be better. Maybe never as well as I was but well enough for us to enjoy life. And I am so thankful & grateful for everything. The Lord has been good to me. I know that.

At home in the bottom desk drawer boxes of old paper of Hyke's. Bring it. Good way to use it. I can use the envelopes.

Take the roses if you want. I don't care. Ben Falk is here too. He always said we would end up our old age in Methodist Hospital together. And here we are after all these years.

I enjoy playing the records. An perdu dans mi corazón. I'm mixed up in my languages. I like him. How's your smoking? Where? Good. It is Bertha, an old house way down on McKinney, a favorite of George Rice's. She is very cute. No club. Beer. Atmosphere and good. Take them to different places. I have to take my treatment. Come back later.

Evelyn—you tactfully (as always) explain to Barbara that she doesn't have to change that thing just wash it in water for one suction. She changes every time she takes it out and it takes so long. That night nurse messed up the UD's last night. She didn't know anything. An RN but—Could I try about a few cc cool sweet tea. I'm sure your husband's family knew Mrs. Gable. She was an old friend of mine.

Well I don't want her to start another one. She's awful. Mr. M fixed it in nothing this am. Cute. How was your day? Tell Jewell to go out and have some fun. I am going to be fine tonite. Thank Jewell and say I will see him tomorrow.

No more secrets. Too late.

You're going into the apartment across the creek? For a while or—Mary Cowan what about your apt? Thinking of selling. Think that would be wise. Beautiful but maybe too much & too expensive as long as you have the farm. You don't really need all that now. Of course I don't need mine. I need it for the family. Anyway you will get more money from home.

The Duchess had the luncheon for Lady Bird today at NASA. Oscar sat next to her, said she is more charming than ever.

You all eat that ice cream, I won't be able to before it spoils. She's lovely—smart capable & kind. When you come tomorrow bring me my wedding ring. I got your letter Mary Cowan it was wonderful. Don't cast aspersions at your self, it was a great letter. Thanks.

Don't worry. The Dr. says I have done something remarkable. I'm glad the children are having a great time. What have they eaten? They look great. Aren't Dora and Emily pretty? Thank you for everything. I couldn't do without you and Jewell, you know that.

I knew there was lots more before but I was too tired. Lets have a small light, brush my hair & wash my face. Dr. S said tea or water, how about a cc or 2 of sweetened tea neither hot nor cold? Prefer something stronger & more fun.

Later.

I didn't tell anyone for some time. I was mad. *But I haven't been able to swallow well recently before this last attack. Will I ever be able to eat again? Otherwise I will be too thin instead of too fat! Normal weight 138–140. When I got sick, 157. What Negroes call fat & pretty! Dr. S. says doing so well. Be careful of mouth. Old dead water, imagine. Tastes good.*

My granddaughters out there? Grandsons? Maybe daughters?

Head doesn't hurt but is uncomfortable. Could I have a small pillow like I have under back?

I want Dora to have that ring.

I have no more words. Like the heroine of MEET MRS. GREER, I can't talk you have to feel. My daughters are sleeping in the room adjoining my hospital one. Mrs. Greer sits here with me. I think this is our last night.

My hands and feet, my legs and arms are numb. I can hear rustling, either inside my own head or around my bed. I will not be coming back. Mary Cowan stands near my head holding one of my blue skeleton-hands, listening to my rasps for breath. Hallie stands at the foot of my bed staring. Oscar sits on the other side of the bed from Mary Cowan, his face funereal. My favorite doctor sits by Oscar.

I know this and I don't know it. My mind is not where it belongs. It is floating over my lips, hovering at my chest. Dr. S.

explains that there is no oxygen getting to my brain and that I will never regain consciousness; my brain is dead. It is my heart beating and going on beating that keeps me here. They will nod now and ask the doctor to pull out the plug of the oxygen apparatus.

My heart is still beating. I can feel its thump raise and lower the skin on my chest. It forces me to gasp breaths within death. It won't prevent the blue from rising up my arms and legs. Mary Cowan holds my hand and thinks that I her mother helped her into this life when she was unconscious coming out of my womb and it is fitting that she help me out of it even though I am unaware of her help just as she was of mine. Hallie's thoughts are paralyzed. Her mind is not where it belongs; it is floating over my chest trying to mix with my mind. Both minds are deafened by the sound of my heart beating—I am doing my part, I am beating beating how long can I go on beating if the rest of you will not help me, I am bound by nature and my Baby strength to keep on beating against all odds in the lap of death for the sake of all of you I will beat and beat and beat, it is my nature to beat until I reach my last beat and even though everything else has given up and I know I cannot endure for long I can make you wait I can make you stand with respect by my beating . . .